Language Learning in Distance Education

CAMBRIDGE LANGUAGE TEACHING LIBRARY

A series covering central issues in language teaching and learning, by authors who have expert knowledge in their field.

Language Learning in Distance Education

Cynthia White

CAMBRIDGE
UNIVERSITY PRESS

PUBLISHED BY THE PRESS SYNDICATE OF THE UNIVERSITY OF CAMBRIDGE
The Pitt Building, Trumpington Street, Cambridge, United Kingdom

CAMBRIDGE UNIVERSITY PRESS
The Edinburgh Building, Cambridge CB2 2RU, UK
40 West 20th Street, New York, NY 10011-4211, USA
10 Stamford Road, Oakleigh, VIC 3166, Australia
Ruiz de Alarcón 13, 28014 Madrid, Spain
Dock House, The Waterfront, Cape Town 8001, South Africa

http://www.cambridge.org

First published 2003

Printed in the United Kingdom at the University Press, Cambridge

Typeface Sabon 10.5/12 pt   *System* QuarkXPress™   [SE]

A catalogue record for this book is available from the British Library

Library of Congress Cataloguing in Publication data

ISBN 052181541 X hardback

To Bruce, Caroline and Rebecca

Contents

Contents

Contents

Thanks

I am indebted to the many teachers, colleagues and students who have discussed their experience of distance language learning with me. Their interest in reflecting on and finding out more about language learning in distance contexts has played a large part in developing the idea of this book. I would particularly like to thank Elisabeth Cunningham, Charlotte Gunawardena, Monica Shelley and Maija Tammelin for their contributions which are included here. I must thank Marina McIsaac, Arizona State University, and Terry Evans, Deakin University Australia, who supported me in the process of gaining a Massey University Research Award in the course of writing the book. I would also like to express my appreciation to Nebojsa Radic, Gloria Cusinato, Lucia Hau-Yoon and Alisa Vanijdee who have contributed in different ways to my understanding of distance language learning. Thanks to Jelena Harding who helped construct many of the figures in the text based on my sketches. I am grateful to Mickey Bonin and Alison Sharpe at Cambridge University Press for their interest and guidance at every stage, and to Cathy Rosario for her careful editing, and to Clive Rumble for overseeing production of the book. I would also like to thank the anonymous reviewers for their valuable comments and suggestions.

I have mentioned Monica Shelley as one of the contributors, but as a colleague and friend she has also provided advice and encouragement and has made many insightful comments on the manuscript – thank you Monica.

Finally I thank my husband Bruce, and my children Caroline and Rebecca, for their love and good humour all along the way.

Cynthia White

Introduction

This is a book about distance language learning. It aims to provide an overview of the field and takes a learner-centred approach to examining key issues within distance language contexts. The book has been written at a time of rapid change: opportunities for distance language learning are expanding around the world, and are attracting the attention of the public, policy makers and new providers. Language learners and language teachers have sensed the convenience and potential of the new learning environments in terms of improved access to and delivery of language learning experiences. While distance language learning creates an array of new advantages, it also places new demands on participants: to acquire new roles, and develop new skills. In spite of the growing presence of distance learning opportunities, and the eagerness to participate in these opportunities, the field of distance language learning remains little known and little understood. It is often narrowly conceptualised as the development of technology-mediated language learning opportunities. Many of the key issues for distance language learning, however, relate to human factors which are common to both hi-tech and low-tech environments – factors that arise as learners attempt to establish and maintain an effective means of working within a distance learning context. The central argument developed here is that in order to understand language learning in distance education, it is crucial to maintain a focus on those who are most involved, the actual learners, and to explore the ways they respond to the demands and opportunities it presents.

Background and purpose

This book is oriented towards developing an awareness and understanding of distance language learning by thinking about learners within the kinds of environments which can be developed through the distance mode. This is not a typical approach. The research literature on distance education has tended to view the subject predominantly from the perspective of providers and to focus on the concerns of institutions. Much of what has been written to date on distance education has related to course provision and the development of learning opportunities, with relatively little attention being paid to language learners, and their response to distance learning contexts. There is a need for a more learner-centred approach within the field to gain an understanding of fundamental issues in distance language learning, and to move away from a preoccupation with the development of courseware as the core or single most important component in providing distance learning opportunities. This angle injects some reality into the teaching–learning process. The sense of control over learning which language teachers may develop in the course of constructing new learning spaces or developing courseware does not take sufficient account of the independent decisions learners make over what will form part of their learning experiences. Course development aspects are important but are considered here as one part of the broader distance learning context, and in relation to the experience and perspectives of learners.

This book offers an examination of elements, processes, issues and challenges within distance language learning, with the experience of learners as the common thread. It is not primarily about the use of technology and the process of innovation in distance language contexts; these issues are discussed but they provide a relatively narrow approach to understanding distance language learning. It seeks to present the advantages, strengths and affordances of distance language learning opportunities alongside its constraints, weaknesses and limitations. Developments in technology have overtaken our understanding of the concerns and issues they raise within distance language learning and teaching environments. In my view the task of making sense of new environments is best guided by an appreciation of distance learning as a unique context which is influenced by a range of factors that are not always immediately apparent or readily discernible to teachers or learners. Many of these concern human and pragmatic factors common to both hi-tech and low-tech distance learning environments.

In writing this book I was always aware of the rate of change and innovation within the field, and also of how short-lived many new courses are. For this reason I have not included many online references, and have avoided screen dumps of current web pages. I draw on examples from across the spectrum of distance education practice, including different paradigms and generations of provision. The contexts I have referred to in some detail provide insights into the continuing practice of distance language learning. Some of the programmes and courses will have changed by the time the book is published but since I have focused on typical examples and standard programmes, they will still reflect what is current practice in distance language learning, and the kinds of issues and lessons that can shape our analysis and understanding of distance language learning.

There is relatively little published research in distance language learning, and most of this exists as accounts of practice or descriptions of language programmes. In particular there is an absence of the kind of 'close' research to investigate what distance language teachers and learners actually do, and how this relates to the development of language skills. There are some exceptions and I draw on those studies quite extensively. Part of the purpose of the book is to identify gaps in the understanding of practices and in our knowledge of the field, and to suggest important avenues for research.

Audience

This book is aimed at language teachers, researchers and professionals with an interest in distance learning contexts. While the subject matter of the book intersects with a number of related fields – such as network-based language teaching and the use of the web for language teaching – I have maintained the orientation of the book towards as complete a representation as possible of distance language learning in all its variability. The concepts and frameworks discussed here will appeal to those applied linguists and teachers with knowledge and experience of instructional contexts and opportunities for language learning beyond those of the conventional face-to-face classroom. It will be of particular interest to anyone who has worked within distance learning contexts – either as a language learner, a language teacher or a teacher educator.

Overview

This book is organised into three major thematic sections, beginning – in Part I – with a background to distance language learning. Chapter 1 introduces the concept of distance language learning, with examples from a range of contexts. Together they illustrate the diversity that exists in the design of distance learning environments, and the different emphases, concerns and issues which arise within particular settings. Matters of definition are considered briefly, then two further ways of introducing distance language learning are presented – through an overview of the landscape of the field, and then by focusing on the challenges for language learners that form part of the distance learning experience. Chapter 2 examines a number of learning systems and movements related to distance education – such as online learning – together with the features of language courses that have been developed within those different forms of provision. Chapter 3 provides a discussion of current trends that are essentially linked to developments in technology. Attention is also given to many emerging issues in the rapidly changing environments for distance language learning; these include participation, access and quality, the development of interactive competence and the emergence of new constraints. The final chapter in Part I provides a theoretical framework for distance language learning. It is derived from student rationalities of the process which place the interface developed between learner and learning context at the centre of the process of distance language learning.

Part II moves to a focus on learners within distance language learning contexts. Chapter 5 argues that a key challenge for anyone working within the distance context is to develop a practical knowledge of distance language learners. The chapter moves from demographic approaches to contemporary approaches which emphasise a more dynamic conception of learners, including a focus on the affective domain and on influences within individual learning environments. Chapter 6 concerns the initial experience of distance language learning and discusses the complex factors and processes involved in adjusting to a new context for language learning. The second half of the chapter explores the knowledge and beliefs learners develop in relation to their experiences of distance language learning. Learner autonomy is the subject of Chapter 7. Emphasis is placed on different representations of learner autonomy – as learner independence or as collaborative control of learning experiences – which stem from different paradigms of distance language learning and their associated goals and ideals.

Part III is devoted to key aspects of the distance learning context: learner support, learning sources and new learning spaces. Learner support is an essential component of distance learning and can best be understood as a response to individual learners rather than as access to information or resources. It fulfils a range of functions integral to the development of effective distance learning experiences. This is discussed in Chapter 8 together with a consideration of the situated nature of learner support, and appropriate forms of support. Chapter 9 looks at the learning sources available within a distance language course. It critically examines the more traditional understanding of course content and presents an alternative view that centres on learners as they actively select and construct content from a range of potential learning sources. It is these sources that contribute to their learning environment and become, in effect, the course. The final chapter looks ahead to the kinds of new learning spaces which are emerging within the field, and to the frameworks which have been developed to understand the nature and affordances of these spaces. To conclude I consider the place of innovation within the field and argue that the way ahead for distance language learning can best be understood if attention is paid not just to new developments, but to developing a broader understanding of distance language learning contexts and of those who are most involved – the learners.

One of the aims in writing this book has been to provide a starting point: an introduction to the field, a foundation for further enquiry and research, a catalyst for continuing interest in the field. To this end I have included an Appendix, which lists resources, journals and newsgroups related to the concerns, issues and contexts that have formed much of the focus of the book.

Part I Background

1 The idea of distance language learning

1.1 Introduction

The last decade has witnessed an enormous expansion in distance language learning opportunities. Rapid developments in information and communications technology, together with societal changes, have increased awareness of and demand for distance education – and now also for online learning, and distributed learning (see section 2.3), to name but two of the more recent incarnations which I will look at in this book. Other forces have contributed to expansion, such as the current growing demand for global education offerings, and the desire on the part of many institutions to reach new audiences or to retain their market share. All this means that distance learning opportunities are becoming an increasingly visible part of educational provision.

Many language learners, language teachers and institutions are coming to distance education for the first time. However, distance language learning is not a new phenomenon. What makes it appear so is the development and wide availability of the new technologies for connecting learners and teachers, the rapid pace at which these have developed, and the widespread publicity they have attracted. More traditional forms of distance language learning, that used print, audio and video materials are being supplemented by opportunities for interaction and collaboration online. The social and technological changes that prompted expansion are also transforming the nature of distance learning. They have resulted in new contexts for learning, new ways of learning and new roles and responsibilities for participants.

There is now broad interest in innovation in distance language learning, both from distance language professionals, and from others who are interested in the possibilities offered by online learning environments. A number of factors have invited new providers to enter the field: a belief in the accessibility and convenience of online technologies, the need to be in the front line of progress, and a perception that distance teaching is time- and cost-effective. A web search on the International Distance

Learning Course Finder showed that more than 1,300 language courses were registered – out of a total of 55,000 distance courses from 130 countries. And the number of providers entering the market to provide online or distance courses for language learners is growing.

While distance education has achieved a new prominence, much about the processes involved and the participants remains little understood. The new technologies provide institutions with access to new audiences, but bring with them relatively little information about these audiences in order to inform their practices. Important aspects of the learning experience are transformed in the distance context, but whereas the tendency has been to focus on technology as the defining feature, experienced distance educators and commentators argue repeatedly that technology *per se* is not as important as other factors such as learner motivation, an understanding of the distance language learning context and of the demands it places on participants, the responsiveness of the teacher, the accessibility of the learning context, and the overall context of delivery.

This chapter introduces the idea of distance language learning in all its diversity. Examples of different contexts for distance language learning are explored, and the ways in which they vary. I then examine the meaning of distance, its relationship to time and place and to learning opportunities. A brief discussion of definitions of distance education and distance learning is used to highlight the difference between a focus on structural considerations as a starting point for understanding distance language learning, as opposed to pedagogical concerns. A brief overview of different generations of distance learning opportunities is given, all of which continue to contribute to current practice. From here I return to an overview of the landscape of distance language learning, and to the particular challenges it presents for learners.

1.2 Distance language courses

The nature of opportunities for distance language learning are diverse and still evolving. Distance language programmes include a wide range of elements and practices ranging from traditional print-based correspondence courses, to courses delivered entirely online with extensive opportunities for interaction, feedback and support between teachers and learners, and among the learners themselves. Here I introduce four distance language courses, which differ in quite distinct ways in terms of how learning environments are designed, the different emphases and concerns within those courses and the issues that arise in course development and delivery. The overview aims to give some sense of the ways in which distance language learning opportunities are inflected in different contexts.

1.2.1 A technology-based course in intermediate Spanish

Rogers and Wolff (2000) report on the development of a distance language programme at the Pennsylvania State University that offers a distance course for intermediate Spanish, developed to meet the growing demand for Spanish instruction. The course is built around a combination of hi-tech and low-tech options. Initial plans were to use a technology package that came complete with a textbook, but a number of compatibility issues emerged. It was then necessary for the course design team to develop their own technology-based support system consisting of:

- e-mail – for asynchronous writing activities;
- chat room – for real-time communication exercises;
- computer-aided grammar practice;
- web-based cultural expansion modules, emphasising reading Spanish.

A principle Rogers and Wolff (p. 47) used in deciding on the kinds of technologies they would use was that 'less is best':

> realising that, with each additional computer-based activity introduced into the curriculum, we were substantially raising the complexity of the course, the probability for technology-based frustrations, and the possibility of instructional failure.

More hi-tech elements were combined with a conventional cassette-tape-and-workbook approach to build listening comprehension skills. Rogers and Wolff acknowledge that in the end they decided to de-emphasise spoken Spanish, because options such as Internet-based audioconferencing were not sufficiently reliable or well-developed to meet the benchmarks they had established for providing quality learning experiences. Of course had the technology met their benchmarks there would still be a host of additional challenges for teachers and learners in learning to work within and derive benefit from what would be a new learning environment.

Rogers and Wolff were also cautious in the way they piloted the course: given that this was a very new undertaking for staff and students, they decided to try it out with a group of students resident at Penn State, so they could change to face-to-face classes if they encountered unexpected difficulties. The lessons they learned from the pilot study were that developing and implementing a distance language learning course requires a substantial commitment of time, energy and money, that technology fails – often when least expected – and the diverse capabilities and shortcomings of students' own computers provided significant limitations on the way and extent to which they participated in the activities. In addition, Rogers and Wolff (p. 51) note that:

> The already steep learning curve inherent in studying a second language became significantly steeper with each new technology that students had to master in order to complete their assignments. In turn, this added pressure increased the probability for learner frustration and failure.

Among the more positive findings were that students, administrators and even future employers expect that available technologies should be part of the delivery of high-quality learning experiences, and they had gone some way to meet the challenge. The team approach they used in developing the course and carrying out the pilot study was rewarding, and also effective 'in anticipating and resolving problems, and . . . it assured the variety of perspectives necessary to create a positive learning experience for both the instructors and the students' (p. 52). Learning to work within a team-based approach is a requirement in most distance language courses, and this, together with the scale of detailed planning required in advance of course delivery, are important areas of adjustment for language teachers new to the distance mode. Based on their experience Rogers and Wolff see the greatest challenges in distance language learning as reduced opportunity for cohort-based learning and immediate, personalised feedback.

1.2.2 A multimode course in thesis writing for graduate students

David Catterick (2001) describes a Writing Up Research course for international graduate students offered by the University of Dundee, Scotland. The course itself lasted six weeks and was multimode: half accessed in face-to-face classes, half via WebCT. WebCT stands for Worldwide Web Course Tools and is software designed for the delivery of distance learning courses, which can be used to create a Virtual Learning Environment (VLE). When the course had been taught as fully classroom-based, scheduling difficulties faced by students from different departments across the university presented ongoing problems. The development of an online learning environment, accessible 24 hours a day, was seen as a viable solution.

The course's first week was classroom-based: the seven students met with the teacher and learned how to use WebCT. The face-to-face orientation was very helpful in enabling students to access and work within the online environment, with the teacher on hand to help with any initial difficulties. Face-to-face meetings at the start of distance courses have been found to be important for motivation, developing a sense of learning community, and in easing access to initial learning events. However, the constraints of time and distance mean that this is not possible in many contexts.

In the Writing Up Research course students accessed materials and completed online tasks early each week using WebCT. They were then required to log on for about an hour – in the university computing labs, in their workplace or from home – on a set afternoon to take part in online discussions. These were based around questions posed earlier in the week and were designed to mirror classroom-based discussions. The text messages could be read by other students who were in the chat room, and the software kept a record of the entire discussion.

The lessons learned included that considerable time and support were required to set up and operate an online course. The response of students to the course was mixed: some appreciated their experience using WebCT, while others preferred 'more class-based teaching'. Overall the evaluations of the course were very positive in terms of its usefulness and effectiveness. In conclusion Catterick notes that the text-based nature of WebCT was appropriate for a writing course, but may be less suitable for other English language courses. In addition language proficiency is an important consideration. Based on his experience Catterick argues that learners with less well-developed communicative ability than those in his study – who were described as being high-intermediate language learners – may lack confidence in their communication skills, and therefore be intimidated by the chat function. Issues relating to interaction and participation in online learning events are discussed further in Chapter 3.

1.2.3 A pre-sessional English for Academic Purposes (EAP) course

Distance language courses are sometimes developed for a small, but significant niche market, and Boyle (1994, 1995) presents a valuable description of a distance learning course as a pre-sessional component in an EAP project. The audience were postgraduate students enrolled in an English-medium school of engineering at the Asian Institute of Technology (AIT) in Thailand. Few staff at AIT are native speakers of English, and 'since students are unfamiliar with the range of idiolects to which they are exposed, many have considerable difficulty in following lectures' (Boyle 1994: 115). While assistance was available for students having difficulty with English when they were studying at AIT, attendance was often difficult because of competing demands from other coursework. In addition, it was not feasible for all students to attend a face-to-face pre-sessional course. Thus a distance course was developed to meet the needs of students. The course had two aims:

- to prepare students for initial course work by sending them recordings of talks and lectures by their future teachers, and by dispatching readings and other materials to aid in this preparation;
- to use the cassette tapes and correspondence to build up a relationship with the students so that they will be prepared to seek the help of language teachers when they arrive at the institution.

(Boyle 1995)

The course was found to be successful in terms of the second aim. The main difficulty in fulfilling the first aim related to a common theme in distance education, namely the demands of course development. Boyle (1994) underestimated the amount of time required for preparation and for managing the production and dissemination of materials. This meant the scope and quality of the work had to be reduced and fell below his expectations. None the less, the initiative by Boyle underscores the role for a distance learning course as a preliminary to further study in English, in response to the evident language needs of students. The Boyle study also represents an early example of the way distance learning contexts can be used to complement or converge with conventional face-to-face education.

1.2.4 A vocational French language course delivered by satellite

Laouénan and Stacey (1999) describe a pilot study into delivering a distance vocational French language course developed as part of a European Union-funded project called RATIO (Rural Area Training and Information Opportunities). The course was developed and delivered by the University of Plymouth to a number of small businesses with an interest in advanced French, focusing on current topics such as politics and innovation in France. It consisted of satellite broadcasts followed by videoconferencing sessions. Materials were sent to learners in advance of the satellite broadcasts, and included an introduction to the programme, additional explanations, reading material and question sheets for listening work. The videoconferencing follow-up sessions were planned around a series of interactive exercises built on the material presented during the satellite broadcasts.

Laouénan and Stacey note that a number of software problems and problems with the link-up between centres prevented the sessions taking place as planned. In addition, 'the delay which occurred between speech and reception made communication difficult, which in a foreign language session is a very serious drawback' (p. 179). Laouénan and Stacey conclude that the potential of the videoconferencing software is considerable, but it proved to be far more complex to use than they had anticipated, and suggest that it is essential to have a technician to hand, at least in the initial stages. The resources required for this type of distance learning are considerable, in terms of both time and costs, and Laouénan and Stacey emphasise that larger numbers of learners would be required to make it worthwhile and cost-effective on a continuing basis.

The course is an example of just-in-time distance learning that is developed for a particular group with specific needs at relatively short notice. It also had a vocational orientation, and as such can be seen as part of the move towards using distance education to deliver opportunities for learning in the workplace. A further feature of the course is that it was group based, i.e., learners came together at a particular time and place to access the classes. There were individual learning opportunities in the materials sent out beforehand, but the main part of the course was based around learning as a group. Laouénan and Stacey describe their work as 'a brief experiment in the distance teaching and learning of French'. As such it reflects much of the published research in distance language learning, which is based on short trials rather than on the provision of distance programmes that have been developed, modified and delivered to groups of learners on an ongoing basis. Research in both types of contexts can contribute to our understanding of distance language learning, but it is important to acknowledge that many of the realities and challenges in providing distance learning opportunities can be understood and addressed more fully in more long-term contexts.

Distance learning opportunities are offered within a range of cultural, educational and institutional settings, each with their own influences, which means that the terms *distance learning* and *distance education* can be applied to language learning programmes with markedly different features. It is possible, however, to identify some common contexts for distance language learning, along the spectrum from individual-based to group-based learning opportunities. These are represented in Figure 1.1.

Figure 1.1 is meant to be illustrative rather than comprehensive in terms of the range of distance language learning contexts. It introduces a number of important dimensions along which distance language learning opportunities vary, including the range of media used, opportunities for interaction, sources of support and individual vs group-based learning. While the distinction between individual- and group-based systems is important, developments in technology have made it possible to combine individual and collaborative learning opportunities. What Figure 1.1 does not show is that many of the most important components of distance language learning deal with people and processes, i.e., the

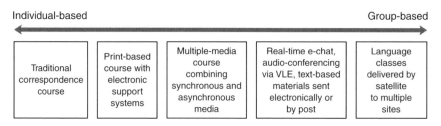

Individual-based   Group-based

| Traditional correspondence course | Print-based course with electronic support systems | Multiple-media course combining synchronous and asynchronous media | Real-time e-chat, audio-conferencing via VLE, text-based materials sent electronically or by post | Language classes delivered by satellite to multiple sites |

Figure 1.1 A spectrum of distance language learning contexts

participants and the means by which effective learning experiences are established on an individual basis within the distance context. This will be an important focus of much of the book.

1.3 Distance, place and time

The traditional model of education is that learning and teaching take place in close proximity, at a particular point in time. However, in distance education the focal point of learning is no longer the classroom but has shifted to the home, or the workplace, or a study context. Learning may take place according to each learner's schedule and in different time zones, or it may take place at set times. Distance can be seen in relation to the two dimensions of time and place. Figure 1.2 shows how particular combinations of time and place relate to different types of learning contexts.

Distance language courses may make use of the same place dimension in face-to-face tutorials or summer schools and through access to regional study centres. Most distance language learning, however, takes place in the different place dimension. It offers possibilities for synchronous learning, when opportunities are fixed at a point in time, and asynchronous learning, which can be accessed at any time.

	Same time	Different time
Same place	ST-SP (classroom teaching, face-to-face tutorials, workshops)	DT-SP (learning centre/ self-access centre)
Different place	ST-DP (synchronous distance learning)	DT-DP (asynchronous distance learning)

Figure 1.2 Combinations of time and place in learning contexts

1.3.1 Asynchronous learning

Asynchronous distance language learning involves learning opportunities that can be accessed at any time, and which make use of, for example, print, video, CD-ROM, e-mail and computer conference discussions. The advent of computer-mediated communication (CMC) has provided a range of possibilities for asynchronous communication, through e-mail, discussion lists, computer conferencing and bulletin boards. In distance language courses that make use of CMC, new opportunities for interaction with the teacher and with other learners counter the traditional and awkward isolation of distance language learners. CMC has also opened up possibilities for interacting with native speakers in tandem learning opportunities (see section 7.6). The advantage of asynchronous interaction is that learners can participate and respond at their convenience, there is time for thought and reflection between responses, and it is possible to revisit discussions at a later date. Lamy and Goodfellow (1999a: 45), referring to the Open University's Centre for Modern Languages, argue that:

> For the Open University's adult distance learners, the form of CMC which has so far proved the most accessible and appropriate to their varied circumstances of home-based learning is the asynchronous bulletin board system, or text-based computer conference . . . Typical of the kinds of interaction generated around these systems is a kind of 'slow motion' conversation in which messages and their responses may be separated by several days.

Asynchronous delivery offers flexibility to learners in that access to the course content or communication can take place at any time, and from different places. Voice mail, for example, has been used in language courses to provide students with listening and speaking practice. Rio Salado College in Arizona offers a distance Spanish course, and as part of this students call up the voice-mail 'kiosk' at least once a week. What they hear is a brief lesson, which prompts them to answer questions, using Spanish, about the lessons scheduled for the week. The responses of the students are recorded, and sent to the instructor's voice-mail box (Young 2000). Asynchronous systems have a number of other practical advantages, in that they are generally cost-effective for the institution and for the individual, and they are not confined to particular schedules or time zones.

1.3.2 Synchronous learning

Synchronous distance language learning uses technologies that allow for communication in 'realtime', for example by telephone or chat rooms.

The time and opportunity for learners to participate is controlled, which means of course that it is a less flexible option. Synchronous systems can be highly motivating in that distance learners feel less isolated and gain energy and inspiration from the learning group. Mason (1998a: 31) notes that this can be further enhanced by the fact that 'real-time inter-action with its opportunity to convey tone and nuance helps to develop group cohesion and the sense of being part of a learning community'. Thus synchronous interactions may feel more like a live conversation, and are more spontaneous. Feedback plays a very important role in dis-tance language learning, and synchronous systems permit immediate feedback by the teacher, as well as providing opportunities for the devel-opment of feedback within the learning group. One of the key challenges in distance language learning is the development of interactive compe-tence, particularly in realtime, and synchronous learning opportunities are important for this (see section 3.2).

However, not all learners respond equally well to the loss of flexibility that is part of synchronous distance learning. While some learners prefer the structure provided by the regular timing of synchronous delivery – to have the course delivered in regular sessions at fixed times and to have their learning paced in this way – others find it a very real limitation.

1.3.3 Multi-synchronous learning

Many distance education providers now combine synchronous and asyn-chronous forms of delivery in order to bring together the benefits of both forms of provision. The term *multi-synchronous* is used by Mason (1998b) to refer to the combination of both synchronous and asynchro-nous media with the aim of capitalising on the advantages of both systems.

This is the most common way in which different media are used in dis-tance language learning – to work together in a complementary fashion. One example is a satellite television Internet-based distance language programme called English Business Communication developed by Christine Uber Grosse (2001). The course brought together the follow-ing elements:

- interactive satellite television linking remote classes (synchronous);
- Internet-based web board for holding chats during office hours (syn-chronous), for posting and reviewing homework and for class announcements (asynchronous);
- e-mail for sending messages, homework and feedback on submitted work (asynchronous);
- face-to-face meetings held at the start of the course as part of an orien-tation week (synchronous).

One of the interesting and under-researched areas of distance language learning relates to the kinds of adjustments that occur as a course evolves with new groups of students, usually in response to the experiences of participants, pedagogical developments, and further refinements in technology. These often include fundamental decisions about the balance between synchronous vs asynchronous learning opportunities.

1.4 Definitions

There is no one definition of distance education. In fact there is no one term to define as the term *distance learning* is also well accepted and widely used. Distance education and distance learning are often used as synonyms or near synonyms in the field. In the European context, distance learning is generally perceived to be a more learner-centered term, and is also used here.

The series of definitions below indicate the range of approaches which have been used in defining these two key terms in the field, all of which emphasise distance – in space and/or time – between teacher and learner.

> The term *distance learning* and/or *distance education* refers to the teaching-learning arrangement in which the learner and teacher are separated by geography and time. (Williams, Paprock and Covington 1999: 2)

> *Distance education* is planned learning that normally occurs in a different place from teaching and as a result requires special techniques of course design, special instructional techniques, special methods of communication by electronic and other technology, as well as special organizational and administrative arrangements. (Moore and Kearsley 1996: 2)

> *Distance learning* is an educational system in which learners can study in a flexible manner in their own time, at the pace of their choice and without requiring face-to-face contact with a teacher. (Shelley 2000: 651)

> *Distance education* implies that the majority of educational communication between (among) teacher and student(s) occurs non-contiguously. Distance education must involve two-way communication between (among) teacher and student(s) for the purpose of facilitating and supporting the educational process. Distance education uses technology to mediate the necessary two-way communication. (Garrison and Archer 2000: 175)

There are several starting points for a definition of distance education; most begin with structural concerns, a few begin with pedagogical concerns, and fewer still begin with learner-based perspectives of the meaning of distance learning. When distance education is approached from the point of view of organisational or structural concerns, definitions generally include the following components, based on the work of Keegan (1990):

- *The separation of teacher and learner* in time and/or place.
- *The influence of an educational organisation* in preparing and delivering materials and in providing support services. This distinguishes distance learning from private study contexts, and learning using open courseware.
- *The use of a range of media* including print, audio, video, and computer-based applications to carry content.
- *The use of communication devices* to facilitate two-way communication. Providing opportunities for interaction is an important challenge, and these are increasingly viewed as integral to distance learning experiences.
- *The possibility of face-to-face contact* usually in the form of tutorials, regional courses, summer schools, and self-help groups. Face-to-face contact serves the function of providing motivation, social contact, group cohesion, and opportunities for support. In some language courses attendance may be mandatory.
- *The provision of a range of support services*, including what is given by the teacher, relating to wider aspects of study and the role of the distance learner. This may include opportunities for interaction and response to individual learners as well as guides such as the Open University UK Toolkit Series produced by Student Services to support distance study.

Richards and Roe (1994), in an introduction to distance learning in ELT, argue that a simple and deceptive conceptual trap in distance learning is to assume that it is the individual learner who is distant, or remote, from the centre of things. They offer the view that it is in fact the teacher who is remote from where the learning takes place. This perspective is important, and is implicit in the theoretical framework of distance language learning developed in Chapter 4.

An alternative approach to defining distance education comes when pedagogical concerns are taken as the starting point, at which point a different set of distinctive characteristics can be identified. According to Peters (1998) these include the extent to which 'written' teaching dominates in contrast to 'spoken' teaching; and so learning by 'reading' is stressed rather than learning through 'listening'. This has important implications for the development of oral and aural skills and interactive competence in distance language learning. In distance learning, pedagogic structures are formed using a range of technical and electronic media and different generations of provision can be identified. The way in which different pedagogical structures – such as those using CMC or Internet audioconferencing – impact on the development of target language (TL) skills is an important, and relatively unexplored, area for research in distance language learning. And the situation in which distance language learning takes place is quite different, in decisive ways, from that of learners in face-to-face settings. The impact of individual learning sites on the learning process has only been recognised more recently. A further point is that specific institutional and organisational conditions are required to provide and develop learning opportunities.

When learner perspectives are considered, the defining characteristics of distance language learning may be found to be markedly different from the perspectives adopted by researchers and theorists. The way in which language learners frame the process of distance learning is the major theme of Chapter 4, the learner–context interface.

1.5 Generations

In the twentieth, and now the twenty-first, century developments in technology have led to many new forms of distance learning (see Table 1.1).

Distance education can be seen as having evolved through a number of successive waves or generations, in response to developments in technology.

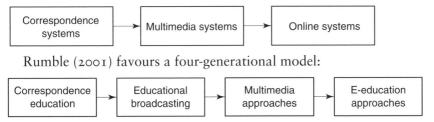

Rumble (2001) favours a four-generational model:

Successive generations have offered the potential for a progressive increase in learner control, opportunities for interaction, and in possibilities for learner choice. More recent models of distance language learning also offer a wider range of opportunities to communicate in the TL, with new possibilities for feedback and learner support. They also raise a number of problematic issues as practitioners attempt to integrate them into distance learning opportunities and these are discussed in later chapters. Here I discuss developments in terms of three generations.

Table 1.1. *Developments in technology available for language learning in distance education*

1940s	Educational radio
1950s	16mm film
1960s	Broadcast television (live and pre-taped)
1970s	Audiocassettes
1980s	Live satellite delivery (one-way video, two-way audio)
	Video compression (two-way video/face-to-face)
	Videocassettes
1990s	Computer-based education (asynchronous)
	Interactive multimedia
	Multimedia conferencing
	CD-ROM
	The Internet
	The WWW
	Web-based video, audio, multimedia
2000–	Broadband technology
	Wireless access

1.5.1 First generation course models

In the *first generation* distance educators used print to carry the educational content to the learners. Interaction between teacher and learners was 'one-way' – usually by post – with a time lag between mailing and response. This print-based model of correspondence learning was the predominant mode of delivery up to the 1960s. Few distance language courses were offered at this stage since it was felt that the context did not support opportunities to develop skills in speaking and listening.

1.5.2 Second generation course models

The impetus for the *second generation* course model came with the incorporation of television into the distance learning environment to supplement print-based sources. The establishment of the Open University UK in 1969 was the first time that a range of media had been used for distance education, even though the dominant medium was still print. In some contexts the telephone was also used to link either individual learners, or remote classrooms, with the teacher. It was at this point that the offering of language courses through the distance mode became a more feasible undertaking: first audiocassettes, and then videocassettes became important components in courses. The second generation is usually characterised as an approach to distance education in which print is combined with broadcast media and cassettes.

1.5.3 Third generation course models

The *third generation* of distance education uses information and communications technology as its basis, and it is these developments which have made interactive distance language learning possible. An early example was a Spanish course offered by Syracuse Language Systems which combined some of the features of third generation distance learning with computer-assisted language learning (Rothenberg 1998). Students used a CD-ROM 'multimedia textbook' supplemented by access to World Wide Web resources. They communicated with the instructors and native speakers via e-mail.

The continuing debate about what constitutes third generation distance education has emphasised the importance of the distinction between technology for distribution purposes and its uses for an interactive exchange between the teacher and learners and between the learners themselves (see Figure 1.3). This distinction is important since an ongoing concern for distance language teachers has been how to improve interactive opportunities for learners, whereas requirements relating to distribution have been met fairly satisfactorily by existing course models.

The opportunities for interaction offered by the emergence of computer-mediated communication (CMC) are central to the third generation model of distance language learning. The hallmark of this model is greater and enhanced communication opportunities between the teacher and learners, and between the learners themselves, either individually or in groups. Within distance language learning a number of third generation course models have been trialled, either as separate from or in conjunction with existing course models. An important body of research comes from the FLUENT Project (Framework for Language Use in Environments embedded in New Technologies) developed by the Open University UK. The project aims to support learners in their development

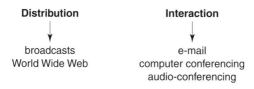

Figure 1.3 Examples of use of technology for distribution vs interaction

of oral and aural competence (Kötter 2001), and involves the development of a virtual learning environment for learners of French and German. The environment is based on voice-over Internet conferencing (where Internet voice technology allows students to communicate verbally in realtime), e-mail and a dedicated project website which is updated weekly (Shield, Hauck and Kötter 2000). Kötter (2001) identifies a number of issues that need further research before the virtual learning environment can be used in mainstream distance language course provision. These will be discussed in later chapters and include:

- the optimal use of tutors' and students' time;
- addressing drop-out relating to technical problems;
- error correction and feedback;
- support for less advanced learners.

All three generations remain in use in different forms of provision around the world. In practice, elements of all three generations are often combined, even within courses which are delivered predominantly online.

1.6 The landscape

An understanding of the landscape of distance language learning can be gained by reviewing commentaries within the field and by looking at providers who have contributed to the development of research and practice in the international context. Both these approaches are taken here.

1.6.1 Perspectives

In 2000 *TESOL Quarterly* published a special issue on TESOL in the twenty-first century. Included in that collection were articles on changes in the global economy and English language teaching (Warschauer 2000) and on the language of computer-mediated communication (Murray 2000). Both included a section devoted to discussion of distance education, and the perspectives they present on key features of the landscape of distance language learning are reviewed here.

Warschauer (2000) places analysis of distance education within a wider discussion of new information technologies in English language teaching. He sees the growth in distance learning opportunities as part of the desire to reach new markets, which in turn is related to the commercialisation of higher education. Of concern is that the expansion of learning opportunities may be motivated by a desire to achieve economies of scale. Warschauer (2000) and Warschauer, Shetzer and Meloni (2000) suggest a number of potential dangers in these developments:

- high quality distance learning opportunities require significant amounts of personal interaction which are expensive to set up and maintain;
- providers may be under pressure to reduce teacher–student interaction, which requires significant resources, and to place more emphasis on individual access to pre-packaged materials;
- administrators may seek intellectual property rights for materials and courses produced by teachers to reuse them in distance programmes;
- as the development of distance programmes may be separated from the delivery of learning opportunities, staff may be employed on part-time, temporary contracts which can have long-term effects on their professional status and standing.

Warschauer (2000: 527) sees distance education as a realm in which the role of technology will be a 'site of struggle' in increasing or lowering the quality of learning opportunities, which could also bring to a head issues about the professional standing of educators within the field of distance learning. The way in which distance language learning will develop remains very much an open question. Warschauer *et al.* (2000: 76) comment that in theory the power of computers and the Internet can allow distance education programmes to be more flexible, interactive and fast-paced, but whether this will prove to be true in practice remains to be seen.

Murray (2000) takes a slightly different perspective in her overview of distance education, beginning with a description of the historical context in which distance learning and teaching evolved. The status of distance education has changed dramatically from what Murray (p. 414) calls the 'traditional stepchild of most educational systems' to become the focus of popular attention in the past two decades. This shift in the positioning of distance education is accompanied by the development of new audiences for distance learning, who are keen to take advantage of the flexibility which comes from the anytime, anywhere functionality of computer-based distance learning. A concern associated with this is that the expanded educational opportunities may not in fact reach the many audiences who do not have access to computers. Murray (p. 415) raises questions about the value of CMC in distance learning and argues that there is little research 'that critically examines either the effectiveness of instruction or the nature of human communication via CMC'. Much has been written about the promise and peril of virtual universities, but little attention has been paid to how learners engage in asynchronous CMC in distance language learning. This question is particularly important because of the significant amount of research in second language teaching devoted to the ways in which teacher–student and student–student interaction facilitates language acquisition. Murray argues that research and discussion on CMC in distance language learning should focus on the outcomes of interaction, rather than on the technology itself.

A scan of the landscape also reveals the diversity in the practice of distance language learning on different continents. In the last decade research and documented accounts of distance language learning opportunities have come from Italy (Cusinato 1996), Finland (Tammelin 1997, 1998, 1999), Thailand (Vanijdee 2001, 2003), Korea (Dickey 2001), Hong Kong (Hyland 2001; Leung 1999), Australia (Möllering 2000) and New Zealand (White 1997, 2000; Garing 2002). Some of these accounts relate to small-scale trials with fewer than ten students; others concern large-scale programmes that have evolved over many years with up to 5,000 learners in a single course. Here I focus on just two providers of distance language learning programmes: the Open University UK, and the Adult Migrant English Program, Australia – both of which have developed a significant body of research and contributed to practice and theory-building within the field.

1.6.2 Providers

The Open University UK

The Open University UK is one of the largest providers of distance language learning opportunities in the world. Each year approximately 8,000 language learners located in the UK and mainland Europe enrol in the distance courses which are offered in French, Spanish and German. It is interesting that while the OUUK has been established for over 30 years it was only in 1995 that the first language course – in French – was offered. The relatively late entry into distance language learning and teaching meant that course developers and tutors were able to draw on the expertise and quality practices which had been developed within the OUUK for course delivery and learner support. The model of distance learning for language learners at the OUUK includes some of the features of traditional methods of delivery; learners are provided with course books, video and audio documentaries, audio activity cassettes, and transcripts of video- and audiocassettes. In addition they are entitled to up to 21 hours of face-to-face tuition at study centres, and students of second- and third-level courses are expected to attend a one-week summer school (Kötter 2001).

The OUUK has been concerned to find ways to improve the learning opportunities which can be made available to distance language learners, and has established a number of important research directions. One of the ongoing issues is that while materials are comprehensive, the amount of synchronous interaction in which learners can participate is very low. Since the delivery of the first French course there have been a number of investigations into opportunities for students to develop their interactive spoken and written competences in home-based environments. Pilot studies include telephone-based audioconferencing, Internet-based audioconferencing, synchronous text chat and audiographics. Shield (2000) observes that the importance learners place on being able to communicate with others on the same course and to participate in events that allow them to share their experiences with other distance learners has been evident in the pilot studies. She adds that the aim is to use ICT to provide learners with a forum in which they can socialise with other learners and overcome a sense of isolation, and also participate in learning activities which allow them to use previously learned vocabulary and structures. The challenge is to match these new learning opportunities with the needs, dispositions and resources of learners who enter distance language courses. A further challenge is to integrate them successfully with established forms of provision.

Other areas of research developed by the Department of Modern Languages at the OUUK include learner autonomy (e.g. Hurd, Beaven and Ortega 2001), changing roles of teachers and learners in online environments (Hauck and Haezewindt 1999), and the development of reflective interaction in online environments (e.g. Lamy and Goodfellow, 1999a, 1999b; Lamy and Hassan 2003). In the writings on distance language learning from the OUUK, the need to find further ways of supporting home-based language learners and developing opportunities for critical reflection and learner–learner interaction are very much to the fore. This overview has been relatively short since I make quite detailed reference to the OUUK distance language learning context in later chapters.

Reflections and experiences

Distance learners of languages at the OUUK

Monica Shelley is a Germanist who has been involved in distance education at the Open University in the UK for nearly twenty-five years. She worked on the production of language courses when the programme began at the OU some years ago. She now works in the Institute of Educational Technology at the OU, and carries out surveys of students on the different language courses.

'What have you learned from your interactions with students about the realities of a distance context for language learning?'

> *Students of languages at the Open University, who are all adults, are generally well motivated and enjoy their courses. For the majority, study at a distance is the only option, often because they are working full or part time, because of lack of local resources or their domestic situation. While this is particularly problematic where learning to communicate a language is concerned – and many often complain about the lack of opportunities for conversation – there are positive aspects such as the flexibility of time and pace possible when studying on one's own, and the availability of high-quality, up-to-date materials and technologies to support learning. Students' contact with the university is based on the course materials provided and feedback on their assignments, plus the opportunity to attend tutorials from time to time, and (in some cases) residential schools. A recent development is the availability of an online tuition system using synchronous voice-over-Internet conferencing and visual workspace tools. Distance learners of languages at the OU bring a wide range of skills and experience to their language study. They often know far more about the country and culture of the target language than school-age or mainstream university students, and have, in many cases, developed language learning skills on the basis of school learning or life experience.*
>
> Monica Shelley, Institute of Educational Technology,
> Open University UK

The Adult Migrant English Program, Australia

The issue of access to English language classes for adult migrant learners within Australia was the catalyst for the development of It's Over To You, a distance language course based thematically around topics relevant to migrant settlement. The course has been offered in various formats since the 1980s and is an important option for adults within the Adult Migrant English Program (AMEP). It aims to ensure that students who cannot attend face-to-face classes – either because of geographical distance, family and work commitments, or cultural factors – do not miss out on opportunities to develop language skills as part of the settlement process. As part of this, emphasis has been placed on the need for distance programmes to provide efficient communication between the teacher and learners, between learners and the TL community and, ideally, opportunities for contact between learners.

Much of the emphasis in the distance AMEP programme is on encouraging learners to interact in the host society, and reflects a task-based and learner-centred approach to language learning. It aims to create opportunities for learners to make their own choices about their learning goals, building on increased awareness of what is communicatively relevant to their own learning and working conditions (Candlin and Byrnes 1995). It's Over To You has now been published by the National Centre for English Language Teaching and Research (NCELTR) Australia, and consists of books, video- and audiocassettes. Additional support materials are available in a variety of languages. An e-learning course is being developed to complement the current programme.

The reports and publications relating to It's Over To You are quite extensive and present accounts from teachers and learners, as well as details about factors that provided the impetus for further developments and revisions. These include the kinds of support required by students (Kopij 1989), student attrition (Harris 1995), the evaluation of technology (audioconferences, audiographics, videoconferences) for enhancing delivery and content of courses (Anderton and Nicholson 1995), and the ways in which an open learning philosophy can usefully inform the provision of distance language learning opportunities offered in the TL country (Candlin and Byrnes 1995). This is an important set of studies because it traces the onset and development of a programme, its character, how it functions and how the experiences of learners and teachers contribute to course development.

1.7 New challenges

Language teaching methodologies have developed largely around the model of synchronous communication – that is, the teacher and the learner(s) working together in the same place, at the same time. This is because of the need to facilitate interaction, to provide feedback, to answer questions and to make adjustments that fit the needs of learners.

Important aspects of the language learning experience are changed within the distance context, and these changes present new challenges for learners. Important limitations of the distance learning context include reduced opportunities for immediate support, guidance, interactivity, feedback and incidental learning. Essentially there is a much greater onus on learners to manage themselves and the learning context.

1.7.1 Immediate demands

When students first begin working in a distance language learning environment, there is a need to respond to a number of new conditions which become evident very quickly. These include:

- isolation, due to the lack of social contact with peers;
- lack of access to regular classroom interactions that can structure and support the learning process – through, for example, providing an occasion to clarify expectations, to gain real-time feedback and to correct misconceptions;
- facing up to problems with motivation and self-discipline;
- fewer opportunities to share perceptions through informal contacts, and for incidental learning;
- experiencing frustration due to hitches, or delays, or when encountering problems with the materials or course delivery;
- the need for effective time management;
- the need to resolve competing demands from study, family, social and professional contexts.

More complex challenges relate to the kinds of roles learners must assume and to the kinds of understandings they develop in relation to the process of distance language learning.

1.7.2 Absence of teacher mediation

Within the distance learning context, the language learner is faced with the task of internalising and gaining control of the language without the same degree of input, interaction, and support provided by conventional face-to-face classes. In the absence of a classroom environment with regular, paced directives from the instructor, distance learners have to establish their own set of learning behaviours. They also need to shape and manage the course of their learning. The teacher is not there to mediate learner interactions with TL sources, and cannot readily adjust these sources based on any perceived response of the learners. Distance learners must also develop the ability to match their learning objectives with the learning sources available in the context, including materials, peers and teachers. Doughty and Long (2002) sum up this aspect of the distance language learning environment as follows:

> . . . the classroom teacher – who is, as noted above, (a) ordinarily the most reliable source on local circumstance, (b) the one who can best make decisions as a lesson unfolds, and (c) a major source of native L2 input and feedback on error – is now removed in space and time from the learners, who may, in turn, be removed from one another.

The absence of real-time face-to-face interaction – and the range of functions it fulfils – is central to the challenges of language learning at a distance.

1.7.3 Awareness and self-management

Prior experiences of conventional classroom learning do not automatically equip distance learners with the skills and self-knowledge required to tackle the new demands of the distance language learning context. They must regulate and oversee the rate and direction of their learning to a much greater degree than classroom learners whose learning is organised by regular classroom sessions. They must also give attention to establishing their own set of learning behaviours and to shaping and managing the course of their learning.

Faced with the demands and opportunities of a self-instruction context, distance learners are compelled to re-evaluate their role and responsibilities as language learners. To succeed in learning the TL, they will need to be more self-directed than in previous language learning experiences, which involves first and foremost developing an awareness of the process of language learning, and of themselves as learners, and an understanding of the need to devise their own means of learning and of managing their learning. Exactly how learners manage to do this will be explored from different perspectives through this book.

1.7.4 Border crossing and the new technologies

A wide variety of learning opportunities are now available for distance courses, which allow learners further choices about where, when and how they learn. While the new learning environments offer more enriched learning opportunities, they also place further demands on learners. The advent of CMC – where available – has had a major impact on the traditional approach to the design of distance education instruction, since it increases the potential for interaction and collaborative work among learners, which was difficult with previous forms of distance language learning. However, the response of learners to these opportunities has proved more complex than imagined, particularly in relation to participation in interactive online learning environments. CMC requires more self-direction, initiative and motivation on the part of participants than elements within more traditional learning spaces. Working within technology-mediated distance language learning contexts requires special, and often new, skills on the part of learners. These learners need to make their own internal adjustments to what is a new context for language learning, while also learning to use the new technologies.

Distance language learning, therefore, is not an easy option. But for many students it is an important means of gaining access to language learning programmes. Having embarked on a more demanding route, there are important benefits reported by learners. Meeting the challenges associated with distance language learning develops their skills in language learning, develops knowledge of themselves as language learners, makes them more engaged as language learners, and more ready to take advantage of other language learning opportunities.

Reflections and experiences

Challenges and opportunities

Elisabeth Cunningham has been involved with the distance teaching of Japanese in Australia for nearly a decade. The strategies used by distance language learners to develop listening and speaking skills were the subject of her MA thesis (Cunningham 1994). Currently she works within the OPAL Japanese distance language programme at La Trobe University.

'What do you see as the main challenges and opportunities in language learning through distance education?'

While distance education language courses can be an excellent alternative to regular, campus-based courses, I always advise prospective students that they should enrol in a regular course if at all possible. DE courses may be appealing because of different presentation, use of technology and flexibility of study time, but the lack of regular face-to-face practice opportunities, particularly in developing conversational skills, is a disadvantage of which students must be made aware. In my experience, DE students tend to develop their writing and particularly reading skills more than oral and aural skills, in comparison to campus-based students. However, the use of CD-ROMs rather than cassette tapes for aural input, and the active encouragement of working with student peers for speaking practice, seems to be very useful in the development of these skills.

I find that I become much closer to my students on a personal level in DE courses than in campus-based courses. I think it is vital to spend time apart from the requirements of the course in getting to know the students, encouraging them every step of the way, and reminding them that we are available to help them. DE teachers must provide a high level of pastoral care.

Elisabeth Cunningham, Department of Asian Studies,
La Trobe University, Australia

While the distance context places a number of what may be new demands for self-direction on language learners, it also presents some exciting prospects. For example, distance learners generally have more opportunities than they would in a teacher-directed classroom to choose what and how they learn. They also have more freedom to determine the kinds and combinations of tasks they work on and to ignore activities or sections of the materials that they do not consider to be personally useful for the development of their TL skills. The particular relationship and tension between demands and opportunities as seen by learners is explored further in later chapters.

For teachers, explicitly recognising and understanding the new demands in the distance learning environment and the skills required is important. If learners understand that they need a range of new skills to work within the distance learning context, and they are supported in acquiring them, resistance can be minimised. And, of course, teachers themselves are challenged to develop many new skills and understandings within a distance learning–teaching context.

1.8 Summary

The idea of distance language learning is realised in a range of highly diverse contexts and systems that stem from different underlying philosophies about the nature of distance education and of language teaching. Traditional distance language learning contexts have mostly been conducted as independent learning experiences, using print, audio, video and broadcast media. Other traditions are group-based, particularly those using satellite transmission, and audio- and videoconferencing. Emerging contexts provide the possibility of a transformed model of distance language learning that allows for communication, interaction and collaboration among participants. Two key dimensions along which distance language learning opportunities vary are place and time – and these exist as group vs individual opportunities, and synchronous vs asynchronous opportunities. Numerous definitions of distance learning and distance education exist, which mostly reflect structural considerations. Having considered more technical approaches to understanding distance education – including a focus on different generations of technology – the final part of the chapter has considered current perspectives on the landscape of distance language learning, and particular challenges associated with learning languages at a distance.

2 Related concepts

2.1 Introduction

Self-access has occupied an important position in language learning for some two decades, along with independent learning centres, self-directed learning centres, learning resource centres, and other resource-based approaches to language learning. They represent, however, more than a collection of materials, a point that Gardner and Miller (1999) emphasise in their definition of self-access as an environment for learning involving resources, teachers, learners and the systems within which they are organised. Distance language learning has some similarities with resource-based approaches to language learning, but also differs significantly from self-access learning. Distance language learning opportunities are not usually fixed in a particular physical location, and they are based around a course of study, with a cohort of learners. Interaction with teachers and learners is mediated by some form of technology, and there is an increasing emphasis on communication and collaborative learning opportunities.

A number of other, related learning systems have emerged alongside distance learning, including online learning, distributed learning, asynchronous learning networks (ALNs), telematics and open learning. These are the subject of this chapter. Some are in general use; others have come to prominence in particular countries. The proliferation of terms is a reflection of a growing and diverse variety of learning systems and of different interest groups and trends within diverse contexts of practice. It is important to acknowledge that many of these terms are used loosely and that the boundaries between them may be hard to establish. Certainly they begin to blur when applied to actual contexts of practice: what Harland *et al.* (1997) refer to as an open learning context for a course in Portuguese in Glasgow University, for example, would most certainly be called distributed learning in the US (a concept explored in section 2.3).

In this chapter I am concerned less with marking out boundaries in any absolute sense, and more with giving a sense of the ways in which language learning and teaching is organised and practised in different systems and of the philosophies that underpin them. Lifelong learning and the Open Courseware movement are discussed here as they highlight and intersect with particular aspects of distance learning. The development of new learning systems and movements also impact on distance language learning in what is a dramatically expanding and changing field. As part of these changes, language teachers may be faced with the task of migrating a face-to-face course to distance or online mode. An example of this process, together with an analysis of the attendant issues, is discussed at the end of the chapter.

2.2 Online learning

Strictly speaking, 'online' implies a live connection to a remote computer. The term *online learning* has emerged more specifically to refer to an approach to teaching and learning that includes the use of Internet technologies for learning and teaching. Learners use the online learning environments not only to access information and course content but also to interact and collaborate with other online participants within the course. The rapid intensification in online delivery has led to the development of a growing array of software systems that combine the functions of delivering web-based course materials with support for other functions needed for the delivery of courses online (Inglis 2001) – mostly interactive, administrative and support functions. They may be used by language teachers to create virtual learning environments. WebCT, referred to below, is one such example; others include Blackboard and FirstClass and are discussed in more detail in Chapter 10.

Here I will discuss two distinct manifestations of online language learning: as an option within a traditional distance language learning programme, and as cyberschools, or 'virtual' language schools.

2.2.1 Online options within distance language learning

Online learning is often used to refer to the delivery of a distance course using online components rather than more traditional methods of delivery, as in Example 1, given by the University of Alberta, Canada.

Example 1

Distance language learning: traditional vs online options

The University of Alberta delivers language courses using two options: the correspondence or traditional method and the online

---

method, also called the enhanced method. They are described to prospective students as follows:

Correspondence method The correspondence method is the traditional method of delivery for this course; it comprises printed course material, in-person seminars, and submitted written work.

Online method The online method is a combination of printed course material, in-person seminars, and participation in online class discussions. The online components are delivered using WebCT (Web-Based Course Tools software) accessed through the Internet. An online discussion, or computer conference, is similar to a classroom discussion. However, there are two major differences: you can participate at a time convenient for you, and you can re-visit the discussion as many times as you wish.

Including online learning components as an option within a distance course is common in the provision of distance language learning opportunities. The descriptors provided by the University of Alberta reflect several other aspects of the way online learning is used for large groups of learners within distance education delivery: the combination of online components with more traditional elements of delivery (such as printed materials), the emphasis on time-independent access, discussion in a text format, and fluid participation patterns.

2.2.2 Online learning in cyberschools

A number of online language schools have been developed, which are available to a global audience. They are also known as cyberschools or 'virtual' language schools, with names such as English Connection, English Online, Cyberlanguages, English by E-mail, and NetLearn Languages. Smith and Salam (2000) evaluated a number of online language schools and identified a common set of characteristics, included as Example 2.

Example 2

Online learning in cyberschools

In a review of online language schools Smith and Salam (2000) note that the following kinds of features are evolving among online language schools or cyberschools:

- The typical school offers a number of specialised courses, ranging from basic English through to English for Specific Purposes and TOEFL preparation.

- Students can work on a number of web pages containing embedded scripts that consist of exercises in grammar, vocabulary and reading, and on listening comprehension exercises using RealAudio (software that makes it possible to play radio and sound files over the Internet).

- For a fee, students can also submit written work by e-mail to a teacher who will e-mail it back with feedback on their writing.

- The school will have a chatroom where students can communicate to each other in English.

- If the school offers access to teachers that consists of more than simple marking of assignments, the school will work within specific 'terms' that may be four or eight weeks in length, and provide students with a number of 'assignments' that have to be completed and submitted by e-mail.

- The more adventurous schools will also offer 'classes' using Microsoft's NetMeeting software and student video cameras.

Smith and Salam note that there are a number of problems inherent in the uses of technology for online learning, which may work against the successful uptake of cyberschools:

1. Level of computer skills

Students who enter cyberschools need a particular level of computer literacy, if they are to benefit from the resources and opportunities that are available. Smith and Salam argue that 'if the concept of the cyberschool is that students can work on improving their English on their own, and at whatever time they like, it is crucial that they are able to operate the equipment without having to call on help each time they wish to use it'. For some language students, working within cyberschools will be a steep learning curve, while more technically advanced students may become frustrated if they perceive the features of the course to be less than cutting edge.

2. Motivation

Motivation is a central issue in distance language learning, particularly that of maintaining the level of motivation learners generally show when they enter a course. Smith and Salam note that motivation becomes an even more complex issue for students working in isolation in a cyber-school, especially if there are no external deadlines for them to work to or a framework that helps them to gauge their progress and guide them to the next stage.

3. Timing

Timing is an important issue in the global classroom, in terms of course dates and synchronous learning opportunities. The first point made by Smith and Salam is that as the timing of academic terms varies around the world, it is impossible to establish the dates and duration for an online language course which will suit all audiences. Timing is even more complex when online language schools include synchronous learning opportunities. Videoconferencing classes, for example, are dependent on having a number of students sitting in front of video cameras linked to their computers at a specific time. Raskin (2001) encountered this diffi-culty when delivering a writing course for a commercial website Englishtown. She offered three chat times throughout the day so stu-dents in all time zones could attend. This solution may not always be feasible in terms of resourcing, and is quite demanding in terms of staff time.

Smith and Salam conclude that the development of online language schools is still in its infancy and that only when they begin to teach to internationally recognised standards, such as the Cambridge Certificate, TOEFL and IELTS, will they make the necessary gains in credibility and become viable. A recent example is a course called IELTS Writing Online, delivered entirely online, which consists of an introduction to academic writing, graded activities, writing tasks, and feedback and support from a personal tutor (Ayers and Brown 2002).

Many new challenges arise for language teachers and learners within online environments. These relate to new forms of interaction and par-ticipation, maintaining motivation and optimal use of learning time. Jegede (2000) argues that consideration should also be given to the various borders learners need to cross in undertaking distance and online learning, and that relatively little attention is given to their socio-cultural environments, which may mediate or inhibit learning. As online learning is increasingly used as the vehicle for the global expansion of offerings to diverse populations in international settings, there is an urgent need to understand how different cultural influences affect the experience of learners in global online language learning environments. Technological developments have overtaken our under-standing of the concerns and issues they raise within online learning and teaching environments. A number of these issues will be discussed further in the next chapter.

2.3 Distributed learning

In recent years *distributed learning* has emerged as a dominant term within the North American context. It is part of a trend to use a mix of delivery modes to complement face-to-face classroom learning opportunities. Part of this mix usually includes the use of multimedia learning opportunities and participation in online discussions, as well as working with print-based sources.

Radic (2001), who taught a course in Italian in both face-to-face mode, and by distance, identifies distributed learning as an important third option. He describes it as the 'middle ground' between the traditional classroom and the 'virtual learning space'. The proposal he develops for a distributed language course in Italian is included as Example 3.

Example 3

Distributed language learning

In a proposal for a distributed language course in Italian, Radic (2001) identifies the following features. The course would require students to come to class for two sessions weekly, to complete real-time communicative listening and speaking tasks. Three further lessons would be delivered each week on multimedia CD-ROM including audio and video files of authentic language use, grammar exercises, communicative listening and writing tasks. In addition, students would be required to take part in online asynchronous tutorials. A course web page would feature links with resources as well as offering possibilities for communication and interaction with Italian native speakers and students of Italian worldwide. Radic describes the learning environment as flexible, multimedia and web-enhanced with opportunities to engage in real-time, face-to-face communication as well as to participate asynchronously in online tutorials.

An advantage of distributed learning is that students have the opportunity to become familiar with the distributed elements of the course in face-to-face settings where they have immediate access to the support of the teacher. Opportunities for interaction in face-to-face classes can also serve the valuable function of developing a sense of community and belonging among participants, which is a major challenge in many distance learning environments. Once the course is well under way, face-to-face classes may be reduced – from, say, three hours a week to two – as learners become familiar with the other distributed elements of the course. However, the teacher is still available on a regular basis, both online and in the weekly classes, to respond to learners' needs as they arise.

A key impetus for the development and use of the term *distributed learning* is to differentiate it from distance learning practices:

> Distributed learning is not synonymous with distance learning. Distributed learning uses IT, both synchronous and asynchronous, to deliver education at flexible times and locations. It has a role at traditional, residential campuses as well as at large, open universities that provide distance education . . . [it] can provide a mechanism to extend class interactions to seven days a week, twenty-four hours a day.
>
> (Oblinger 1999: 1)

Inglis (2001: 89) argues that in order to understand the significance of distributed learning it is necessary to remember that 'in the North American context the term "distance education" generally refers to a remote classroom mode of delivery mediated by audio or video conferencing'. This distinction is less important in countries outside North America because the term 'distance education' is not used in such a narrow sense, and encompasses many of the elements of distributed learning. The main benefit of distributed learning systems is that they are flexible and can provide interactive learning opportunities that extend those offered in face-to-face classes.

2.4 Asynchronous learning networks

Proponents of *asynchronous learning networks (ALNs)* have pointed to the limitations of learning environments based around the provision of multimedia software with no teacher or learning group. Instead they emphasise the development and use of group networks established by learners and teachers. The other defining feature of ALNs is the emphasis on asynchronous elements, which do not require learners to synchronise their schedule with anyone else or any other event.

The ALN language programme described in Example 4 was developed, according to Almeda and Rose (2000), to reach students in their own contexts and to provide access to a learning community that can be accessed any time, any place.

Example 4

ALNs for language learning

The University of California Extension offers an English as a Second Language course within its ALN program. The course is delivered asynchronously on a rolling-enrolment basis, and students have up to six months to complete. The primary objectives of the ALN format for the course are communication, interaction and access to resources. Course materials include an online syllabus, and links to study resources. Other materials are posted to students when they enrol. The course itself requires individual study, one-to-one interaction with the course instructor, and online contact with other students, including group activities online. Students submit course assignments to the instructor and participate in class discussion on the course message board. Online interactions and discussions are graded and comprise part of the student's final course grade.

(Almeda and Rose 2000)

A number of features of ALNs are attractive for language learning: the emphasis on learning networks with a teacher and cohort-base, the combination of self-study with opportunities for asynchronous interaction, and the flexible learning environments. Of course the different elements associated with ALNs are not uncommon as part of a distance language course, but the emphasis on the dual features of asynchronicity and learning networks are particular to ALNs. The key ingredient, therefore, of an ALN is this capacity for learners to learn any time, anywhere, and yet to be part of a community of learners.

The teachers at UC Extension who worked within the English language programme raised a number of important issues about language teaching in an ALN format. They were used to face-to-face settings for language teaching and noted a number of changes in their roles: the need to provide lots of motivation for students, the amount of writing they needed to do to engage students appropriately, and the additional amount of time needed for teaching online. Given the emphasis on communication and interaction, an important strategy reported by teachers in the ALN programme was to encourage students to bond with each other so the class felt more like a community, and less like a private tutoring session. Teachers liked the closer and more intense dialogue with students, and judged that those who participated really 'stretched themselves'. More negative features or concerns included frustration with not being able to see students, the added instructional time required, lack of participation, and students' expectations for fast responses. The lack of face-to-face interaction emerged as the most pervasive theme of concern among instructors, and was judged to be the key obstacle to more widespread adoption of ALN for language learning and teaching. Teachers also felt there was a need to develop a stronger network of support and training for themselves. In response to this an instructor website was in the process of development, which would be a resource centre and also 'a kind of faculty club where instructors can meet to share ideas about ALN' (Almeda and Rose 2000).

2.5 Telematics

The term *telematics* is used in the Netherlands and several other European countries (Collis and Moonen 2001; De Kline 1999) to refer to the application of information and communications technology for particular purposes. The technologies that are currently used in European educational telematics settings are also used in many of the other systems we have referred to earlier:

- audioconferencing;
- videoconferencing;
- chat;
- screen sharing;
- e-mail;
- video-mail or audio-mail;
- news groups;
- bulletin board systems (BBS);
- computer conferencing.

Example 5

Telematics-mediated language learning

Maija Tammelin developed a telematics-mediated English language learning environment for an Environmental Communication course that aimed to integrate the learning of subject matter with the practice of communication and argumentation skills in English (Tammelin 1999). Students were in two groups some 250 kilometres apart – one group at Helsinki School of Economics and Business Administration, the other at the University of Technology in Lappeenranta. They communicated via computer conferencing, e-mail and videoconfer-

---

encing. The main meeting place for participants was the online classroom on the World Wide Web – which included access to course information, course material, writing tools, links to websites and completed course projects. A café conference was available for students for informal interaction. Another section was used for the discussion forums where students and tutors developed understanding of the topics. The two groups had face-to-face sessions with their respective tutors and three videoconferences were held between the two groups. A videotaped recording of the conference was analysed by students who then wrote a report on the conference, and on their own performance within it.

The description given in Example 5 is similar to that of other technology-mediated distance language courses. However, in the European context, what is distinctive about telematics is the broad application of the term: it is not limited to the educational arena. The discussion and critical debate about telematics brings together a range of socially oriented concerns about the use of technology, which could include reference to tele-working, global markets and the interrelatedness of the issues of employment and education, for example.

Something of the flavour of the debate surrounding telematics can be gained from looking at issues relating to the division between production and delivery of products, as for example in distance language learning. One of the major consequences of the telematics revolution is that a number of services can be provided from a location that is distant from the market (Mitter and Bastos 1999). This brings both challenges and opportunities for the educational sector. The nature of educational provision has changed in response to telematics, and a number of European commentators have commented critically on this, in relation to such issues as outsourcing. There is a concern that a number of negative scenarios within the telematics revolution will become a reality within Europe and the developing world. In particular, the need for correct assessment of markets, the appropriate use of technology and close interaction between providers and learners are underlined. These issues in relation to distance language learning are recurrent themes throughout the book.

2.6 Open learning

Candlin and Byrnes (1995) present a comprehensive discussion of the distinction between distance learning and open learning. They are concerned to identify the range of issues facing a move from a more conventional distance language programme to one focused on an open learning philosophy. As part of this they argue that the distance learning of languages has a traditional dissemination model of education at its base. Even though learners may be physically separate from teachers, they argue that the conduit metaphor still holds. A key challenge for a distance language course, according to Candlin and Byrnes, is to facilitate language learning as a personally meaningful activity in the distance context. The approach they adopt is based on an open curriculum for language learners, which involves identifying learning experiences and using the TL within the community, according to their contexts and needs.

Open learning has often been associated with highly innovative projects within existing teaching institutions, many of which have been developed on a trial basis, and which attempt to influence more conventional teaching–learning contexts. In Australia the Adult Migrant English Program (AMEP) distance learning course It's Over to You, is grounded in the learner-centred principle of open learning and aims to offer a language learning experience equal in quality to classroom experience for a group of learners faced with a range of settlement issues and with no access to ESOL provision. Candlin and Byrnes (p. 8) note that the AMEP developed through several stages, reflecting 'something of the movement from the delivery-focussed perspective of distance learning towards the more negotiative and learner/learning focussed philosophy of open learning'. They argue that real understanding emerges when learners try to do something on their own – and in line with that the AMEP course encourages learners who are resident in TL communities to engage with resources in the community, to set their own learning goals and to assess their progress towards these goals.

A number of principles underpin open learning: optimising or extending learner choice, focusing on the needs of individual learners, not the interests of the teacher or institution, and the gradual diffusion of decision-making to learners. But however desirable these are seen to be, they are more difficult to realise in practice. Open learning is less of a technique and more of an educational approach, which differs quite widely in its practices according to the contexts in which it occurs. Bruce King, writing from the Australian experience, emphasises this point:

> What is key to our understanding of open learning, however, is the acknowledgement that it is not a distinctive form of educational delivery but the assertion of certain value positions in relation to education that are primarily student centered in their orientation.
>
> (King 2001: 59)

Open learning is embedded in concerns about social equity, especially in relation to those groups previously under-represented in education.

Consequently the notion of open access is important, and one way to help achieve this is explored in Example 6.

Example 6

Open language learning

MiraCosta College, San Diego developed an open entry course for ESL students based around the Crossroads Café video series. A key feature of the course was to provide flexible learning opportunities which included possibilities for interacting with an instructor. The course is based around the 26 half-hour videos and associated work-texts and photo-based materials. New learners are able to go to the drop-in learning center at any time during programme hours to receive an orientation to the program, to receive instructional assistance or to check out new videos. When the center is not busy they are able to receive one-to-one help. The atmosphere at the center is informal: people are able to bring their children along, and spend time talking with other learners. The development of individual support networks is an important part of open learning. Opportunities to interact with others in the MiraCosta course are still limited, compared to the equivalent evening class, so teachers encourage learners to form their own learning community among family and friends.

(Ramirez and Savage 2001)

The commonalities between open learning and distance learning may be difficult to identify in practice across language programmes. This was an important finding of the EU Socrates Programme entitled *Best Practice for Second Language Learning and Teaching through Open and Distance Learning*. In the course of developing the project the three project partners from England, Portugal and Denmark found it necessary to reorient their project to focus exclusively on open learning:

> Though we started to discuss distance language learning . . . in the end what we have written about is open learning. This came about as most of the provision we were able to observe in order to draw up the Guidelines was open rather than distance learning. For anyone who is keen to research distance learning for second language learners, there is still much work to be done.

This finding is not surprising. The contexts and practices of open learning centres in the EU study are very different from those experienced by distance language learners. It is not easy to access the practices and contexts of distance language learning since, for the most part, they take place in individual settings rather than in learning centres.

The two following sections discuss lifelong learning and the open courseware movement. They are movements rather than learning systems, and are both related to distance learning.

2.7 Lifelong learning

Distance language learning needs to be seen in the context of current trends towards lifelong learning, which focuses on the social and economic gains that may come from the allying of information, education, work and technology. While language learning has always included individuals who are diverse in age and goals, it is also now influenced by what Tuijnman (1999) calls the 'silent' explosion of adult learning and lifelong learning initiatives in Europe and elsewhere.

The renewal of interest in lifelong learning has two main components: one relating to the high priority placed on the knowledge economy and the knowledge society, and the other relating to the need to realise individual potential within evolving societies. These are reflected in increasing participation rates in tertiary and general education, and the growth of learning and leisure programmes for adults who are enjoying longer lives in retirement or semi-retirement. As Tuijnman (1999: 158–9) observes:

> All OECD societies are experiencing an increasing demand for learning opportunities that lead to professional development and the realization of individual potential. Individual expectations are rising, influenced, in part, by the opportunities opened up by the new information and communications technologies . . . and by the frequent changes of skills and competencies demanded at work. As populations age and leisure time increases for a large number of people, new and varied demands for personal fulfilment are likely to emerge.

With the growing need for lifelong learning, the student population is increasingly composed of adult working people looking for flexible, effective, and efficient educational solutions. These changing demands represent a challenge that cannot be readily met by conventional educational structures and institutions.

A number of distance language learning initiatives are workplace based and are linked to ongoing professional development opportunities (Grosse 2001; Laouénan and Stacey 1999). Fox (1997, 1998) provides a more detailed account of the vocational distance language course he developed within the Language Learning Network Project. The aim of the project was to promote lifelong learning by developing and delivering courses based on increased flexibility of access for learners. Three companies participated in Fox's distance French language course, and 12 employees began the course which could be accessed from work or home from multimedia PCs. The impact of the vocational context on the course was evident at several points. Only six learners completed the course as a series of job changes and redundancies depleted the numbers; participants were reluctant to ask for technical support because of existing time pressure within their work context. They also felt their companies had not given them sufficient support to make full use of the course. Fox (1998) argues that there was in fact a disparity between the employers' expressed commitment to lifelong learning and workplace-based training, and the level of resourcing available for employees to support study. The significant impact of learning sites and roles on distance language learning is not always understood in the move towards online workplace-based training, or in lifelong learning initiatives, and this is discussed in Chapter 5.

2.8 The open courseware movement

In April 2001, the Massachusetts Institute of Technology (MIT) announced its commitment to make the materials from virtually all of its courses freely available on the World Wide Web for non-commercial use. The move by MIT brought to prominence the open courseware movement and has focused attention on an important tenet in distance education: course content alone does not equate to the course itself, nor does it reflect the sum total of input and influence on the learners. Many people new to the field of distance language learning tend to equate the key aspects of practice with courseware. However, a distance language course is complex in totality. It involves interaction, guidance, feedback, support, the development of a learning environment and of relationships within that environment. All these conditions, and others, significantly affect the quality of the learning experience for individual learners.

In language teaching it has long been understood that materials – whether textbooks, institutional materials, or teacher-prepared materials – represent *plans* for teaching (Richards 2001: 270). They do not represent all aspects of the complex process of teaching whereby teachers mediate between learners and the available sources of the TL. Access to content within a textbook does not of itself constitute an educational experience nor the entirety of a learning context either in a face-to-face language classroom or in the distance context.

This point is developed by Laurillard (2002: 212) as she emphasises the importance of the organisational context in the distance learning process:

> students respond primarily to the institutional context as they perceive it. The demands and constraints it imposes . . . will have a greater effect on what students know than will any ingenious pedagogic design.

Laurillard uses the term the *context of delivery* in arguing that the development of learning materials is important but that delivery is paramount. The context of delivery takes in the support systems which help learners to derive maximum benefit from their learning experiences. The context of delivery also plays a significant part in the way in which fluid course elements develop, that is those which are based on interactions between participants in the course (including the teacher, learners, tutors, mentors and so on). The open courseware movement serves to draw attention to the crucial contribution of the context of delivery to the experience of individual distance learners.

More institutions are now contributing to open courseware projects: they provide a means for sharing knowledge and also serve as a 'shop front' for institutions in a highly competitive market. The open courseware movement renews the challenge to the field of distance education to continue to enhance the ways in which it provides a high-quality context of delivery to distance learners. This emerges as an important issue in transferring a face-to-face course to another learning system such as online learning.

2.9 Adapting a face-to-face EAP course to online delivery

It is not uncommon for language teachers to be faced with migrating a face-to-face course to another mode, for example to distance, online, or open learning. The focus tends to be on using existing resources to be modified as necessary. When this happens, however, the crucial role played by the teacher in the face-to-face classroom – in structuring the material, in interpreting instructions, in providing feedback – tends to be overlooked, or undervalued.

Phil Garing has provided a practical case study of the processes involved in adapting a face-to-face English for academic purposes/study skills programme to an online format. Here, I concentrate on three aspects of the process, followed by a brief outline of the online course and a commentary on the issues which are raised.

2.9.1 Climate of adaptation

When individuals or institutions decide to offer an existing face-to-face course in an online or distance format, it is important to acknowledge the kinds of pressures that may impact on the process in unexpected ways. Garing (2002) identifies some of the pressures as:

1. *Competing budgetary constraints*: developmental initiatives often compete with other special projects in an environment of reduced and uncertain funding.
2. *Organisation-wide change*: the move to online learning may take place alongside other organisational changes such as restructuring and the internationalisation of education.
3. *Institution-wide IT systems*: existing IT systems have generally been developed to support administrative, rather than teaching or training functions. Where delivery software is purchased, the decision may be based on cost and ease of integration within existing systems, rather than on suitability for the pedagogical aims of the course.
4. *Resourcing*: 'Getting a course going' has been seen as the job of the teacher. While additional resourcing may be made available, this tends to be seen as a cost to be minimised.
5. *Time pressure*: pre-determined course start dates often dictate small development timeframes.

2.9.2 The design process

These pressures may mean that there is a tendency to minimise the complexities involved in moving from a face-to-face course to developing an online course. As Garing (2002) suggests, a design process similar to the one outlined in Figure 2.1 is often followed. According to this model, at the first stage of selecting a delivery tool the focus may be on the 'best fit' for existing course resources, or on lowest implementation cost, or on a decision which minimises the need for staff training. Subsequently the 'path of least resistance' may involve collating existing resources and

Figure 2.1 A common design process used to adapt a course to online delivery

adapting them for online delivery. These first two stages are particularly problematic. The final stage is to extend the core of the course through the provision of communication opportunities, feedback and support – all of which are crucial in any online course.

When the focus is on working from existing resources, new resources that are available in the online environment – such as online dictionaries and related Internet resources – tend to be added on at the end rather than integrated into the course. In following this model, a number of 'conversion problems' inevitably emerge, and these are outlined below.

2.9.3 Conversion problems

A number of key elements in face-to-face teaching may be taken for granted and are not necessarily evident within the course resources. In particular, many of the roles carried out by the teacher may be over-looked in the online course format since they do not appear in the face-to-face course materials. Phil Garing (2002) identifies the following:

- Much of the content of the course is often in the head of the presenter, not on paper.
- The role of the presenter as motivator may be missed out in the process of adapting the course for online delivery.
- The ability to provide immediate feedback to learners' concerns or problems is part of the face-to-face environment. Good online delivery needs to develop extensive feedback resources that are immediately available to learners.
- Much of the value of face-to-face learning is derived from the types of activities and interaction that take place. Simply adapting resources does not necessarily result in effective learning activities or in the level of interactive engagement that brings about deeper learning.

A more appropriate approach in developing an online course is to develop a clear learner profile which is used to inform the way in which course features are articulated, the forms of learner support used, the choice of technologies and so on. Part of this process is referred to below.

2.9.4 The learners and the course

The online course TESS2000 – Tertiary English Study Skills – has been developed by Toucan House Ltd. It aims to prepare students for the kinds of skills they will need when they enter tertiary level study. Throughout the process of online course development, the needs of the learners were kept to the fore and remained the focal point for the online course. TESS2000 was designed for learners with the following profile:

- English language ability equivalent to IELTS 5.5 level;
- motivated to enter mainstream tertiary study;
- access to a computer with a CD-ROM drive and a 33K Internet connection, or better, with basic ability to navigate within a common browser;
- varying levels of ability to study independently;
- from a variety of backgrounds: secondary school students; language school students; mature age students; students who are learning English in their country of origin.

One example of how the learner profile informed the process of course development relates to technology. CD-ROM based resources were developed based on the technology profile of the learners: reliable Internet connections could not be assumed and learners would not necessarily be able to stay online for extended periods. Thus the bulk of the learning was CD-ROM based.

The online course has three main components, which fulfil particular functions as outlined in Figure 2.2.

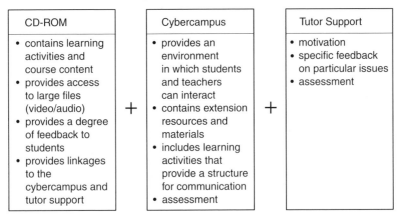

Figure 2.2 TESS resources (Garing 2002)

In attempting to build quality into the online course, Garing identified a number of quality indicators such as adequate and timely feedback and consistency between objectives, content and assessment, and then design strategies were adopted to meet the indicators.

2.9.5 Commentary

Many recently published books include detailed descriptions of how to convert face-to-face courses to online delivery (Duggleby 2000; Moore *et al.* 2001; McVay Lynch 2002; Weller 2002). However, few focus on the kinds of issues raised by Phil Garing concerning what can be lost, overlooked, or discounted in the process. The emphasis has tended to be on streamlining course conversion, rather than on addressing how factors such as learner support, feedback and the social context for learning change dramatically in online environments. The issues outlined by Garing are a useful starting point in prompting teachers to reflect on the complexities involved in moving to the online delivery of courses.

1. Resourcing for course delivery

A number of pressures are usually associated with the move to online courses. These can have unforeseen effects on the course developer. One point mentioned by Garing related to resourcing of the process. Frequently a single sum of money is made available for the development of a course, but this does not take account of the extra time, energy and training needed for course delivery and maintenance. The almost exclusive focus on course development means that the equally important, and very different, teaching and learning skills needed once the course is under way are ignored or discounted. This can have a serious impact on the online teacher who finds him or herself attempting to deliver the course in a new medium requiring new skills and new roles. For the learners too, learning online may be new, and the teacher needs to be able to provide support, and to model appropriate ways of communicating and learning online. Staff development at the course delivery stage needs to be resourced adequately.

2. Quality

A certain scepticism about the quality of online courses is often based on a view that face-to-face environments are of consistently high quality with regard to such things as interaction and learner-centredness, and that online environments will invariably be found wanting by comparison. Significant losses in quality in adapting a course to online delivery tend to centre around two common pitfalls identified by Garing: overlooking the contribution of the teacher to materials used in the face-to-face context; failure to recognise the need for structure, interaction and feedback for learners. There is the very real danger of an overemphasis on presentation formats during the process of converting an existing face-to-face course to an online format. Much attention may be paid to the appearance of material, rather than to thinking about ways of incorporating the 'teaching voice' of the instructor or providing for interaction and feedback.

Currently there is an ongoing debate about quality in online learning, which includes acknowledgement that this is a complex issue. In the US context there is a call for new standards to be developed which recognise the particular nature of online courses (Palloff and Pratt 2001). This comes at a time when fears are growing that quality standards may be bypassed in the push to online learning. Others believe that quality standards should be developed through student feedback and institutional responsiveness rather than having more national accreditation standards. These approaches involve quality assessment only when a course has been developed and delivered. Ongoing course evaluation is important, but should not be a substitute for attention to quality during course design and delivery phases. An argument for building good quality into courses rather than auditing quality when the course is delivered was first advanced by Koumi (1995) and has been influential within distance education. The approach taken by Garing was to focus on the former – on building quality into the course at each stage of constructing TESS2000. The development process was set around a number of quality indicators for that particular course and learner profile. They are consistent with the overall focus, which is concerned as much with critical reflection on the processes being used as with the final product – an online course.

3. Course ownership issues
A further reality in the move to course delivery online is that intellectual property and course ownership issues have become paramount (Palloff and Pratt 2001). A key question in journals and on discussion lists is 'Who owns the courses developed by staff for online delivery?' When face-to-face teachers leave an institution they generally take their materials with them. Someone else is employed to teach the course and that person usually introduces some of their own interpretations, approaches and materials. Palloff and Pratt argue that because online courses are generally housed on a university server and can be archived the question of ownership has become a bone of contention. There is a growing trend for the institution to claim ownership of the course, and the concern is that 'experts' will be hired to develop courses which will then be delivered by others, who are generally paid significantly less. This means that once again course delivery is undervalued, and that the teachers who are providing the facilitation and the support have little or no input into many parts of the course, which is run as an intact unit. The term for this used first by Warschauer (2000) – *a bifurcated system* – is particularly apt, and represents a situation which is less than ideal.

2.10 Summary

Opportunities for distance language learning have expanded dramatically over the past decade, and are linked to the development of related ways of organising language learning and teaching. A number of these have been discussed here, with an emphasis on both common and distinctive features of different forms of provision – between, for example, distributed learning, asynchronous learning networks and online learning. Another important emphasis has been on the different philosophies associated with particular learning systems, and the issues they raise, especially in relation to course delivery. Important interrelationships have been identified between distance learning, lifelong learning and the open courseware movement. The next chapter focuses in more detail on a number of key issues and trends associated with providing distance language learning opportunities within what continues to be a rapidly changing field.

3 Issues and trends

3.1 Introduction

There are many emerging issues in the rapidly changing and diverse environments of distance language learning. New technologies, new learners, innovations in practice, and new ideas about access and quality provision all require new ways of thinking about approaches and practices within distance language learning. At the same time, they raise new challenges. Developments such as the use of CMC place longstanding issues relating to participation and interaction in distance language learning in a new light. Further to this, the issues and trends that are identified and discussed as pertinent to distance language learning reflect different positions in terms of what is important within the field. The early part of the chapter reflects more of a concern with technology and its place in distance language learning. The latter part focuses on issues of access and quality, and the emergence of new constraints within distance learning environments. A number of these issues and trends are discussed in the context of a recent venture into distance language teaching using interactive television (ITV) in Victoria, Australia.

3.2 Interactive competence

Learning and using a language is both an intrapersonal or mental process and an interpersonal or social and interactive process (van Lier 1996). The learning opportunities provided in distance language courses have traditionally been based on written and recorded course materials, presented in the form of workbooks, video-, audiocassettes, CD-ROMs, and television or radio broadcasts. Such resources provide somewhat limited experiences for learning and using the TL. Teachers have spent a lot of time in attempting to devise ways of providing interactive opportunities in the TL, including the use of telephone courses (Dickey 2001) and voice mail (Ramirez and Savage 2001; Young 2000).

Most distance language courses provide a range of face-to-face opportunities for practising speaking and listening in interactive contexts, including summer schools, weekend courses and local tutorials (Baumann and Shelley 2003; Vanijdee 2003), but factors relating to distance, time, money and competing commitments mean that not everyone can attend. Shield *et al.* (1999) describe the constraints of the distance learning context offered by the Open University UK as follows:

> Traditionally, as a result of their geographical distribution, it has been difficult to offer home-based language learners extensive speaking and listening practice. While CD-ROM technology has addressed this issue to some extent, it does not allow learners to interact synchronously – in real time – with each other and their facilitators via voice.

In other contexts the limitations are acknowledged and students are encouraged to see the distance language course as just one learning source, which they can supplement through interactive opportunities with native speakers or in subsequent learning opportunities. The Adult Migrant English Program, for example, encourages distance learners to engage with interactive opportunities in their communities as part of the course materials. Learners are supported by the teacher in this, and encouraged to critically reflect on these learning experiences (Candlin and Byrnes 1995). In addition, they are encouraged to form learning networks with other learners as a means of accessing further ways of learning and using English.

New possibilities for addressing the issue of interactive competence have come with the development of the Internet. An important discussion of this has been developed by Kötter (2001: 328), based on his observation that:

> Distance learners have few opportunities to write in the foreign language for an audience other than their tutor. But they normally have even fewer chances to test and improve their speaking skills in authentic communication.

Two important pilot studies were carried out at the Open University UK in which students met online once a week with their tutor to complete a series of tasks designed to help them improve their interactive competence and their confidence in their TL skills (Kötter 2001). In providing opportunities for spontaneous interaction within a distance language course, key challenges relate to orienting learners to use the TL in what is a very new learning environment. The pilot studies were part of the FLUENT project referred to in section 1.5.3. The learning environment included Internet-based audio conferencing with a text-chat facility which allowed users to talk with each other in realtime. It was available for small-group and plenary sessions and learners could work in different virtual 'rooms' without being interrupted (Shield 2000). It was possible for learners to 'invite' tutors into their rooms if they needed help. E-mail was also used and a website containing both technical and pedagogical information. Learners were able to meet and socialise online with each other, and participate in collaborative learning activities.

On the basis of the two studies Kötter, Shield and Stevens (1999) and Kötter (2001) note the following:

Response to the new environment: learners were initially reluctant to take risks in an unfamiliar setting with reduced context cues, and took time to accommodate to the new learning environment. They overcame what was described as initial apprehension about having to talk to 'disembodied voices'. The issue of participation, however, remained: learners found it harder to contribute, and easier to 'hide' in the anonymous environment.

Response to learning opportunities: learners became increasingly aware of the gaps in their current level of competence in the foreign language; they received a substantial amount of collaborative support from other students in interacting in the TL, and appreciated the opportunity to practise speaking, and to receive rapid feedback from their peers.

Support and proficiency: different types of tutorial support appear to be required among learners with different levels of proficiency; learners with basic or intermediate competence in the TL required more tutorial support than anticipated. Communication and fluency-related tasks are ideally used in an online environment with learners of at least intermediate competence in the TL.

Persistence: about one fifth of learners dropped out for technical reasons; this would be a major concern in a regular course.

Important conclusions from the pilot studies are that further research is required in relation to task design, online correction and the optimal use of tutor and learner time before distance language courses can move to a completely online environment.

The focus of these research directions intersects with current research interests in networked language learning (Kern and Warschauer 2000; Donaldson and Kötter 1999; Ortega 1997). However, the context of delivery is very different when technology is used in a distance learning environment, compared to a classroom or face-to-face context. Particular challenges that arise include the fact that the teacher is not physically present to assist and orient learners in the use of the technology; online activities may be perceived as time-consuming, especially in the initial stages and if they are in addition to other course work; problems with technology may be difficult to manage for all learners;

challenges relating to maintaining motivation need to be addressed. Opportunities for the development of interactive competence in distance language learning will be discussed at later points in the book in relation to such issues as learner autonomy, congruence between the distance learning environment and the individual learners, and the roles of teachers and learners.

Reflections and experiences

Issues and challenges in online learning

Charlotte N. Gunawardena is Professor in the Organizational Learning and Instructional Technologies Program at the University of New Mexico, Albuquerque. Her recent research examines knowledge construction in online learning communities, social presence theory and its impact on learner satisfaction, cultural factors that influence online group dynamics in international distance education, and the design and evaluation of distance education systems.

'What do you see as the main emerging issues and challenges relating to online learning within the USA?'

I believe that the theoretical challenges for distance education will centre on issues related to learning and pedagogy in technology mediated online learning environments. One such issue is understanding and evaluating knowledge construction in online collaborative learning communities. Increasingly we are subscribing to a knowledge construction view of learning as opposed to an information acquisition view, as we design web-based distance learning environments. The knowledge construction perspective views computer networks not as a channel for information distribution, but primarily as a new medium for construction of meaning, providing new ways for students to learn through negotiation and collaboration with a group of peers. The challenge, however, is to develop theory to explain how new construction of knowledge occurs through the process of social negotiation in such a knowledge-building community.

A related area of theoretical challenge is to determine how the social dimension of an online learning environment influences learning. The online learning environment has been described as a sociotechnical system incorporating both technical and social aspects. Unique aspects such as the time-independent nature of an asynchronous environment can create communication anxiety, or the lack of visual cues in a text-based medium can give rise to the development

---

of emoticons (icons that express emotion, such as ☺) to express feelings. Research on social presence is one way of looking at this social dimension. The online environment forces us to reformulate the way in which we view the social dimension and how learners actively influence each other's knowledge and reasoning processes through social networks.

With the expansion and acceptance of the Internet and the World Wide Web across the globe for education and training, the significance of culture and its impact on communication, and the teaching and learning process at a distance will provide an impetus for further research and theory building. If we design learner-centered learning environments, how do we build on the conceptual and cultural knowledge that learners bring with them? How does culture influence perception, cognition, communication, and the teaching–learning process in an online course? How do we as instructors engage in culturally responsive online teaching? These types of questions need to be addressed in research and in theoretical frameworks as we move toward making distance education a more equitable learning experience.

Charlotte Gunawardena,
University of New Mexico, Albuquerque

3.3 The advent of CMC

The impact of computer-mediated communication (CMC) on thinking and practice in distance education is a common theme in the research literature (Kötter 2001; Murray 2000; Warschauer *et al.* 2000). The advent of CMC in the 1980s was hailed as providing 'a new learning domain which enables us . . . to develop qualitatively new and different forms of educational interactions' (Harasim 1989: 62). Bates (1995) argues that CMC has revolutionary implications for distance education, providing the means to free students from the centralised control of pre-determined and constricted curricula as they develop their own learning opportunities through discussion online and collaborative learning experiences. CMC has made it possible for learners to raise questions and take part in collaborative learning opportunities to complement access to more fixed course content in the form of prepared materials. The advantages of CMC are seen to accrue not only in terms of interaction, and opportunities for reflection on learning, but in terms of motivation and overcoming a sense that distance language learning is an impersonal experience; it can give participants a sense of being part of a cohort of learners, even a community of learners.

CMC uses text-based systems for interaction between learners and teachers. In distance language learning the most common forms of CMC are, in order, e-mail, computer conferencing, and real-time chat systems. CMC has been singled out in the literature as a key development in distance learning, because it is seen as providing the following:

- a means of support: learners can support each other both directly and indirectly, by sharing their experiences, insights, concerns and reactions to the course;
- a sense of being part of a cohort of learners, thus reducing a sense of isolation;
- a way of learning from others' questions, as well as responses;
- a source of alternative perspectives;
- opportunities to ponder the points raised, and to have time to formulate a question or reply;
- access to earlier discussions, which are available for review;
- variety;
- motivation to keep going;
- a 'voice' for learners within the course, which is under their control.

The primary use of e-mail for distance language learners is to ask questions of the teacher, for example administrative questions, course-related questions, queries about the TL, or requests for support. An additional use is the electronic submission of course work and as a means of providing feedback to learners. Distance language learners may use e-mail to communicate with individual learners, groups of learners or the whole class. A difficulty teachers face in using e-mail for announcements and course information in many distance language courses is that not everyone has access to e-mail, in which case e-mail is used alongside more traditional forms of communication.

E-mail was an important part of a distance writing course developed by Janet Raskin (2001) for an Internet school called Englishtown, with students enrolled from many countries. New students entered every two weeks, so the lessons were designed as independent modules, which were sent to students by e-mail each week. The study guide included the URL of a website containing reading material relevant to the writing topic, which in turn was linked to exercises in the study guide. Students were expected to write 150–300 words on the weekly topic. E-mail was also used for interaction with peers. Each student was assigned a partner, and they were expected to use e-mail to clarify ideas together, to motivate one another to write, and to provide feedback on each other's drafts. Pairings changed each week to allow interaction with different students in the course, and to develop a sense of community.

Synchronous chat was also used by Raskin as part of the Englishtown course in a weekly one hour session – three sessions were held at different times during the day so students in all time zones could participate. One feature of chat is that messages appear at varying speeds so questions and answers are not necessarily consecutive. Chat functioned mainly as a means of socialising, and also to discuss questions distributed in the weekly study guide. The overall aim was to get inspiration for the writing assignment.

Computer conferencing systems also have a place in distance language courses. Lamy and Goodfellow (1999a) used them to promote reflective conversations among distance learners of French (see section 7.7). Weller and Mason (2000: 363) note that the strengths of computer conferencing as a means of interaction within distance learning are also its weaknesses:

- it doesn't require fixed times for study, but consequently other demands on one's time easily take precedence;
- it maintains a record of all interactions – but this makes many people wary of committing their ideas to such a public forum;
- it allows everyone to be 'heard', but this can lead to an overload of messages which many people find completely overwhelming.

They go on to note that for many people this is a new medium and it takes time to learn appropriate skills. Computer conferencing requires substantial self-direction, motivation and initiative on the part of learners. The teacher is required to become an effective facilitator, placing the student at centre stage in the learning process. In the absence of body language and some of the other cues of face-to-face contexts, the teacher must work harder to stimulate and sustain discussion and to help the group develop a sense of community.

For distance language teachers working with e-mail, computer conferencing and chat systems is a time-consuming process, and can become all-consuming. For example, Christine Uber Grosse taught a class for English Business Communication for executives, which had an enrolment of 116 students (Grosse 2001). The students lived in Mexico, while the course was offered from the Arizona Campus of Thunderbird, the American Graduate School of International Management. Noting that by the end of the initial course she had sent about 3,000 messages, she declined to assume sole responsibility for the next course which had a similar enrolment.

The demands associated with CMC can also stem from institutional policy. Given the importance of timely response to student queries or concerns, some institutions have a requirement that facilitators reply to students within 24 or 48 hours, which can place enormous demands on staff. And, of course, this does not recognise the fact that a quality response, in many cases, cannot always be delivered within such a tight timeframe. Some staff have met the requirement by providing an automatic acknowledgement, which then gives more time to develop a fuller response should that be required.

All of this points to the fact that it is critically important to establish clear protocols and expectations for learners, and to orient them to practices within CMC, particularly for computer conferencing. Weller and Mason (2000) suggest that it is important to frame expectations of students as the immediacy of the medium can sometimes lead to unrealistic demands. One of the key things for a language teacher to negotiate with learners is the amount of attention that will be paid to accuracy, to the content of the discussions, and the kinds of feedback that will be given. The expectations of teachers and learners may be different in this regard, and may vary at different points in the course. Learners may choose to focus on assessment, or on questions about their own performance, or may seek detailed explanations of grammar points – none of which may coincide with the intended use of the list by the moderator.

One of the important claims in relation to CMC for language learning is that it is an ideal medium for students to benefit from interaction because the written nature of the discussion allows greater opportunity to attend to and reflect on the form and content of the communication (Kern and Warschauer 2000). In a review of the literature on CMC and language learning Kötter (2001: 328) notes the following findings:

- CMC encourages discussion among learners by giving them more opportunities to express their ideas than would be possible in an oral discussion of equal length;
- CMC secures fast transmission and allows participants to receive instant feedback, and to save and revisit their data;
- CMC facilitates language learning by giving students more time to reflect on their fellow students' contributions and to develop and refine their own responses; this may lead to greater precision and sophistication of expression;
- the written exchanges are informative to students who participate in a discussion and to those who follow but do not actively contribute to a particular thread.

More research is needed on the value of different forms of CMC in language learning, as Murray (2000) and Doughty and Long (2002) discuss, and on the contribution it makes as a component within distance language learning programmes.

3.4 Participation, interaction and online learning communities

3.4.1 Participation and interaction

Two significant issues in distance language learning relate to interaction and participation within different learning environments. The detailed treatment of interpersonal dynamics and group dynamics in classroom language learning (e.g. Ehrman and Dörnyei 1998; Dörnyei and Maldarez 1997) has not been matched by a similar body of research into the significant features of interaction and participation in the new distance language learning environments. A central issue in distance language learning is how to maintain sufficient learner contact and ongoing interaction. This challenge applies to all forms of distance learning, but the challenge has become particularly apparent at a time when the focus is shifting from independent learning, as in first generation distance education, to interconnected learning and the ideal of online learning communities.

CMC has made it possible for language learners to integrate independent learning experiences with opportunities for interaction and collaboration. The crucial question now is how to arouse and maintain in distance language learners a desire to interact online. This is no easy task since they need to perceive the value and the relevance of the online learning environment, and need to be willing to interact meaningfully with the opportunities it provides.

Mason (1998a) reflects on the way in which text-based interaction was received when it was first introduced into distance learning. She notes that practitioners were struck by the novelty of the medium and 'fell into the trap of thinking that providing students with a user-friendly system and a lively tutor/moderator were the keys to successful, educational discussions' (Mason 1998a: 57). However, as experience accumulated it was evident that learners did not readily participate in interaction, particularly sustained interaction. The characteristics often associated with CMC – interactivity, collaboration and reflectivity – are of course not inherent within the medium but can result from it, depending on a range of factors such as design, moderator roles, participation patterns and involvement (Eastmond 1993). The problems associated with getting some language learners to participate in face-to-face settings are all the more complex and acute in distance environments. An important outcome of experience with CMC has been the recognition that facilitation of learning in online environments requires very different skills from those of the conventional distance tutor, and intensifies the need for new orientations to distance learning.

In a proposal developed by the universities of British Columbia and Auckland for an International Business English Course to be delivered by distance, a major challenge to implementation was identified as learner engagement in the online community of the course (Curtis, Duchastel and Radic 1999). Participation in collaborative learning opportunities was seen as important since the aim of the course was to enhance students' communication, problem-solving and team-building skills in the context of English for business. Curtis *et al.* (1999: 44) note, however, that 'some language students, particularly those who are accustomed to teacher-centered approaches may believe they cannot learn from their peers or from a more collaborative style of learning'. This is, of course, an issue in some face-to-face language classrooms where students are reluctant to participate in group work or collaborative work, but it is a more complex challenge in distance learning because the teacher is not physically present to encourage students and to deal with incidental queries or concerns. A consistent finding in studies about interaction in distance education is that individual preference for levels of interaction varies greatly and that this preference is the greatest single influence on the level of interaction that takes place (Miller and Webster 1997; Kearsley 2000).

The question of learner volition in relation to participation is currently contested within the field. On the one hand, there is the view that individuals should be given control over the extent of interaction, the form of interaction, and whether they interact at all (e.g. Sutton 2001). On the other hand, in the face of reluctance on the part of some language learners to contribute to CMC discussions, a number of teachers have adopted the approach of requiring regular – for example, weekly – contributions, and of assessing these as part of the grade for the course.

The contribution of interaction to the affective dimension of distance language learning experiences is also the subject of much debate. Providing a range of options for interaction has been found to be important to overall satisfaction with the experience of distance learning. The research of Fulford and Zhang (1993) and others, has shown that when learners perceived that there was a high level of interaction and possibilities for interaction in the course as a totality, they were satisfied, even if they did not, or in some cases could not, interact personally. Kelsey (2000: 72) considers the concept of vicarious interaction, in tandem with anticipated interaction, to be useful in explaining the relationship between interaction and satisfaction, noting that a 'variety of opportunities for interaction did not increase actual interaction among participants, but it did serve to increase student satisfaction'. The contribution of vicarious interaction to distance learning processes has not as yet been the subject of research, but it is a worthwhile avenue for enquiry, focusing on the ways learners interact with TL sources created by course participants.

3.4.2 Online learning communities

Interaction and participation are integral to the educational ideal of online learning communities within distance learning. Language learners are encouraged to interact, not only with the teacher, but with one another. The distance language teacher's role has been expanded to include the role of a facilitator in an environment where interconnected learners are expected to negotiate meaning through multiple interactions among participants. A theoretical framework for developing online learning using CMC leading to the development of online learning communities has been developed by Salmon (2000). Salmon identifies a five-step model (see Table 3.1) that reflects what she calls a positive progression in the quality and intensity of interaction between members of an online community.

Table 3.1. *Model of learning online through CMC*

Stage	Features
1. Access and motivation	Individual access and ability to use CMC is essential for participation.
2. Online socialisation	Participants establish their online identities and find others with whom to interact.
3. Information exchange	Participants contribute course-related information.
4. Knowledge construction	Course-related group discussions occur and the interaction becomes collaborative.
5. Development	Participants look to more benefits from the system to help them achieve their personal goals, explore how to integrate CMC into other forms of learning and reflect on the learning process.

Source: Salmon (2000).

The five-step model is based on a constructivist model of learning and has as a key aim: the development of critical thinking skills of participants. Salmon's theoretical contribution to understanding CMC as a learning tool is derived principally from her work with MBA students at the Open University UK. The applicability of the research to the distance language learning context has yet to be determined, but certainly the initial stages of her model reflect closely the kinds of issues that confront both teachers and learners new to CMC. A very important challenge is how to integrate CMC into the other forms of learning and experiences within a distance language course. Unless this integration takes place – both integration within the course, and integration for each learner in terms of congruence between learning experiences – it is unlikely that participation in CMC will be perceived as adding value to the process of distance language learning.

Moore (2002), writing from the perspective of a language teacher, acknowledges the theoretical contribution of Salmon's model, and the links which are made to practice, but questions the assumptions made relating to constructivism, participation, access and motivations of learners. The notion that 'constructivist learning is effective, desirable and real, and that it can best take place through participation' needs careful consideration (p. 23). He goes on to note that while constructivism is intuitively appealing, it remains largely a philosophical position, rather than an empirically supported approach, and that within such a position participation is presented neutrally as effective for learning while the cultural and political issues relating to participation are not acknowledged.

The motivations and needs of distance learners and their responses to learning through CMC also need to be understood, acknowledged and used to inform our view of the role of online learning communities within distance language learning. Further challenges include overcoming barriers to participation related to technology, including access, reliability and learner disposition, and understanding more about the affordances and limitations of different uses of CMC for distance language learning.

Reflections and experiences

Collaborative Learning Opportunities in Online Learning

Maija Tammelin from the Helsinki School of Economics (HSE) is a lecturer in English Business Communication. She has been involved with the use of distance teaching technologies in language and business communication education for the past fifteen years. Currently, she is in charge of departmental network-based development projects in the HSE's Department of Languages and Communication.

'What kinds of collaborative learning opportunities have you introduced into your distance language courses? How have learners and teachers responded?'

In Finnish higher education, language teachers are mainly using distance learning technologies either to enrich campus-based, face-to-face teaching or to offer various types of hybrid course formats, ranging from online modules within a course to entire courses, which include some or no classroom sessions. There are growing pressures for arranging the latter types of study opportunities as students struggle with their busy timetables in which they also have to find room for obligatory language studies.

As for collaborative learning opportunities in my own online courses, I would like to mention two in particular. First, in my course focusing on writing, instead of the students getting feedback from only their teacher on their writing assignments, I now use a peer feedback system in which the students are in small online groups of three or four and comment on each other's reaction to paper assignments. On their longer final paper they also get comments from at least one student reviewer. In addition to their own writing assignments, their course-work assessment thus covers their reviews of and comments on other students' work. This seems to have an uplifting effect on the quality of the students' performances. I have been particularly surprised at the depth and quality of the students' comments on each other's work.

The second collaborative learning opportunity is of a different kind. In my course where my students have videoconferencing sessions with a group from another university, they prepare collaboratively for the videoconferences by exchanging messages in their online course platform. This collaborative preparation places the focus more on the students' collaborative effort rather than individual performances. This in itself can for instance reduce the shyer students' anxiety during the videoconferences. All in all, students have enjoyed the videoconferences very much.

Maija Tammelin,
Helsinki School of Economics, Finland

3.5 Social presence

In face-to-face language classrooms the establishment of a positive social climate and cohesion within the class are considered an important part of the teacher's role, and integral to good practice. As part of this, language teachers and learners in face-to-face classrooms make use of a number of social, linguistic and context cues to understand and contribute to the dynamics of the classroom. The absence of physical presence in distance language learning contexts means the loss of cues which are available in face-to-face classrooms to support interaction and the social and affective dimensions of learning and to maintain engagement between those present. There is also a reduction in teacher immediacy, that is in the verbal and non-verbal behaviours and routines which help to establish relationships between teachers and learners and which are important in creating a learning environment.

The climate of 'social presence' and how it is created is a key difference in language teaching and learning in distance and face-to-face contexts. Social presence in distance education serves a similar function to phatic communication in conversation. It is based on an acknowledgement and awareness of other participants within the learning environment. If learners feel socially present in a mediated situation, they feel part of the larger social context which in turn affects motivation, attitudes and social cohesion (Gunawardena and Zittle 1997; Tammelin 1998; Tu 2000). Social presence is seen as contributing to interaction, collaborative learning and learner satisfaction.

The notion of social presence is in line with a long-standing theory of distance learning developed by Börje Holmberg, who was the first theorist to focus on distance language learning. His conversational model of distance learning emphasises the importance of interaction, emotional involvement in the learning process and feelings of personal relation between participants in distance contexts. It provides a useful counterbalance to views of distance learning that emphasise organisational dimensions, or to a view that once technology is in place, interaction and social presence will emerge. If language teachers have little or no experience of working within technologically mediated language learning environments they may not be aware of the existence and the potential significance of social presence in mediated environments that may exclude face-to-face interaction partly or completely (Tammelin 1998).

The absence of visual cues – such as nods, gestures, and eye contact – presents a very real challenge within synchronous distance language learning environments, such as telephone conferencing (Stevens and Hewer 1998) and Internet audioconferencing (Kötter *et al.* 1999). Turn-taking routines are affected by the absence of these cues, which can have an alienating effect on participants, and inhibit their participation in conversation. This is a particular issue in group conversation as opposed to one-to-one interaction. In addition the loss of social and contextual cues, which are an integral part of face-to-face interaction, can have an impact on learners. Uncertainty about the larger social context that they are part of, and expected to contribute to, may result in reluctance to participate or to take risks, both of which are important for language learning. Kötter *et al.* note that the learners in their pilot project at the OUUK (sixteen students of German and fourteen students of French) were able to become used to the absence of social context cues, and it became customary 'to allow three to four seconds after the end of one turn before beginning their own' (p. 58). These issues may be resolved more readily as participants become more familiar and more comfortable in using different online environments.

Maija Tammelin (1998, 1999) has investigated the role and development of social presence in telematics-mediated distance language classes. The English language course in Environmental Communication – described briefly in section 2.5 – takes place in a network-based learning environment using computer conferencing, e-mail, videoconferencing, a café conference and a course site on the WWW. Students on the course are at two different tertiary institutions in different parts of the country and communicate by computer conferencing and videoconferences. The importance of providing a range of communication channels is emphasised in Maija Tammelin's research, as students' sense of social presence was found to arise from a range of opportunities related to different media. For example, the café conference was established as a space where participants could demonstrate their own social presence and sense the presence of other participants (Tammelin 1998). It was distinct from the threaded discussion forums, which focused on the actual context of the course. The café conference was supported: the course assistant was responsible for monitoring the café conference and for initiating new threads if contributions were coming to an end. Students visited and contributed to the café conference, and it was seen as important in developing cohesion and solidarity within the course. Tammelin (1998: 225) includes the following reflection on the café from a student's final course report:

> Naturally the café was the most popular forum. It was a great idea to start this kind of discussion space so that everybody could say something, anything, because that really played a major role in creating the common atmosphere of this course.

The text-based environment for interaction suited some students who remained relatively quiet in the face-to-face sessions and videoconferences. Tammelin refers to one student in particular who was seemingly serious and quiet in face-to-face settings, but whose text-based messages were important in creating a positive social climate online – and humour played a part in this.

While participating in a text-based environment was important for some students in developing a sense of social presence, other students were reliant on face-to-face sessions and videoconferences for social presence and motivation, as in the following student report from Tammelin (1998: 227):

> I feel that at least a few group meetings face to face are needed to create a certain atmosphere. A course where several communication channels are used is very different from a course where only, for example, e-mail would be used to communicate

between the participants. If you never see what the others really look like, it somehow makes it all much more distant and so there will not be the same kind of connection.

It is important for distance language teachers to be aware that students may have distinct preferences for the way in which they develop a sense of social presence within a course. An important conclusion that Tammelin draws from her work is that it is possible to either overestimate, underestimate or perhaps completely neglect the impact that the use of various media may have in fostering social presence. It is also important to acknowledge that teachers' perceptions and understandings of the affordances of different environments in terms of the development of social presence may not coincide with learners' perceptions and preferences. This is an important avenue for research.

How is social presence developed in different distance learning environments? Warschauer, Shetzer and Meloni (2000) suggest that one avenue for online language learning research is to look at the linguistic features of communication. An important question then is whether in text-based computer conferencing it is possible to develop social presence by attention to the form of language that is used. Some important insights into this come from the work of Rourke, Anderson, Garrison and Archer (2001) and Garrison, Anderson and Archer (2000) who have investigated how the construct of social presence is realised in text-based computer conferencing. Based on the analysis of transcripts, they suggest that social presence consists of three categories: affective responses, interactive responses and cohesive responses. For each of these categories there are a number of indicators of social presence.

3.5.1 Affective responses

Affective responses involve the expression of emotion, feelings and mood. Indicators of affective responses, with examples, are given below in Table 3.2.

The role of affect in language learning has been underlined in research (see, for example, Arnold 1999), but many of the ways affective elements are attended to in face-to-face interaction in language learning contexts are eliminated or changed in text-based interaction. In computer conferencing affect may be expressed through self-disclosure, humour and emoticons.

3.5.2 Interactive responses

Computer-assisted conversation does not always follow the normal rules of turn-taking since a number of people may be writing at once. This can

Table 3.2. *Affective aspects of social presence*

Indicators	Definition	Examples
Expression of emotions	Conventional expressions of emotion, or unconventional expressions of emotion, including repetitious punctuation, conspicuous capitalisation, emoticons	'I just can't imagine . . .' 'I am really and completely confused!!!!'
Use of humour	Teasing, cajoling, irony, understatements	'Who's on stage this week?'
Self-disclosure	Presentation of details of life outside of class, or expression of vulnerability	'Where I work, this is what we do . . .' 'I am not so good at this sort of exercise.'

Source: Adapted from Rourke *et al.* (2001).

result in a series of asocial monologues rather than interactive discussion (Warschauer *et al.* 2000), though this may be less likely in asynchronous mode. One of the key features in promoting socially meaningful interaction is evidence that other people are attending, listening, and engaging meaningfully with what is being said. A number of cues, responses and rejoinders in face-to-face settings offer support to the speaker and encouragement to keep going. Interactive responses can be provided in a text-based medium such as CMC (see Table 3.3).

Students have a need to have their contributions acknowledged, which also helps maintain further attempts to use the language and to sustain interaction. Negotiation of meaning and feedback in face-to-face language classes are both based on an acknowledgement of the contributions of learners. The challenge is to develop interactive responses in different CMC environments.

3.5.3 Cohesive responses

Rourke *et al.* (2001) define cohesive responses as those which build and sustain a sense of group commitment, of cohesive ties within the group, of association and affiliation. They argue they can be defined by three indicators: phatics and salutations, vocatives, and addressing the group as 'we', 'our' or 'us' (see Table 3.4).

The idea of phatics will be familiar to most readers, that is communication that is not so much concerned with the communication of ideas

Table 3.3. *Interactive aspects of social presence*

Indicators	Definition	Example
Continuing a thread	Using a reply feature of software, rather than starting a new thread	Software dependent, e.g. 'Subject: Re' or 'branch from'.
Quoting from others' messages	Using software features to quote others' entire messages or cutting and pasting selections of others' messages	Software dependent, e.g. 'Martha writes:' or text prefaced by 'less than' symbol <.
Referring explicitly to others' messages	Direct reference to contents of others' posts.	'In your message you talked about . . .'
Asking questions	Students ask questions of other students or the moderator	'Anyone else had experience with WebCT?'
Complimenting, expressing appreciation	Complimenting others or contents of others' messages.	'I really like how you describe . . .'
Expressing agreement	Expressing agreement with others or content of others' messages	'I was thinking the same thing . . .'

Source: Adapted from Rourke *et al.* (2001).

Table 3.4. *Cohesive aspects of social presence*

Indicators	Definition	Examples
Vocatives	Addressing or referring to participants by name	'I think John made a good point.' 'Emma, what do you think?'
Addressing or referring to the group using inclusive pronouns	Address the group as *we, us, our.*	'Our textbook refers to . . .' 'I think we are off track.'
Phatics, salutations	Communication that serves a purely social function: greetings, closures.	'Hi everyone.' 'That's it for now.' 'We're having the most beautiful weather here.'

or information, but that aims to establish a mood of sociability or to confirm ties. Vocatives involve addressing participants by name – something which is important in the face-to-face language classroom as a means of acknowledging both the identity of the individual and, indirectly, their membership of the group.

The template proposed by Rourke *et al.* was developed in content-based distance courses, rather than in a language course. It provides, however, a means of investigating and reflecting on the level of social presence in distance language learning environments and can perhaps point to ways in which the climate of text-based computer conferencing can be enhanced for learners. Without attention to social presence, interactions in online learning environments can appear terse and pragmatic, and learners may have a sense that other participants are less approachable. Support needs to be provided for language learners in online environments to encourage them to participate and to attend to the contributions of others. A key starting point in all of this is a heightened awareness of social presence on the part of language teachers, who can then model ways of interacting that contribute to an optimal level of social presence. Of course, we do not as yet know what is an optimal level of social presence – too much may be as inhibiting as too little. An important avenue for further study includes further analysis of CMC, audioconferencing, and videoconferencing as unique social contexts. Another is participant perception of social presence and its value, among distance language learners from different linguistic and cultural backgrounds, and in different TL environments.

3.6 The technology challenge

Technology is a major issue for language learning and teaching in distance education. In some contexts it is *the* major issue, not only because of the new possibilities offered by technological changes, but because of the range of attendant issues for learners and teachers and for the future directions of the field. Distance learning is linked essentially to technology – never more so than at the present time – and it continues to evolve as new developments in technology emerge. The major attraction that has led to the alliance between technology and distance education is the need to 'take the distance out of education' and to enhance its interactivity (Bates 1995).

As the influence of the new technologies becomes more pervasive, it draws attention to the need for shifts in the practice and conception of distance language learning. Distance language learning can now involve a new learning context, that is an interconnected community of learners rather than an isolated series of individual learners. It can now take place within new mediums, such as the WWW, and text-based computer conferencing. And it involves new ways in which learners go about learning, with higher levels of interaction and collaboration (Morgan and O'Reilly 2001). This means there is both change and a degree of uncertainty within the field of distance language learning, especially as the use of technology is more than just a technical issue. It raises fundamental questions about target groups, language teaching methodologies, the role and purpose of interactions and, most importantly, the question of what constitutes a quality learning experience. While the new and emerging technologies provide opportunities to reduce the reliance on presentational and broadcast approaches in distance language learning, attention also needs to be focused on the overall context of delivery of a distance language course. It is the context of delivery – including learner support systems, the responsiveness of the teacher and the quality of interaction developed within a course – that enhances or diminishes the benefit students derive from distance language learning courses.

One theme running through worldwide experience is the impact of the new technologies on the key participants in the process, that is distance language teachers and learners. Important questions within this issue – some general, others specific – include:

- How can we avoid mistakes in the choice of technology?
- How sustainable are particular learning environments, i.e., can they be integrated successfully into mainstream provision of distance language learning opportunities? Will they survive?
- How scalable are particular learning environments, i.e., can they be extended for use with larger numbers of students?
- Will technologies be used to create quality learning environments or simply to enhance presentation quality?
- How do language learners respond to the new technologies?
- Will language learners make use of technologically enhanced learning environments?
- Is there a gap between the anticipated and actual use of particular technologies by language learners?
- What do we know about the complex process by which learners take to using new technologies as part of their language learning environments?

A number of authorities have, however, expressed qualms about the close relationship and intertwined development of technology and distance learning. Robinson (2001) has pointed to the need for distance educators to understand more fully the contexts of learners and to build better bridges into and out of the learning cultures of individuals. Burge and Haughey (2001) emphasise the importance of focusing on a wider range of issues in relation to the role of technology in distance education including concerns and issues within an international context, and with a diverse range of participants. And Jegede (2000) observes that the push to adopt the new technologies is often combined with a push to participate in global education through the export of courses to new markets. In all of this, he argues, the learners' views are hardly considered – nor are their motivations to learn or their socio-cultural environments, which may mediate or inhibit learning. In addition, distance learning environments using the new technologies require learners to cross a number of cultural borders in order for learning to occur:

> There is the culture of the content being learnt and the cultural framework through which it is being presented. Then there is the native culture or the culture of the immediate environment of the learner. Finally, there is the culture of the use of technology and of the particular communications technology chosen to convey instruction to the learner at a distance.
>
> (Jegede 2000: 52)

Jegede argues that consideration be given to these various cultural borders that distance learners must cross in order to make learning meaningful within their immediate environment.

A further crucial issue is that of equity and universal access to distance language education. It is important to think about technology in the context of the home-based learner. If web-based technology is made mandatory for distance study, existing inequalities between students are likely to increase (Kirkwood 1998). A number of vulnerable groups have been identified and cited in the literature, including ethnic minorities, older students, women, rural learners and those from poorer socioeconomic environments (Burge and Haughey 2001). That distance language learning opportunities should be available to all individuals is still axiomatic for many of the established providers of distance education. Until computers and Internet access become sufficiently commonplace and affordable, the issue of access to technology will remain a sensitive and potentially divisive area within distance language teaching.

It is also important to emphasise that distance language learning is not synonymous with the newer technologies, and proceeds in many contexts that make limited, if any, use of information and communications technology. Referring to a collaborative distance language course for language teachers – developed by the Hellenic Open University and the University of Manchester – Fay and Hill (2003) argue that while much can be learned from the rapidly expanding literature on new technological environments, it does not provide us with a sufficiently broad conceptualisation to understand distance learning. The challenge faced by distance language practitioners and theorists is to come to an understanding of the place of technology in distance language learning.

3.7 Teacher roles and responsibilities

The role of teachers within language learning has been revisited and reconstructed many times over the last two decades. Brumfit (1984: 60) noted that the teacher's role was moving towards that of a facilitator and participant in the learner's learning and that 'learning will be partly dependent on the teacher's ability to stop teaching and become simply one among a number of communicators in the classroom'. His emphasis on the communication skills of the teacher, and on the teacher as learner are two key features of the role of distance language teachers.

As many language teachers begin to use distance environments for the first time, they face unfamiliar tasks and responsibilities. There are three broad areas that will be unfamiliar to them. These are new forms of communication and interaction in distance environments, the need for new kinds of awareness and skills, and the scale of processes in distance language learning (adapted from Moore and Kearsley (1996)).

3.7.1 Communication and interaction

Most language teachers have developed a knowledge of their craft in settings that include a substantial component of face-to-face interaction. Distance language teachers need to become competent communicators within teaching–learning relationships that are sustained by using a range of technologies. For example, language teachers in face-to-face classes have developed a repertoire of strategies to remediate boredom, lack of engagement and so on, and have learned to respond to students in a variety of ways. Distance language teachers need to develop similar tacit knowledge about how to interact appropriately at a distance, and how to orient learners to working within unfamiliar environments.

3.7.2 Awareness and skills

The range of roles required, and how they are realised in distance environments mean that language teachers need to develop new kinds of awareness and skills. If teachers have little or no background in distance education, they may not be aware of the issues that arise and of the adjustments that are required. They may also have difficulty in identifying and articulating the kinds of support and training they need.

Referring to the FLUENT project developed at the OUUK, Kötter, Shield and Rodine (1999), quoted in Hauck and Haezewindt (1999: 50), note that:

> The learning environment changes the roles of the tutor to that of a facilitator, co-learner and activity co-ordinator, and allows learners and tutors to participate equally in the design process.

Some of the other roles distance language teachers assume in mediated environments include those of modeller and motivator. Aspects of these roles will be familiar to language teachers, but not as they can be enacted in online environments. Thus, flexibility and a shift in mindset are required. The ability to develop understanding of a new language learning context, the use of new mediums (e.g. course delivery tools), and new ways of learning and teaching is crucial.

3.7.3 The scale of processes

The extent and scale of the planning, development and delivery processes involved in distance language learning will exceed the expectations and experiences of many language teachers. A further crucial process is that of in-depth evaluation, linked to the design and development process before the course is actually implemented – to be then followed by ongoing evaluation.

A detailed study of the competencies required by distance language teachers is a high priority within the field. It would provide a useful source of information for novice teachers, and could be used as the basis for professional development and training. The competencies below are those I have identified based on experience. These are the ability to:

- adjust to the new distance language learning settings;
- help learners to adapt as well;
- identify the characteristics and needs of language learners at distant sites;
- provide ongoing support for learners in a new learning environment with often unfamiliar elements;
- respond to a range of issues and affective states in relationships with learners, beyond what may generally emerge in face-to-face settings;
- motivate learners at a distance;
- support students at a distance in taking responsibility for their learning;
- work as part of a team, with, for example, technology experts and learning support staff;

- understand the advantages and disadvantages of new language learning environments, and develop appropriate strategies and relevant
responses;
- work within a context of ongoing change and innovation.

What does the research tell us about teachers' experiences in distance
contexts? Hauck and Haezewindt (1999) report on tutors' perspectives
of their role in a pilot study of Internet-based synchronous voice conferencing carried out as part of the FLUENT project at the OUUK. The
online tutors were working within what was for them a new context, and
it is this feature of the study that is important here. Placed within the
environment, the tutors identified the following:

- the importance of confidence in the use of online tools;
- the ability to adapt their teaching style to suit often rapid and unexpected changes in the ways the learning environments develop;
- the need to develop strategies that require learners to take a more
active role in working online;
- the need to manage multiple roles within online environments – for
example facilitator, coach, co-ordinator – alongside student demands
for individualised feedback.

These broad areas have parallels in face-to-face teaching. However, what
is less available to distance language teachers is a repertoire of appropriate responses and strategies in technology mediated environments. We
can look forward to more research focused on how teachers are affected
by the new learning environments and on the evolving roles and responsibilities that are now emerging for them.

The context for innovation is also important to the individual distance
language teacher in terms of how she or he works with new roles and
responsibilities. Individual initiatives may take place in an organisational
context which is mostly concerned with face-to-face teaching, this is the
case for the distance language teaching initiatives discussed at the end of
the chapter. Introducing distance learning in such contexts can be
demanding for teachers, largely because the institution may be slow or
reluctant to make the changes needed to support the innovation. This is
a key issue since the introduction of distance language learning involves
changes at many levels: course development and delivery, course administration, support for learners, and the nature of professional development needs. Organisations that do not value the rather different demands
of distance teaching *vis-à-vis* conventional face-to-face teaching can
place unrealistic demands on teachers.

Equally prevalent is the situation where organisations have a policy that
supports and encourages distance learning initiatives. While initiatives

may receive institutional support they may then be met by scepticism and resistance by staff. Nebojsa Radic (2001) makes mention of the impact of the social and political climate that can surround the introduction of computer-mediated language instruction at a distance. He refers to the pattern first noted by Jaffee (1998) that organisational change is contingent on social and human factors and dynamics that are difficult to manage, together with the established practices of staff.

3.8 The emergence of new constraints

The major constraint within distance language teaching and research has been seen as distance between learners and teachers – physical, temporal and psychological. However, *time* has now emerged as a significant constraint for both learners and teachers that may be growing rather than diminishing in new and more complex learning environments.

3.8.1 Constraints for learners

Looking first at the situation of learners, time has always been an important consideration, because individuals who take up distance language learning are usually part-time learners who need to fit study in with the range of demands of adult life.

A recent example of this comes from the FLUENT project trial reported by Hauck and Haezewindt (1999). The distance learners of German and French were provided with opportunities to collaborate with each other in synchronous interactions in an environment which used an audioconferencing client (with a text chat facility), e-mail and a website. Language students were able to create their own spaces where they met in pairs or small groups to engage in real-time interaction. Students were also encouraged to work in self-organised groups at a time that was mutually convenient, to prepare for the weekly scheduled session.

In the course of the trial it was found that students could be suddenly or unexpectedly absent due to conflicting demands. Absenteeism emerged as a significant constraint when not all learners could take part in all scheduled meetings. It was then necessary in the tutor-facilitated sessions to set up groups on an *ad hoc* basis once everyone was online. This was found, on the whole, to be satisfactory, except, as Hauck and Haezewindt note, that it has some repercussions on community-building. Learners felt disappointed that they had collaborated with others who were not present during the scheduled sessions. While distance had been bridged in this language learning environment, issues relating to time affected participation. Time and timing are important in any synchronous distance language learning environment, and language teachers must be prepared to adapt and respond to new configurations and demands.

In online courses students complain about the amount of time they need to spend especially in the first few weeks of a course, familiarising themselves with activities, requirements and opportunities available to them. Weller and Mason (2000) note that the kinds of elements which are notorious for taking large amounts of time include:

- browsing the web;
- interacting in computer conferences and working in groups online;
- getting to grips with a personal computer.

They note that learners new to distance learning can spend a disproportionate amount of time on such tasks.

There is also now a concern that there may be a connection between time pressure and the increasing number of media in new courses. A number of distance language learning environments offer multiple learning sources, and an enriched set of resources. At the same time they are more complex, often requiring language learners to navigate their own path through the materials, to co-ordinate multiple sources and to keep track of a range of learning materials. These new opportunities may have a very real down-side for some learners. Thorpe (2001: 128–9) argues that when learning technologies are added to the resource base of learning programmes they may increase the study time required in two ways:

1. When several media are used the student must expend time and effort figuring out what each medium carries and how best to use it. This can add considerably to the time language learners spend getting started and establishing their own means of learning.
2. The technologies may present further resources or optional resources. This can be an advantage for some language learners but a distraction for others, who may spend time learning more than they need to – or simply get hooked on an optional extra and spend longer using it than the course designers intended.

Neither of these is a deficiency in itself, but responses from learners suggest that in more complex learning environments some may find it difficult to identify and focus on essential areas.

Kötter (2001) notes that in the second phase of the FLUENT project, the Internet-based audioconferencing environment referred to earlier was used with a trial group of learners who were at the same time enrolled in the more traditional OUUK distance language course. The aim was to assess how learners from French and German distance language courses would cope with the online environment while simultaneously completing their current course work. Kötter notes (2001: 337):

> The single most important factor accounting for student dropout, particularly during phase II of the project, was time. Learners claimed that they spent an average of four to five hours per week on project-related activities such as online meetings, reading and responding to e-mail, the preparation of their contribution, and on revising vocabulary and grammatical structures. While this was practicable for some students, others found that they spent too much of their time on this extra-curricular activity.

Research into the demands and opportunities of new distance language learning environments needs to take into account the issues of time and time pressures for learners, and to consider the effects of more complex and more varied learning sources.

3.8.2 Constraints for teachers

It is easy to misjudge the time commitment for teachers in distance language learning. While the new technologies have vastly improved opportunities for communication and interaction, they have also introduced a number of work-related concerns, including significantly greater workloads and increases in the speed of work. Course planning and development are now more complex as the range of options in terms of learning sources and learning spaces has increased dramatically (see Chapters 8 and 9). More time is required for the different stages of course planning, design, development and evaluation. This is still often underestimated by novice distance language teachers, and by management.

Once the course is under way, person-to-person communications can be time-consuming, particularly in contexts which have a substantial element of CMC. It is important to access the course site regularly, to follow and orchestrate discussions, to respond to enquiries and to problems, and to co-ordinate other course functions. Since many language learners start working online at evenings and weekends, it may be necessary to be available at less conventional times. There may be an expectation of the 'permanent' availability of the teacher to interact and respond to queries 24/7. There may also be an expectation of individualised feedback on language used in collaborative work online, and again the teacher needs to negotiate parameters in relation to when, how often, how and why this feedback will, or will not, be given.

Part of the difficulty is that this is a new field and language teachers are developing skills in how to work within the medium of CMC. It is not intended as a medium where learners can be left to work independently for long stretches of time, but teacher participation needs to be carefully managed. Laurillard (2002) points out that we have developed formal mechanisms to protect tutors in the traditional place-based mode – offices, office hours, appointments, timetables, and so on. Similar mechanisms will need to be developed for the electronic environment if workloads are to be sustainable.

3.9 Quality

Concerns about quality, quality provision and best practice are very much to the fore at a time of rapid change, expansion and diversification within distance education. Robinson (2001) highlights the ways in which a lack of resources – financial, personnel, time, facilities – often accompanies commitments to produce 'low-cost' distance learning opportunities. She also points out that innovation in distance learning may face even higher levels of risk because of its uncertain status and relative unfamiliarity in some contexts – that is learners, teachers and other participants may have little sense of what a quality distance learning experience should entail.

An important study carried out by Smith and Salam (2000) has focused on the issue of how to assess online language schools. They note the uncertainties potential learners face when they first investigate an online school. While a number of websites that claim to be 'virtual' English language learning centres are free, an increasing number demand payment for enrolment. These schools, Smith and Salam argue, are a manifestation of distance learning and can be examined within the kinds of frameworks developed relating to quality issues. In an evaluation of sites they looked for the following:

- a clearly defined syllabus and teaching approach;
- the range and levels of learning materials offered;
- evidence of instruments for student assessment;
- the ability to access a teacher when required;
- the quality of teaching material, including the design of teaching materials, adequate variety and sufficient workload for the type of programmes offered;
- the existence of any form of face-to-face teaching;
- the nature of help available for students (not only for ways to learn, but also what to do with the task in hand);
- value for money, which includes educationally effective materials and an adequate quantity of materials;
- an indication of the length of the course.

The positive characteristics they identify of online language schools were reported in section 2.2, but a number of negative features were also identified by Smith and Salam. These include what they describe as a serious image problem relating to sites which are unwelcoming in format, have few graphics and lack a sense of social presence or human face. Many of the sites offer little information, or only give further information after the student enrols. While in some cases a sample of free exercises was available, there were no examples of the kind of personalised instruction they could expect. A final point is the number of hidden costs that can emerge in relation to online language schools: in addition to computer, software and Internet costs, it is possible that students would need to purchase additional equipment such as a sound card or video camera. A key conclusion they draw is that the future viability of online language schools, cyberschools and virtual English schools depends on the credibility of what they offer.

3.9.1 The attributes of quality

Of course the notion of quality in any teaching or learning context is always subject to reinterpretation, particularly at a time when the notion of absolute standards has been relaced by context-based approaches:

> Quality in education is socially constructed and reflects the constructions of different periods and places . . . the attributes constituting quality can refer to intrinsic criteria (learning or performance as an end in itself) or extrinsic criteria, that is, goals or objectives external to the educational process.
>
> (Robinson 1992: 12)

The current educational, social and political climate in many countries, and in many contexts, emphasises lifelong learning and ongoing educational opportunities. In these terms, equality of access and extension of access may be regarded as important attributes in quality distance language learning opportunities – as in the conclusion to a study carried out by Epstein (2001) mentioned in a moment.

Various criteria have been applied to assessing best practice in distance learning. The following is based on the work of Calder (2000) and Mason (1998a):

- learner support;
- the level and amount of engagement with the course;
- ongoing evaluation over the life of the programme;
- the content, structure and context of provision;
- the use made of media;

- the teaching approach;
- the management of provision;
- contact opportunities;
- feedback options;
- level of services and resources.

Epstein (2001) evaluates two distance language teacher education programmes – one in Canada, the other in Thailand – in terms of a number of quality indicators. She argues that because distance education differs in many ways from conventional education, it must be evaluated, and understood, on its own terms, not in comparison with face-to-face instruction. The following quality indicators, developed by the University of Wisconsin-Extension (2000), are used in her study:

- knowing the learners;
- creating confident and committed faculty;
- designing for active and effective learning;
- supporting the needs of learners;
- maintaining the technical infrastructure;
- sustaining administrative and organisational commitment;
- evaluating for continuous improvement.

A number of the indicators would not necessarily be key indicators of quality in face-to-face contexts, but are very much to the fore given the nature of distance learning. These include indicators relating to creating and maintaining commitment within the institution, in the administrative and technical infrastructure and among teaching staff. Epstein argues that quality indicators can be used to raise awareness of the inherent components and challenges of distance education so that teachers can be better prepared to address them, both proactively and systematically. The following conclusions drawn by Epstein (2001: 139) focus on the importance of knowledge relating to learners and attention to the context of delivery in providing effective and appropriate distance learning opportunities:

> Providing a high-quality learning experience for learners from different geographic regions involves familiarity with the learners, their goals and needs, and the programme content. It also involves awareness of what is feasible within a given context and implementation of a design and delivery system that will be effective in the environment where the programme will be delivered. This will perhaps mean thinking critically about the latest trends that favor advanced technology and using a more reasoned combination of delivery options that ensure reasonable costs to institutions and assured accessibility for learners.

3.9.2 Diversity and expansion in the global context

A number of critical commentaries relating to quality within global distance education have been prominent in the last four to five years. For example, Daniel (1999) observes that there is a danger in everyone clambering onto the self-directed, technology-mediated bandwagon. He identifies economic and political pressures, the lure of the new technology and the hype of the new millennium as three potent, and possibly perilous influences on education. Together they can easily lead to quick-fix solutions – such as the wholesale conversion of courses to digital form – which can expose students to courses of questionable quality.

Calder (2000: 2) emphasises that issues surrounding quality provision in the global context are all the more significant because of the motivations of policy makers:

> The development and introduction of many open and distance learning initiatives may be driven by a desire to achieve simple, low-cost solutions to complex social and economic problems. In such contexts, the quality of provision may appear as a fragile afterthought rather than as fundamental to its development.

Mason (1998a) points out that the enormous task of establishing quality practices and benchmarks within the new domain of global distance education is also particularly complex given the diversity of practice which characterises distance education.

3.10 Access

The tensions between access and quality in distance learning continue to be explored in the field. Here I will consider the issue from two angles: the potential divide between access and quality provision, and the tensions between accessibility and the quality of the educational experience.

In the 1970s and 1980s, open and distance language learning was driven to a large extent by a commitment to access and equity. Latterly, however, a number of new economic imperatives drive education. There is a concern that open and distance learning systems may come to fall into two camps: those delivering high-quality language learning experiences using a range of presentation formats and offering a high degree of interaction, and those of lesser status and quality for language learners who are less well resourced in their individual contexts. This issue is becoming increasingly prominent in the global context, and there is a very real danger of a gap emerging between the haves and the have-nots around the issues of access and quality provision. The challenge for the field now is to be aware of the danger of a divide between access and quality, and to guard against it in practice.

The second angle focuses on pedagogical aspects and philosophies of learning, and is most fully developed in the work of Garrison (2000). He places the issue of access alongside that of the quality of the learning and teaching process in the distance context. Transmission approaches to education are equated with a dissemination model of distance learning with an emphasis on information and distribution, rather than on communication and interaction. The argument he develops goes as follows: the more accessible the content in the distance context (e.g. through broadcast television, radio, print), the greater the number of learners who access the content and the more sporadic and patchy the interactions between teachers and learners. Of course it is possible to have opportunities for interaction and sustained discourse in courses that can be accessed by large numbers of learners – if there is a sufficiently low student:teacher ratio. The reality in a number of contexts is that institutions seek a high-intake, low-cost approach to providing distance learning opportunities, with an emphasis on access to content. It is possible to argue that the greater the accessibility, the poorer *may* be the quality of the language learning experience. The tensions between access and quality remain, and are given new prominence as CMC becomes an integral part of a distance language learning environment.

I now want to consider issues and trends as they relate to a particular context, namely recent initiatives for the development of distance language learning opportunities in Australian schools.

3.11 Distance language learning by interactive television

Interactive television (ITV) for language learning has mostly been a feature of US distance education systems, as noted in Chapter 1. Here I focus on the use of ITV in the Australian context, largely because of the issues that have been raised and explored there in relation to ITV distance language learning opportunities in schools – issues that are common to many distance programmes. Two aspects of the research are of particular interest. First there is the detailed tracing of the way in which ITV was put into operation – how it evolved and how it receded into something far removed from the original conception (Evans *et al.* 2001). Second, and related to the first aspect, is a consideration of how teachers and learners responded to opportunities for interactive language learning from remote sites, and how they responded when the interactive elements were discontinued. The early stages of the research were carried out by Terry Evans and Karen Tregenza, and Elizabeth Stacey also participated in some of the later projects. All three are researchers at Deakin University in Victoria, Australia.

3.11.1 Background

The impetus for the use of distance teaching within conventional class-room settings in Victoria, Australia was nested in a new policy called Schools of the Future in which schools were equipped with new technology. Distance learning opportunities were effected by satellite transmitted interactive television (ITV) in key curriculum areas, which included languages. At the same time, the Government had placed new emphasis on language teaching within schools: at least one Language Other than English (LOTE) was to be taught in primary schools, and at least two at secondary schools. There was a shortage in teacher expertise, so the transmission of language instruction via satellite to schools became one of the key areas of the SOFNet programme, the acronym for Schools of the Future Network. The introduction of group-based distance language education within the US school system was also based on expanding foreign language programmes beginning in elementary school, and was seen as a way of compensating for the lack of district-level resources (Glisan, Dudt and Howe 1998).

3.11.2 The SOFNet programme

The SOFNet programme was first developed in the mid 1990s. The reports of Evans, Stacey and Tregenza (1999, 2000, 2001) indicate that the programme included the following features:

* the languages covered were: Italian, Indonesian, Mandarin, Japanese, French and German;
* programmes were developed for the primary (elementary) level, and for the secondary (high school) level: Primary Access to Languages via Satellite (PALS) and Secondary Access to Languages via Satellite (SALS);
* broadcasts ran for 30 minutes weekly and were conducted mostly in the TL;
* broadcasts consisted of live one-way television transmission;
* interaction within each broadcast was sustained by live telephone link, fax or e-mail;
* broadcasts were supported by materials distributed to schools, which included: a list of resources required for each programme, the expected student outcomes, a brief summary of the programme format, and detailed descriptions of the activities to be undertaken;

- opportunities were provided for teachers to give feedback and suggestions to the programme makers through evaluations and in-service days;
- an estimated 100,000 students learned another language via SOFNet (Victoria Department of Education quoted in Evans *et al.* 2001).

Interactivity was incorporated into the programmes in a number of ways including:

- the producers nominated different schools to create live interaction for each programme;
- interaction included live-to-air question and answer sessions, or the discussion of tasks that the children had completed and faxed to the presenter;
- classes were encouraged to interact with the programme through e-mail queries, for example, which would be included in later sessions.

Evans *et al.* (2001: 3) note, however, that 'after 1998 the opportunities to interact were ceased or greatly curtailed to the extent that SOFNet became more of a video distribution network for schools to record their own video-cassettes of the programs'. The reason for the decline in interactivity, and the subsequent implications for the learning experiences of participants, are important aspects of this study.

3.11.3 The role of the ITV classroom teacher

The contribution of the teacher to the success of the programme is very strongly indicated in this study. As mentioned earlier, the programmes were conducted mostly in the TL – the aim was to give an immersion experience – and they proceeded apace. Teachers needed to prepare the learners for the language broadcast, and to give them the tools for what was an intensive language experience. In particular they needed to focus on vocabulary if the learners were to be able to join in a song, answer the presenter's questions and so on. The follow-up lessons were also important as part of this sequence, and time needed to be set aside in class for these.

Linked to this were issues of teacher confidence and proficiency:

> The program design elements . . . relied more on the capability of the PALS supporting teacher for their effectiveness. Students with teachers who were not competent with the language being taught and who did not apply a timetabled preparation lesson as well as a regular follow-up lesson, were ill-equipped for a dialogic process in an immersion program.
>
> (Evans *et al.* 1999)

Other organisational skills were required of the teachers. Since the language programmes were part of a synchronous learning environment, the teacher needed to ensure that the weekly timetable allowed the class to be available in a particular room at a particular time. This was not always possible, and many teachers took to videotaping the programmes, which then eliminated many of the interactive opportunities.

One of the difficulties experienced by teachers within a distance context arises when the production and delivery of courses is separated from other teaching functions. In the case of the SOFNet languages scheme this was the case: teachers had very little control over the content of the language classes. Language programmes were designed, developed and broadcast by one group, and teachers then facilitated interaction with the class based on the programme. Learners found the pace of the programmes too fast and the level of vocabulary too advanced. Though adjustments were made after teachers provided this feedback to the producers, the requirements of the programme still exceeded the proficiency of learners. Ultimately this meant that learners were less motivated, and less able to sustain participation. Thus while teachers were given opportunities to influence the nature of the material broadcast to their classrooms, in practice they felt that their feedback was having little effect:

> There was a less responsive cycle of evaluation and comment between the teachers and ITV teams, and the frustration with this had resulted in some of the teachers treating the lessons as passive television viewing.
>
> (Evans *et al.* 1999)

In short, teachers struggled to match the programme to the needs of their learners.

The ability to work together as members of a team, and to take ongoing course evaluation seriously are key competencies for *all* professionals within distance language learning environments, including course designers and producers. This includes responding to ongoing course evaluation. When this was not attended to, the teachers did not feel a part of the evolving learning environment and so they were less engaged than was ideal.

3.11.4 Interaction and participation

The interactive elements in the SOFNet programme, as originally conceived, were attractive and valued by teachers and learners. The importance of interactional opportunities for the overall satisfaction with a distance learning experience was confirmed in this context, and included:

1. *Motivation*: students focused quite intently on the interactive parts of the ITV programme and were motivated to prepare responses and to focus on responses provided by others. Evans *et al.* (2001: 8) note that 'in both secondary and primary classrooms it was a motivational highlight for the children to talk to the presenters and to be an audible part of the satellite transmission or to fax questions or class work during or after the program and to have it acknowledged by the presenters subsequently'.

2. *Reference points*: the interactional parts of the programme allowed the teachers to gain a sense of how learners and teachers in other classrooms were working within the programme.

3. *Learning community*: a sense of community developed among participating schools as each one became familiar with the others who were taking part in the programme. Evans *et al.* (2001) report that teachers contacted one another after they 'met' through SOFNet. Since many of the participating schools were in isolated rural areas, this sense of being part of a larger learning group was valued. Networks were enhanced during the stages when the programme makers would shoot scenes at particular schools or within participating communities.

4. *Momentum*: synchronous learning opportunities can provide a framework for learning since a fixed schedule must be followed. When the language programmes were interactive, there was a sense of the immediacy of the learning experience. At the point at which the interactive elements declined and lapsed, teachers reported that it was easier to miss out on some of the sessions, and then, inevitably, to fall behind. Thus the structuring and momentum provided by the synchronous learning opportunities were largely maintained by the live, interactive opportunities.

3.11.5 Sustainability of distance learning environments

Many aspects of the SOFNet programme could not be maintained as originally conceived. Beginning in late 1999 there was a gradual downscaling of the interactive elements within the language programmes. The school location shoots declined, the interactive segments were reduced and eventually previous programmes replaced live presentations. The response of the teachers was noted as follows:

> The teachers thought the quality of programs on video had deteriorated and was repetitive of earlier programs with the teachers having to edit them for class use. Students had lost interest and were bored with the programs with the interactive element removed, as without the network of communicating schools and

presenters, the activities seemed lacking in authentic 'real world' purpose. Teachers thought that few newcomers to SOFNet would persist with the programs in their new format.

(Evans *et al.* 2001: 10)

SOFNet eventually became a static resource rather than an interactive medium. The rhetoric and intended use of SOFNet did not match realities within the contexts of use. Opportunities for interaction and exchange have also shifted in some distance foreign language instruction in schools in the USA. Oxford *et al.* (1998) note a trend to move from satellite mode to video mode in order to contain costs and to overcome scheduling difficulties. The loss of opportunities for interaction and exchange with 'remote' teachers and 'remote' learners represents a move to focus on the delivery of content rather than communication and interaction.

3.11.6 Commentary

1. Course development

One of the key issues highlighted by the fate of the SOFNet programme is the difference between the development of content or courseware and the context of delivery – and the implications of lack of sufficient attention to the context of delivery. Much time, energy and expense were devoted to producing the programmes and providing corresponding learning resources for use in classes both before and after the broadcasts. However, insufficient attention was paid to other key aspects of the context of delivery – such as the timing constraints imposed by synchronous delivery – and this impacted severely on the programme. In particular the need to gain support from the administration within the schools to enable the teachers to make the language programme schedule a priority was not sufficiently recognised. This detracted quite markedly from the viability of the programme.

The context of delivery fell short of the ideal in terms of the pacing of programmes. Teachers reported that the classes, particularly at the primary level, were moving too quickly in their demands on vocabulary development, and that the learners could not keep up, especially in an immersion context. While channels were provided for feedback, the feedback did not impact sufficiently on the producers of the course, so the gap between the level of learner proficiency and the demands of the programmes continued to widen. There was ample evidence within the studies that a workable balance between attention to course development and attention to the context of delivery was not achieved, resulting in a lack of sustainability in the programme as a whole.

2. Roles and responsibilities

The study also draws attention to the issues that emerge as teachers enter distance learning environments for the first time. The unanticipated roles and responsibilities inherent in the new context had a particularly strong impact on the SOFNet programme. Working in a synchronous learning environment with limited prior information about programme content, the teachers were unable to prepare themselves or their classes adequately. Once the broadcast began they had little ability to control the course of the lesson and their prior teaching experience had not equipped them for a situation in which they themselves were essentially learners in two domains, that is as learners of an unfamiliar language and learners in relation to satellite-based teaching. On the occasions when the course materials did not match the scheduled programme, the teachers were put under extra pressure.

The inherent uncertainty within many distance learning–teaching environments, and the need for all participants to be able to tolerate a range of ambiguities, present major points of adjustment. I referred earlier to some of the broad areas that would be unfamiliar to teachers new to distance teaching environments. These included the ability to orient learners to working with new technologies in unfamiliar learning environments, to develop new understandings of learning and teaching environments, to be prepared for uncertainty, ambiguity and some loss of control, and to adjust to engaging in planning and evaluation processes that are different in timing and scale to those they have used in the classroom. An additional difficulty for the primary-level teachers in this study came from competing demands: the languages programme was only one of many subjects that they taught within an already crowded curriculum. While the teachers reported that they enjoyed developing language skills themselves and gained considerable personal satisfaction from this part of the curriculum, the range of other roles and responsibilities that they had to assume within their everyday classroom contexts meant that they were limited in the time and attention they could devote to developing skills for working within the ITV learning environment.

3. Access and quality

The study also revealed issues relating to access and the quality of the learning experience. The interactive opportunities, as originally conceived, were a highly effective and attractive part of the programme; many schools and many individuals were given access to the course content, but in the course of the project the interactive opportunities began to wane, and then faded altogether. While broadcasts maintained access to TL content, the quality of the programme decreased dramatically as possibilities for real-time communication were removed.

4. Interaction

The central issue raised by the SOFNet study, as I see it, is that of interaction. Distance learning involves more than being given access to content. The range of interactive opportunities, such as on-site interactions in schools during the filming of the programme, and the response to and discussion of tasks submitted by participants, were highly motivating for the learners and created a learning community among the participants. The importance of vicarious interaction was also noted in the study, which confirmed previous findings that the perceived level of total interaction in a course is more important for individual satisfaction than the level of personal interaction. However, the study also indicates that the interactive elements of the programme were considered less important than the 'fixed' course content, and came to be viewed over time as dispensable. This had a dramatic effect on the viability of the programme as satisfaction decreased once it switched from ITV to pre-recorded programmes. The vulnerability of more fluid aspects of distance education, particularly interactive elements, are highlighted in this research, and it is these elements that make an essential contribution to the quality of the learning experience from the point of view of the participants.

3.12 Summary

The issues and trends outlined in this chapter reflect the ways in which distance language learning is an evolving field. Language teachers and researchers continue to address such issues as the development of interactive competence, and participation and interaction in online learning environments. Current shifts and developments within the field are impacting on the roles and responsibilities of teachers, and are resulting in concerns about access and quality and the emergence of new constraints. The intertwined development of technology and distance language learning opportunities runs through the kinds of issues and trends explored in the early part of the chapter. Current issues and trends within the field affect many of the decisions, processes and emphases within distance language teaching programmes. A recent move to deliver ITV language learning opportunities in Australian schools illustrates how decisions and subsequent changes in a distance programme relate to broader issues of participation and interaction, roles and responsibilities of teachers, access and quality.

4 The learner–context interface

4.1 Introduction

This chapter provides a theoretical framework for understanding the essentials of distance language learning. It is based around the notion of the learner–context interface (White 1999a) which places the individual learner's capacity to construct an effective interface with target language (TL) sources in the learning environment at the centre of distance language learning. According to this view the establishment of an effective interface between each learner and his or her learning context is the crucible for distance language learning. The notion of the learner–context interface and its role in the distance language learning process originates from learners' reflections and perspectives on the meaning of distance language learning and its unique characteristics White (1999a). It is further informed by the insights of distance language teachers and current thinking within the field.

In this chapter I begin by drawing attention to the need for complementary perspectives in conceptualising distance language learning, that is the use of models of the process which include the insights and experiences of the learners as key participants in the process. The three main dimensions of the interface-based framework – namely, the individual language learner, the context and the interface – are discussed. The remainder of the chapter brings together commentaries from distance language learners and teachers that link features of the interface to the practical realities of learning within the distance context.

4.2 Conceptualising distance language learning

As part of an examination of 'visions of language learning', and the meanings those visions assume for both learners and teachers, Tudor (2001: 77) puts forward the following observation:

> If we were to ask the imaginary lay person . . . what he or she understands by language learning, the response is less easy to predict than with respect to language, which is . . . 'out there' . . .

86

Language learning, on the other hand, is something that we do not 'see'. It is a mental process which cannot be 'observed' in any direct or tangible manner.

The question 'What is language learning?' is an important one to pose in relation to distance language learning. The answer(s) to this question form the substance of this chapter. They represent what Tudor calls 'student rationalities' of language learning, which may include individual rationalities or rationalities shared by a larger number of students. An understanding of student rationalities is necessary since 'effective teaching depends crucially on teachers being able to tune in to the meaning which language learning has for their students both as individuals and members of a learning group' (Tudor 2001: 34). It is particularly important in distance language learning since the needs, concerns, situations and rationalities of learners are less easily discerned. What is presented reflects the views distance language learners hold about the learning process. While these rationalities were diverse they centred on the notion of a learner–context interface, 'the hallmark of which is *a belief in the primacy of the unique dynamic established between the learner and the context in the process of self-instruction*' (White 1999a: 449).

4.2.1 The need for complementary perspectives

While a number of theoretical models of distance education have been put forward over the last 30 years (see, for example, Moore (1993), Peters (1998), Keegan (1993)), none has been developed specifically in relation to distance language learning. They are based on the distance learning of content subjects such as history, economics, psychology. The other abiding concern has been with systems theory of distance learning. And until recently, very few of those theoretical models have been informed by students' perspectives of distance learning. The focus has been on distance education as a system for developing and delivering study opportunities to learners.

The theoretical framework which I develop in this chapter is derived from a complementary approach to understanding distance language learning, which incorporates perspectives offered by learners, teachers and researchers. It is congruent with the descriptions of distance language learning put forward by many distance language researchers and teachers. For example, Kötter *et al.* (1999) see the nature of distance language learning as requiring students to develop a level of strategic competence that will enable them to learn without the daily or weekly guidance of a teacher. Harris (1995: 44) argues that the distance language learners who had succeeded in the AMEP in Australia 'had found ways to re-create for themselves the "study-nurturing" environment needed for success'. She adds that distance language learning can be a 'viable or productive option for learners who are able to match the level of the course and teacher support with their own self-supporting strategies' (Harris 1995: 52). Hurd *et al.* (2001: 342–3) argue that in order to be able to succeed in the distance context 'the distance learner . . . must not only find out by trial and error which strategies seem to work, but also learn the skill of assessing personal learning needs, including strengths and weaknesses, and have some idea of how to address them and monitor progress. In order to develop these skills, learners need to be self-aware and knowledgeable about their own perceptions, attitudes and abilities'. Emphasis on the ways distance language learners need to respond and act in order to benefit from learning opportunities is also a feature of the learner–context interface framework developed here. The following representation of language learning in distance education serves as background to the learner–context interface framework.

4.2.2 A representation of language learning in distance education

Context plays a key role in language learning, and different contexts afford certain possibilities for learning and offer certain constraints (Gibson 1986; Greeno 1994; Barnes 2000). One of the affordances of the distance learning context relates to choice, that is learners are able to make a range of choices about what will constitute their learning experiences. These may relate to the content of learning, the use of particular media, the amount of interaction, and the sequence and pace of study. Such choices all influence the precise interface that is developed between learner and learning context. We can think of learners not so much as *entering* a course or learning environment, but as *constructing* the course according to the affordances of the learning environment and their own contributions as learners. The challenge for each distance learner is to establish their own effective interface with the learning environment.

4.3 The interface-based theory of distance language learning

The following report was given by a learner of Spanish after six weeks' experience in the distance context:

> Now I see it basically as me and the language: that's it. I'm there, with these materials in a 'raw' form. I somehow have to make

them come alive for me. I guess I hadn't quite thought of it that way at first . . . I have to make the first move, to somehow work into those materials, to create a sort of dynamic between me and the materials, so something happens for me. That's really what it's all about. Once you get that dynamic going, you're well on the way, and the whole thing begins. I'd like to know how other people made contact with all the materials, set something up for themselves that works.

(Quoted in White 1999a: 449)

The points made in the report illuminate one aspect of a broader view of the distance language learning experience. According to this view, the key issues for distance language learning revolve around the development of an effective interface between each distance language learner and their particular learning context. How learners define the context, how they define themselves as learners, how they act on that knowledge – all are central to the process of distance language learning. In other words, how learners construe the context and their actions within that context is critical for the development of the interface.

The idea of the learner–context interface as the nucleus of distance language learning is derived from student rationalities of their experience of the process. Learner conceptualisations of distance language learning were investigated in an in-depth longitudinal study (for details of the study see White 1999a). The concept of the learner–context interface represents the first attempt within the field to provide a theory of distance language learning and also to identify essential aspects of distance language learning. It has three dimensions: the individual distance learner, the learning context and the interface between the two.

4.3.1 The learner dimension

The *learner* dimension comprises the characteristics and attributes that an individual brings to language learning. The aim here is not to present an account of learner factors in distance language learning – there is a lack of research in this area – but to draw attention to the kinds of areas of difference in terms of what learners bring to the distance learning process. The learner dimension includes any prior knowledge of the TL, of how to learn a language and of the distance learning context. It also includes knowledge and skills related to learning in other contexts, and the knowledge individuals have about themselves as learners. Alongside knowledge are the beliefs and attitudes learners have developed within particular educational, social and cultural settings, which also influence the ways in which they approach and experience distance language

Table 4.1. *The language learner dimension*

Learner attributes, conceptualisations and affects
• Innate language acquisition capacity
• Psycholinguistic processes
• Gender
• Age
• Aptitude
• Cognitive style
• Learning disabilities
• Personality
• Self/social/cultural identity
• Agency
• Metacognitive knowledge
• Beliefs
• Attitudes
• Motivation
• Constructs of self as learner, of teacher . . .
• Conceptualisations of learning environments

Source: Adapted from Breen (2001: 9).

learning (for more on this see Chapter 6). Learner characteristics such as age and gender may also be relevant alongside affective aspects including motivation, tolerance of ambiguity, and locus of control (White 1999a). The work of Breen (2001) on learner contributions to language learning is useful here. He suggests that learner contributions can be seen as the attributes of individual learners and the conceptualisations and affects they apply to language learning experience (see Table 4.1).

4.3.2 The context dimension

I have also broadly defined the second dimension, *context*. The context dimension comprises features of the distance learning course (e.g. the nature and opportunities for interaction, support, flexibility, learner control), of the TL learning sources, and of the environments in which the learning is carried out (see Table 4.2). Distance learners play a key role in *selecting* and *structuring* elements within the learning context to provide an optimal learning environment for themselves. A number of important aspects of distance language learning contexts – learner support, learning sources, learning spaces – are presented in the final chapters.

Table 4.2. *The context dimension*

The distance learning context
• Learning sources (including the course and other TL sources) • Learner support • Learning spaces • Opportunities for interaction • The teacher(s) • The distance learning community • Features of the learner's immediate learning environment • Other resources (human and material)

4.3.3 The interface between learner and context

The third dimension, the *interface*, is both the place *at* which and the means *by* which learner and context meet, interact and affect one another. The interface is developed (vertical strands) as each learner interacts with the learning context (horizontal arrows) (see Figure 4.1). As learners become more accustomed to engaging and interacting with

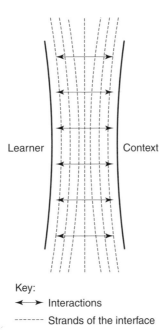

Key:
◄───► Interactions
------- Strands of the interface

Figure 4.1 Model of the interface forged by interactions between learner and context

the distance learning context (through interactions with the course materials, with other learners, or with the teacher) to develop TL skills, these same interactions contribute to the development of the learner–context interface. The vertical strands of the interface can be seen as representing the development of preferred ways of learning, the ability to match learning needs with resources within the learning context, knowledge about how to proceed within a distance language learning context and skills in self-management and in establishing a home-based or work-based language learning environment.

The interface facilitates the interchange between what a distance language learner may already know and understand – about how to learn a language, about the TL, or about distance learning – and what there still is to know and understand.

The interface is not a fixed attribute. The way in which it develops with individual learners depends on factors relating to both the individual learner and to the context. In some contexts, with some learners, the interface may be enhanced by the new technologies, such as by online discussions or opportunities for e-mail partnerships with native speakers of the TL. In others, it may be improved by particular support structures, such as opportunities for telephone advisory sessions, or by peer support. In others changes within the learner prompted by the particular learning experiences may develop the interface. The challenge for the learner is to develop an interface with the learning context that provides the opportunity to discern and explore the affordances of each situation.

Learners must develop the interface in order to develop TL skills within the distance context. In face-to-face classrooms the teacher mediates between each learner and the TL, by planning, providing instructions and directions, monitoring understanding and performance, providing feedback, answering questions, providing further guidance, and evaluating the effectiveness of particular classroom activities. There is much less need for classroom learners to develop, monitor and maintain their own means of working with and within the learning context. This key facet of distance language learning has tended to be overlooked.

The interaction that occurs between each learner and the learning context may enhance or inhibit the development of the interface, depending upon the extent to which those interactions contribute to meeting the needs of individual learners. So, for example, interactions with the course video may be deemed to be useful by a learner for practising pronunciation and dialogues, and become at that point an important part of his or her learning experiences and ways of working in the distance language learning context. On the other hand, if a learner encounters difficulty in understanding what is required in a writing task, posts a question on the discussion list, and is referred to more instructions on the course website, rather than a personalised response with opportunities for dialogue, that interaction may impact negatively on the development of the interface. Two further points are important here:

- distance language learners must devote mental resources to developing an effective interface between themselves and the learning context;
- they may already have mental models based on prior experiences of training and instruction. They may not be prepared for or have had experience of the kinds of processes involved in developing an effective interface with a new learning context.

Of course, how each learner develops the interface, and acts at the interface, will also depend upon a number of individual and contextual factors as outlined earlier.

4.4 Features of the learner–context interface

The concept of the learner–context interface has a number of features which are elaborated on here. They bring together current thinking within the literature and the reports of learners and teachers. They were first identified in the longitudinal study of White (1999a), as learners were asked in an iterative data collection cycle to elaborate on the conceptualisations of distance language learning which emerged in the study. The excerpts from learners included in this section are taken from previously unpublished data from the study reported in White (1999a). Those from teachers are drawn from an extension of that study to investigate how distance language teachers responded to the conceptions held by learners in relation to distance language learning (White 1999c).

4.4.1 Distance learners are key agents in the construction of the interface

The term 'key agent' is taken from Esch and Zähner (2000), who identify a set of principles to inform the development of a network-based language learning environment. They are concerned with how Information and Communications Technology (ICT) may be evaluated by learners as relevant contributors to their language learning experiences. One of their main arguments is that:

> Individual learners, with the help of their teachers, are the key
> agents of the process whereby particular ICTs are identified as
> potential tools for language learning; they analyse their potential

in terms of their specificity and of their own requirements; they test them, then build them gradually into their language learning environment.

(Esch and Zähner 2000: 6)

This analysis of learners as key agents in the construction of language learning environments is particularly relevant to the distance learning context, and to the idea of the learner–context interface. Distance learners are key agents who select elements within the context to be part of their learning environment. They may select from TL sources, tasks, interaction patterns with the teacher and peers, forms of support, and the format of study sessions, for example. The teacher may, of course, prescribe and monitor the presence and use of some elements within the distance learner's environment, such as requiring learners to contribute to discussion lists on a regular basis. Learners must then still decide how and when to operate on those requirements. For the most part it is the learners who must select, configure and manage the interface between themselves and the learning context.

Obviously some individuals are more able than others to identify how to create a productive interface with the learning context; some are better informed in terms of knowledge about themselves as learners and affordances within the learning environment. And some enjoy the opportunity to take responsibility for these aspects of their learning. However, even for the most skilled learners, the construction of the interface takes time, involvement, initiative, commitment, confidence and a degree of trial and error.

Learner commentary: Learners as key agents in the construction of the interface

When you are studying at a distance you make judgements all the time about what you will do, how you will do it, and the amount of attention and focus you will give to that particular word, task, assignment, or whatever. You really have to decide all of these things for yourself. Sometimes I find I have worked a lot on something which turns out not to be so useful, relevant, productive or whatever. I also have to decide on how I am carrying out my learning, the habits I am setting up for myself, and whether they are working or not. At the moment I think I can decide what is right for me as I learn, but that may get more difficult. I still keep a lookout for other things that might help too.

(White 1999a)

> **Teacher commentary: Learners as key agents in the construction of the interface**
>
> This student has obviously worked out a key part of adjusting to the distance learning environment. That is, making decisions about what is appropriate for themselves, and thinking about how to set that up. Also, they are aware of the ways in which particular sources help with developing abilities in the language. The face-to-face teacher makes decisions about the kinds of tasks which might suit most people in the class. So does the distance teacher. However, in the distance context students have influence in terms of the elements which are brought into their experience and learning environment.
>
> (White 1999c)

4.4.2 *The interface is essentially dynamic*

A socially oriented approach to second language learning views the relationship between the individual learner and the social context of learning as dynamic, and constantly changing (Mitchell and Myles 1998). The idea of the learner–context interface expressed by learners reflects a view that the interface is developed and reconstructed through the ongoing experiences within distance contexts. Learners themselves vary in terms of their preferences, needs, experiences, skills and the attributes they bring to the development of the interface. And different aspects of the learning context, including different aspects of the course, assume significance for particular learners. Further to this, the learner–context interface itself is also variable. The interface changes according to the background, goals, skills and so on of individual learners and the particular requirements and affordances of the context, and because of the divergent ways learners incorporate aspects of the context into their learning experiences.

The nature of the interface between learner and context changes over time, in response to a range of factors. The factors that may play a role in the ongoing changes include:

- learners' ideas about their needs and preferences;
- perceptions of the learning context;
- perceptions of the usefulness of TL sources within that context;
- familiarity with distance language learning;
- knowledge and skills in self-management;
- the demands of 'the course' (e.g. assessment demands);
- successful and less successful learning experiences;

- feedback from within the learning context;
- the kinds and extent of interaction preferred by learners;
- preferred learning environments.

Learner commentary: The interface is essentially dynamic

I have really changed how I go about learning in this course. I hadn't realised how much my way of working would alter, and how much I would have to modify how I go about things. I spent five years learning languages at school, and thought I knew pretty much how to get into the language by myself, but the context here is very different, and you can't operate in the same way. I still do keep changing how I set things up, how I manage them, the kinds of things I select, but the changes are much smaller in myself and how I go about things. I notice that when things get difficult, I begin a rethink of what I am doing.

(White 1999a)

Teacher commentary: The interface is essentially dynamic

One of the interesting things about working with distance language learners is the degree of change they experience in the way they manage themselves and their learning environment throughout the course. This is not something they are usually prepared for. At the outset they tend to expect things will unfold in a fairly straightforward way, and they do not always foresee the ongoing adjustments they will need to make in order to get the best out of themselves and the learning context. I find it very satisfying when students report how much they have learned, not only in the course, but about how to make ongoing adjustments to the learning context. It is quite difficult when students are not happy with the need to really work with the learning context and themselves to get the best result. This is where support structures and opportunities for learning from other students are important.

(White 1999c)

It takes time and persistence to develop a means of working at the interface between learners' own resources and resources within the context. Learners must adjust and modify their interactions, fitting their own characteristics to those of the context. These adaptive interactions require both confidence and flexibility.

4.4.3 *The interface gives rise to mutually interactive effects*

Van Lier (2002: 17) makes a case for approaching the classroom teaching/learning setting as an ecology in which:

> the learners' and teacher's interactions make available sociocultural affordances that provide opportunities for learning. This presupposes an active learner whose actions cannot be prespecified in the way that methods traditionally attempt to do.

This perspective extends the view of learning as socially constructed, to focus on the complementarity between learners and the environment. The view of distance language learners was that the interconnection between themselves and the context had a number of mutual effects – mutual to both themselves and to the environment that they create. Learners change as a result of interaction with the context, and they can take actions which modify the context as part of developing their own learning environment. According to this view, learners are influenced in new ways by the solo learning context, to extend and develop their learning skills and knowledge about themselves as learners. At the same time, learners exert an influence on elements within the context, as they approach them, engage with them and accommodate them into their learning experiences.

Learner commentary: The interface gives rise to mutually interactive effects

I have learned a lot about myself, what works for me, and what I am capable of. I hadn't really expected that this course would have such an influence on me. I think it is because it is quite difficult starting to learn this way – then you can be surprised what you find. What really changed me was having to make decisions and to manage things for myself. It took me a very long time to set the course up the way that suits me. I am really interested to know how other people have gone about this – about the choices they have made – I wonder if their ideas about the course are the same as mine.

(White 1999a)

Teacher commentary: The interface gives rise to mutually interactive effects

Distance language students are not always prepared for how much they will need to adapt to the context – at the same time, of course, there is a very positive side to this as they develop knowledge about

> themselves as language learners. The pity is that they may not rec-
> ognise the long term value of developing an understanding of them-
> selves. I think often the demands of getting through the course
> obscure these other aspects . . . The other thing in all of this is that
> students shape the context to suit themselves. And it is critically
> important that there are opportunities in the course for this shaping
> to take place. There needs to be the time for this, and also the course
> structure needs to be open enough. If students are to really learn
> about how to optimise learning experiences in the distance context
> you need to keep all the options open for them to make choices in
> relation to themselves and the context.
>
> (White 1999c)

The extent to which learners are proficient in developing the interface will impact on progress in the TL. The extent to which they understand and feel comfortable with this role also has an impact on progress and a sense of enjoyment or satisfaction. This is true even for experienced language learners; they still need to take time to set up a means of working with features of the learning context as an integral part of the process of language learning, and of developing a learning environment appropriate for their needs.

Developing a productive interface between learner and learning context is central to success in distance language learning. Learners must ultimately do this for themselves – since the interface must be viable in terms of their learning needs – and must continue to maintain the interface in each learning experience. The teacher, however, also plays a critical role.

4.5 The contribution of the teacher

Distance language learning changes the teaching–learning relationship that students have been confronted with for much of their lives. If learners are to become full beneficiaries of, and active partners within, distance learning environments they need to be supported in finding ways of effectively managing themselves and their learning experiences. Distance learners may not be aware of the time, energy and mental resources they will need to devote to establishing an effective interface with the new learning context. The contribution of the teacher includes:

• awareness of the importance of the development of the learner–
  context interface;

- preparedness to assist learners, wherever possible, in accommodating to the process of developing the interface;
- responsiveness to the particular interface each learner develops;
- flexibility in tailoring aspects of the context (e.g. learner support) to fit with the means of working developed by learners;
- willingness and ability to set up and improve conditions in the context, which are conducive to enhancing the learner–context interface;
- guiding learners in the ongoing enhancement of the interface.

4.6 Summary

The theoretical framework developed here is derived from student rationalities of language learning. The notion of learner–context interface places the relationship between learner and learning context at the centre of the process of distance language learning. The key issues for distance language learning take place at the interface: the point at which learners need to establish for themselves a working mode through which to derive learning experiences from the context. How learners define the context, how they define themselves as learners, how they act on that knowledge – all are central to the process of distance language learning. In other words, how learners construe the context and their actions within that context is critical for the development of the interface. While the view of learners as active within the learning context is widely held, the view of learners as active in constructing an interface with the distance learning environment is relatively new. The concept of the interface emphasises distance learning as the relationship and interaction between learner and learning context, rather than the delivery of learning materials. Naturally course preparation and delivery are very important, but they should be informed by an understanding that the critical processes for distance language learning occur at the interface. The challenge for practitioners is to make it possible for learners to develop an appropriate interface between themselves and all aspects of the context in which they pursue their learning.

Part II Learner Dimensions

5 Developing awareness of distance language learners

5.1 Introduction

A major challenge for anyone teaching languages at a distance is to develop a knowledge base about distance language learners that can be used to inform course design. Further understanding is required once interactions begin and the course is under way; at this point the teacher needs to support learners in developing an effective interface with elements in the learning context as the basis for acquiring skills in the TL. Both these types of knowledge – one to inform course design, and the other to inform course delivery and interactions – are critical. More important still is an awareness of the contextual and affective factors which influence the way learners relate to and proceed within distance learning environments.

In this chapter I explore different approaches to building awareness of distance language learners, beginning first with the types of knowledge that are needed for course design and the idea of learner archetypes or learner profiles. A 'practical knowledge' of learners is also needed once a course is under way to guide the teacher in the various roles she or he will undertake – and to enhance and personalise interactions within the course. The different aspects of this knowledge that may be drawn upon by the teacher are outlined. More recent approaches to developing awareness of distance language learners presented here include a focus on the environment in which the learning takes place, the affective domain and the depiction of learners as dynamic individuals within the distance learning experience. What emerges throughout this chapter is the importance of using a variety of approaches to developing a knowledge, understanding and awareness of distance language learners in context.

5.2 Learner awareness: challenges and constraints

Language teachers, whether at the stage of course design, lesson planning, or classroom interaction, usually have in their mind's eye an idea
of who their learners are, what their needs will be, what their preferences
might be, what might motivate them and so on. Such knowledge is also
a critical issue for distance education, but presents a number of challenges in the kinds of learning–teaching contexts associated with distance
language learning opportunities.

Doughty and Long (2002) identify developing knowledge of learners
as one of the key issues in adopting a task-based approach to language
teaching in the distance context. A task-based approach draws on and
reflects the experiential and humanistic traditions in language teaching,
in which the point of departure is a collection of tasks rather than functions, or situations, or topics, or a grammatical syllabus. The results of
pre-course and ongoing needs analyses are the foundation for syllabus
design and many pedagogical decisions taken in the course of task-based
teaching. This approach has significant implications in terms of the practicalities of developing an understanding of learners, and emerging
learner needs in the distance context. Doughty and Long argue that programme developers need to confront this as a fundamental issue: how
can needs analyses be carried out in distance language learning? A focus
on learner needs becomes all the more important, according to Doughty
and Long, as distance education shows signs of mass commercialisation,
and as staff may be pressured into providing language courses that are
packaged into ill-fitting courseware management programmes. This
argument parallels earlier debate within second language teaching that
challenged a unitary approach to syllabus design and course development in which 'learners were fed an undifferentiated linguistic diet –
regardless of their communicative needs' (Nunan 1999b: 148). From this
debate it became axiomatic that rather than fitting students to courses,
courses should be designed to fit students.

Candlin and Byrnes (1995) are also concerned with how to move away
from a more delivery-focused perspective to a more 'learner/learning
focused philosophy' in distance language learning. Unlike Doughty and
Long they are writing from the perspective of their professional involvement in an existing distance language programme for adult migrant
learners of English in Australia. The prevailing approach within distance
language learning is described by Candlin and Byrnes (1995: 11) as
follows:

> ... the delivery of distance learning programs has generally been
> characterised by mass production of materials, a centralization

of decision-making about learning and a pervasive requirement for programs to accommodate to rapidly changing technological advances which have their own particular orientations to learning.

Within this approach, traditional distance learning materials and delivery modes have paid less attention to factors such as motivation, individual differences, and learner attitudes. A more learner-focused approach to distance language learning recognises:

• the importance of flexibility and negotiation;
• the centrality of highlighting and developing cognitive and attitudinal processes;
• the importance of learner motivation.

(Candlin and Byrnes 1995: 9)

A practical knowledge and awareness of distance language learners is crucial in facilitating such an approach, and of the changing needs of individual learners as they progress through the course.

Both Candlin and Byrnes, and Doughty and Long, are concerned to identify and raise matters for debate, rather than to offer any set of solutions to what can be called the 'educational, philosophical and disciplinary issues' (Candlin and Byrnes 1995: 19) facing the move towards a more learner-centred distance language programme. The issues also relate to questions about the degree to which different aspects of distance language learning – syllabus design, pedagogical decisions, choice of technology, course development, course delivery, learner support – can be informed and influenced by a knowledge of the needs, preferences, interests and responses of learners.

These questions are particularly important when we reflect on the emergence of distance education as borderless education in which the pool of learners who access such education comes from an ever-widening range of countries. Much of the rhetoric focuses on the many *potential* audiences for distance learning in the global context, with relatively little knowledge of the *actual* background, experiences, expectations and so on of those learners.

5.3 Knowledge of learners for course design

A commonly-used approach to developing a distance language course is to begin by focusing on technology and course content – both of which are often seen as the most complex and most influential aspects of the course design process. The learners come into the picture once the course is set up. This approach, however, is far from ideal. Needs analysis, which has been an important principle in face-to-face language teaching since the 1980s, is also highly relevant to distance contexts – before, during and after course development. Potential learners and their needs should be considered right at the beginning of what is a highly complex process of course planning for distance learning, whether it relates to decisions about curriculum, materials development, delivery mode, opportunities for interaction, assessment and so on.

Emphasis placed on what Richards (2001: 54) calls an 'a priori' approach to needs analysis is particularly significant in distance learning because of the complexity of course design, which is a time-consuming, and therefore expensive, process. The time taken to develop a distance language course is many times that of developing a face-to-face course. Radic (2000) notes that the design and development of an Italian language computer-mediated distance language course took a team of professionals 4,500 working hours to complete. Given the long lead time between beginning course development and actual delivery of the course, the development process tends to be based on planning for potential learners. The approach most commonly used in distance language learning is to invest – often a considerable amount of time – in developing a profile or, more likely, profiles, of learners for the course. This is considered not only good practice, but essential if the course is to be viable. It is difficult to realign a course if it is found to be unsuitable for the eventual audience. The learner profile developed at this stage should also be used in pre-course counselling to advise students as to whether the course is appropriate for them or not.

Obviously, the notion of learner profiles, sometimes known as learner archetypes, does not claim to be an exact model of the actual learners in the course; the information tends to be of a generic rather than specific kind. The process of compiling learner profiles requires course development teams to reflect on, and develop, some clarity about, important aspects of the background of potential learners. They may include:

- demographic knowledge about the student population (e.g. geographical distribution, age, gender, employment);
- learner needs and goals;
- knowledge about how learners are likely to respond to particular approaches, methodologies and tasks within a distance language course;
- learner characteristics and expectations;
- access to technology (e.g. computer, Internet);
- access to TL resources (e.g. native speakers in the community);
- knowledge about how learners are likely to respond to different

aspects of the distance learning context, such as familiarity with the use of online discussion groups.

One important element to include in developing learner profiles is to ask learners also to provide information about themselves that they think is important or relevant. This aspect could easily be overlooked, yet it is often the most informative about the kinds of expectations, concerns, and background factors that students identify with. They may be highly individual factors, and as such may not be typical of the eventual body of learners in the course, but they add to the store of knowledge about the kinds of things that distance students think are important. Some examples are given in the *Reflections and experiences* section below. The comments identify learners' perceptions of the centrality of course content, and the portability of that content, and the isolation of some study contexts. They also identify the clear goals and high motivation of some learners, as well as the constraints of time, location and competing commitments.

Reflections and experiences

Reflections on learner background

Here are responses given by three individuals who were planning to take a distance language course in Spanish at Massey University, New Zealand, which was at the very early planning stages. They were asked to reflect on 'other' things they felt they would like the course designer to know about themselves.

I am pleased I am going to be able to learn Spanish through a course. I haven't studied formally for many, many years, so I feel a bit unsure of myself. I will be working entirely on my own – I have no access to other classes or to native speakers – and I don't know anyone else who has learned Spanish. So I will be completely reliant on this course to develop my skills in the language. I live on a farm so I am quite isolated. But I am very keen and I have plans to put all this to use by going to Latin America in three years' time with my husband.

I am a flight attendant and will carry my materials with me – to study in between flights. My Spanish is rusty, so I hope more study will bring the language back to life a bit. That's what I really want out of the course because I have forgotten so much. I think I am a fairly independent learner, but I need the structure of a course to motivate myself. I am not sure I'll be able to attend the campus course because my schedule varies so much.

> *The main thing for me is to find the time to do this course. To complete the course I will have to work on the essentials. I don't have much time but I learn quickly. For me learning is a very individual thing. I am highly motivated and I have learned a language before – I am looking forward to this Spanish course being offered.*

In creating a proposal for a computer-mediated language course to be delivered at a distance, a profile was developed of the target group. The International Business English course was to be taught and administered by two institutions – the universities of British Columbia (UBC) and Auckland (UA). In a collaborative environment it was considered particularly important to identify and reach agreement on the nature of the target group. Curtis, Duchastel and Radic (1999: 39) note that the International Business English course is designed for:

- Students who wish to study business at the undergraduate or graduate level at an English speaking university but do not meet the language requirements for acceptance in regular programmes.
- Some of the applicants may already be in the workforce but will not have experience in the business world. Applicants who are business professionals are advised to take the English for Executives programme.
- The target group is relatively heterogeneous; there is likely to be an even mix of men and women, and while the majority of students will be in their early 20s, some may be older individuals who are considering a change of career.
- The course is expected to attract students from all over the world. However, an attempt will be made to serve the large immigrant populations in both countries.
- Course participants are expected to represent a wide variety of cultures, which would facilitate cross-cultural exchanges.
- Students should have a minimum of 550 (TOEFL) or 6.0 (IELTS) to enrol.
- Students need access to a computer with a CD-ROM and should have basic computer skills, i.e., a familiarity with Windows, simple Word Processing, and web browsers.
- In all likelihood few students will have taken a technology-based distance course before.
- Most students will have experienced the teacher-centred approaches to learning characteristics of the traditional classroom. It is expected that there will be a variety of learning styles among the target group.

The profile covers a number of areas from demographic factors to access to technology, cultural background, language proficiency and prior learning experiences. It has been developed in such a way as to be useful for both course development and advisory sessions with students who are contemplating enrolling in the course.

It does not make sense to present a template which can be used to develop learner profiles for the design phase of all distance language courses since a number of other factors influence the kinds of knowledge needed to design a distance language course. These include the institutional context, the level of the course, perceptions of the teacher's role and that of the learner, the modes of delivery available within the institution and the availability of resources. These factors are what Richards (2001) includes under situation analysis – that is an analysis of factors in the context of a planned programme which may impact on the project. In distance language learning it is important that situational analysis focuses not only on the immediate context of the institution, but on the particular contexts in which the learning is carried out, which are, of course, remote from the teacher. The importance of individual learning sites is expanded upon later in the chapter.

How can knowledge about distance learners be acquired? In my own institution, the impetus for developing new language courses has traditionally come from existing distance learners, or from members of the public who enquire about possibilities for distance language study. Through such enquiries and interactions, the course designer has, in the first instance, been able to build up in an informal way a profile of the kinds of learners who are likely to enrol in the course. Students are also sometimes appointed as representatives of the potential student group to the design team with a brief to keep the design team informed of learner perspectives, needs, interests, etc. Key sources of knowledge about learners also come from discussions within the institution, with colleagues, with other distance learners and experience of broadly similar learners. To return to a point made earlier in the chapter, the wider the potential pool of learners, as in 'borderless education', the more complex are the issues relating to course development informed by knowledge of learners.

5.4 Knowledge of learners at course entry

It is considerably easier to acquire knowledge about learners during the course, rather than at the course design stage. This is obvious since the individuals who together constitute the class have already enrolled and some information is available through the enrolment process. Learners can be asked to post an introduction about themselves and/or to complete an online questionnaire that can form the basis of an overall class profile. Such a profile would give the class a sense of the diversity of people who are enrolled in terms of age, occupation, location, interests and so on. Privacy issues must be respected in any information distributed to the class. Again, online technologies have simplified this considerably since learners themselves can choose to release or withhold information. Two examples of how distance language teachers approach issues relating to knowledge of learners are given in the following Reflections and experiences section.

Reflections and experiences

Knowledge of learners online

Establishing a pilot project for distance learners of German and French working online at the OUUK, Markus Kötter, Lesley Shield and Anne Stevens considered the most appropriate ways in which participants could provide information about themselves working in an online environment.

'We did not include photographs or students' self-descriptions in our web pages. Even though this might have supported student bonding, we believed that this kind of information could also have had intimidating effects on the students. So, while students were free to volunteer some personal data during the warm-up activities, we left it up to the participants to decide what and how much information they wanted to share with their peers.'

(Kötter *et al.* 1999: 57–8)

A different approach was taken by Maija Tammelin in the English for Environmental Communication course described in section 2.5. She was interested in the issue of social presence within the course environment. Here she refers to the course website and a café conference for social interaction.

'. . . at the beginning of the course, the participants' home pages were placed on the course WWW site . . . Many of the HSEBA students mentioned in their final reports that . . . it gave them a chance to learn more about each other . . . the main purpose of the café conference was to establish a space where the participants could demonstrate their own social presence and sense the presence of the other participants . . . through a café conference participants feel fully represented as human beings on a system that welcomes them

---

teacher to adapt to the different backgrounds of students, to foster interaction, to personalise interactions, develop appropriate feedback, to address student concerns, to provide support and so on as the course unfolds.

A practical knowledge of distance language learners is needed for pedagogical decision-making, and to enhance the quality of learner–teacher interaction. More specifically, the following roles for the distance language teachers identified by Candlin and Byrnes (1995: 13) will require the teacher throughout the course to draw on the knowledge base about learners which she or he has developed:

- select learning experiences that encourage choice and expand learning options;
- provide a supportive climate for learning;
- encourage risk-taking in making efforts to change;
- provide constructive judgements and evaluations;
- involve learners actively in posing problems;
- provide repetition, recycling and variation;
- present language and content through a range of sensory experiences.

The above roles are intended to relate to teacher–learner interaction throughout the course, rather than at the materials design stage.

A distance teacher's knowledge base about individual students extends as the course progresses. It is built up through interactions (by telephone, e-mail, discussion lists), submission of course work, queries and requests, reflections on their progress, notices that learners post on the bulletin board and so on. As a result of the more frequent contact between learners, and between the teacher and learner, that is made possible by e-mail and online discussion lists the teacher gains a more detailed view of how learners are responding to the distance learning environment. This was much less the case when the means of interaction were fewer, less immediate and less accessible. This developing knowledge base can provide insights into how learners are responding.

What teachers actually learn from the dynamics of responses of language learners has not, to date, been explored. Neither do we know how they use the knowledge they gain, nor how it adds to their practical theory of distance learning. An analysis of the nature of a teacher's practical knowledge of distance language learners – and its contribution to practice – is an important avenue for research.

The approach taken thus far has not dealt with a number of broader issues that are part of developing a more complete awareness and understanding of distance language learners in context. The three areas I will focus on for the remainder of the chapter reflect trends in second language teaching research and in the distance education literature in which:

- the environment in which learning takes place has achieved growing prominence;
- an increased emphasis has been placed on the affective domain of distance learning;
- learners are depicted increasingly as dynamic individuals within the distance learning experience.

An appreciation of these aspects is essential for distance language teachers in understanding the challenges faced by learners, in involving and supporting learners in the decisions they make about their learning experiences and in developing their sense of themselves as distance language learners. Each of these aspects is now discussed.

5.6 Learning sites and roles

5.6.1 Learning sites

An important yet often overlooked characteristic of distance students is that the primary site of learning is the home or the workplace. Learning takes place in a context that is located within personal and/or professional environments. The significance of these contexts as sites of education is just beginning to be recognised. Until recently in distance learning, space and time were considered to be inert features of the learning environment rather than key influences on the process. Relatively little account was taken of the multiple environments in which students pursue their learning and the way they contribute to, or detract from, the development of an effective interface with the distance learning context.

More attention is now being paid to the milieu of learners and the role of that milieu in learning. The major work in this area has been carried out by Gibson (1998) who uses ecological systems theory to examine the complex relationship between the developing person and the environment. Gibson (1998: 116) underlines the need to:

> . . . remain mindful that the context, both proximal and remote, can invite, permit, or inhibit progressive development over time in interaction with the individual's characteristics which encourage or discourage interactions with that environment . . . ecological systems theory helps us to go beyond the conception of a decontextualised or single-context learner to recognising the learner in multiple contexts.

Gibson highlights the ways in which individual learners seek to evoke a response from, alter or create an external learning environment in order to develop conditions conducive to learning. In particular, Gibson shows how others within the distance learner's environment(s) contribute either positively or negatively to the resolution of these demands and difficulties. This is a helpful approach to understanding the ways in which students work with and restructure aspects of their learning environment to establish more optimal learning conditions. Working with the external learning environment may mean establishing a physical study space, or choosing which aspects of the course to focus on, or deciding on the extent of participation in online text-based interaction with the teacher or course members. It can also include whether they seek out other students or native speakers to practise with, and how people and relationships within their professional or personal contexts enhance or detract from learning goals. Gibson's work has a generic focus on distance learning, and has not been applied to distance language learners in their individual learning contexts. However, ecological systems theory has much to contribute to our knowledge of how distance language learners develop an effective learner–context interface from within their environment. Van Lier (1996) and Tudor (2001) have also used an ecological approach to understanding the process of language learning and teaching, and I refer to their work in the next chapter.

5.6.2 Life roles

While the *learning site* is significant to an understanding of distance learners, so too is the role of each language learner in relation to other *life roles*. Much has been written about the philosophy that underpins lifelong learning, and the development of the knowledge society, but less attention has been given to associated changes in practice in adult lives as study is fitted into existing responsibilities and activities. Distance students have typically engaged with a number of life roles (worker, spouse, parent) and have a range of personal, professional, family and community responsibilities. These multiple roles are a major influence on the student experience, which distinguishes distance learners from full-time, on-campus students, who can enjoy a relatively more exclusive relationship with the learning context and the learning process. Distance learners often express a concern that their ability to develop an effective learning environment and to engage with the TL is compromised by the complex context in which they study as part-time learners.

Part-time study combined with other life roles can also be an advantage. When learners are alternating between studying the TL in the distance course and using it in their work, home life or other roles, this inevitably has an influence on the learning culture within a programme. Many language teachers have reported that the interplay between language learning and language use is particularly rewarding in the distance context (Grosse 2001; Radic 2001). Students seek not only to extend their skills, but to develop competence in areas which are directly useful to their current context. They are more likely to initiate questions, to bring forward aspects of the TL for discussion, and to provide feedback on how their language learning is going in terms of their TL language use. The relationship between the context of work and the context of learning was an important feature of a case study carried out by Nunan (1999a) in a distance Masters programme in TESOL. He notes that the students constantly referenced insights and research outcomes from the course against the realities of their working situation. He also argues that knowledge was situated and contextualised.

To respond effectively to the concerns expressed by learners it is essential that distance language teachers understand the impact of students' circumstances on the learning process. This idea is developed in the next section concerning knowledge of the affective domain of distance language learning.

5.7 The affective domain

That language learning is a complex task susceptible to a range of emotions such as motivation, anxiety, self-esteem and inhibition has long been acknowledged (see Arnold 1999 for an overview of affect in language learning). Distance language learning is subject to a similar range of influences relating to the affective domain. However, further demands on the affective resources of both learners and teachers arise from the more isolated study context, separation from peers and the teacher, and reduced or altered forms of social contact and interaction. The affective aspects of distance language learning need to be considered very carefully by language teachers, since studies show that students' affective experiences within distance learning may not always be favourable (e.g. Harris 1995). This is of concern since affective factors are now seen as critical to effective learning (Nunan and Lamb 1996: 208). Two affective factors in particular – motivation and empathy – are to the fore in writings on distance language learning, as contributing either positively or negatively to involvement and persistence with distance learning experiences.

5.7.1 Motivation

A recurrent theme in the reflections of distance or online language teachers is that individuals enter their course of study with high initial motivation, but that the motivation to enrol in the course and to begin learning is not always maintained (see, for example, Harris, 1995; Smith and Salam 2000; Curtis, Duchastel and Radic 1999). This observed decline in motivation is linked with a number of factors: loneliness, isolation, competing commitments, absence of the structuring aspects of face-to-face classes, and difficulty in adjusting to a distance language learning context.

Numerous references have been made in the literature to the loneliness of the 'long distance language learner'. Certainly students often find distance language learning to be a somewhat isolated experience with relatively few opportunities for social interaction. It may also be difficult for learners to maintain motivation in the distance context without the structuring effect of face-to-face classes. Smith and Salam (2000) note that this becomes all the more difficult in the context of online language schools if there are no external deadlines for students to work to or a framework that helps them gauge their progress and guide them to the next step of learning.

One of the ongoing challenges identified in the distance course developed by the Adult Migrant English Program in Australia relates to maintaining high levels of motivation among learners who missed the peer support and social aspects of face-to-face classes (Candlin and Byrnes 1995; Harris 1995). In a detailed study of learners in the AMEP Harris (1995) found that those who managed to remain motivated were able to match features within the course with their own self-supporting strategies. They actively created for themselves a study-nurturing environment, which they saw as similar to the learning environment a teacher would develop within a face-to-face language class. This self-supporting strategy was a crucial element in maintaining study impetus. It is another expression of the importance of the individual distance learner's capacity to establish and maintain an effective interface with the learning context.

Learners, too, identify the importance of affective factors – and of motivation in particular – for 'success' in distance language learning. As part of a longitudinal study of novice learners of Japanese and Spanish studying by distance, White (1999a) asked participants to identify conditions that they felt were important for success as a distance language learner. Nine conditions were identified in the reports of learners: motivation, confidence in one's capacity to cope with distance learning, quality of course materials, amount of time studying, persistence, quality of interaction with tutor, amount of interaction with tutor, knowing how you learn best, and the optional face-to-face elements in the course. When all participants were asked to rank these conditions in the next phase of the study in terms of their importance for success, two affective factors – namely motivation and confidence in one's capacity to cope with the challenge of distance learning – received the highest rankings. Developing awareness of distance language learners includes understanding what they consider to be important for success, and in this affective factors play a key role.

5.7.2 Empathy

In language learning, empathy is also seen as an important contributor to success – this includes an emphasis on encouraging empathy in language learners particularly towards cross-cultural empathy (Arnold and Brown 1999). Empathy takes on a further dimension in distance learning, namely that an empathetic approach on the part of the teacher is fundamental to learners' satisfaction with distance study. Empathy relates to interpersonal aspects of distance language learning, and has been judged to be an essential ingredient in learner–teacher interactions (Holmberg 1986, 1995). Holmberg has long advocated a teaching style within the distance context which is informed by an empathetic approach on the part of the teacher to the context, situation and characteristics of each student. This approach has been highly influential in informing the design of teaching materials – with the principle that the 'teaching voice' in the materials should, as far as possible, be personalised and empathetic.

Both theoretical considerations and practical experiences have shown that matter-of-fact communication rarely meets student needs and demands. Van Lier (1996) writes of the negative effects on language learning when the teacher is primarily a transmitter of information, and argues that when relationships between teachers and students are depersonalised and kept programmatic and brief, what is lost is the development of extended and transforming relationships. Empathy and encouragement – both of which require an appreciation of learners and their circumstances – are essential components to effective interaction in distance language teaching.

5.7.3 Affective strategy use

Affective strategies are those that 'serve to regulate emotions, attitude and motivation' (Richards and Renandya 2002: 121). Distance language learning requires more self-management of learners in terms of their affective responses to learning, more than would perhaps be demanded of them in face-to-face contexts. One might expect distance learners to make wider and more frequent use of affective strategies since their isolated context may foster anxieties and concerns about their progress. In addition, the relative isolation of their study contexts may also mean they have to provide themselves with motivation, reinforcement and encouragement.

In a comparative study of classroom and distance language learners enrolled in a dual-mode institution, White (1993) found that distance learners used a wider range of affective strategies than classroom learners and also used them more frequently than their classroom counterparts. The strategies learners used included a particular type of self-motivation strategy. Self-motivation can be differentiated from other affective strategies as involving an explicit focus on the means learners use to keep themselves going, other than the arranging of rewards after an activity has been completed (*self-reinforcement*), beyond saying positive things to oneself (*self-encouragement*) or apart from using techniques in order to feel competent to carry out a task (*self-talk*). The *self-motivation* strategy can be defined as providing an impetus to keep going by reminding oneself of reasons for or advantages of continuing with the course. The following is an example of a self-motivation strategy from a distance learner of Japanese:

> Once I have got a certain amount of work done I remind myself that the big incentive is to keep going otherwise I am throwing away all the advantage.
>
> (White 1993: 157)

The use of self-motivation strategies means that learners keep in mind particular goals or incentives that can easily be called to mind to maintain study impetus. In the study self-motivation was the most frequently mentioned affective strategy used by distance language learners. Distance learners used affective strategies to encourage themselves, to reduce anxiety, to reassure themselves they could tackle the work and to motivate themselves. An understanding of the affective domain of distance language learners makes an important contribution to the knowledge base of distance language teachers.

Affect is of course a complex phenomenon in language learning. Tudor (2001: 102) makes the point that it arises out of:

> the dynamic interplay of what students bring with them to the classroom (not just as language learners but as individuals), the methodology and materials that are presented to them, how these fit in with their preferences and goal structures and, last but by no means least, the human relations that exist in the classroom both among students and between students and teachers.

Within a distance language programme it is important to add one further critical dimension that impacts on the affective experiences of learners, namely the circumstances in which they pursue their learning, including learning sites, life roles, and support structures within their learning environment.

5.8 A 'dynamic' conception of distance learners

While it may be useful to understand the characteristics of a cohort of potential learners, this approach is also essentially limited. And even for an individual learner, any profile must be tentative and dynamic, rather than static (Thompson 1998). A number of studies have examined the changing nature of learner characteristics. Gibson (1992, 1996) focused on changes in learners' self-perceptions as they progress through their distance programmes. The interplay of students' predisposing characteristics and changing life circumstances with institutional factors needs to be recognised as well as changes in students' willingness and ability to exercise control and/or self-direction. Understanding the dynamics of distance learner characteristics has profound implications not only for the design of courses and learner support, but for the individual distance language teacher. One of the key competencies required of a distance language teacher is the ability to develop an understanding of the contexts of distance language learners, of the realities of distance study, and of the shifts which take place in their perceptions, experiences and circumstances. This is the subject of the next chapter.

The study discussed in the next section was carried out at the OUUK and aimed to build up knowledge about learners who chose to enrol when a German language course was offered for the first time.

5.9 A profile of learners of German in a large-scale distance language programme

A study carried out by Uwe Baumann and Monica Shelley (2003) at the Open University UK illustrates some of the practical aspects of developing an initial understanding of the learners in a newly developed German language course. Information that was available to staff was based on earlier surveys of potential learners, and any background knowledge gained during the developmental testing phase. The research carried out by Baumann and Shelley aimed to develop an understanding of the distance learners who entered the course, and to document any shifts that occurred in their general understanding of Germany and the German people as part of studying the language. Here I will focus on some of the aspects of learner background that they identified as important.

5.9.1 The course

The context for the study was an improvers' German language course. Baumann and Shelley describe the language programme as a mixed-media course, consisting of course books, authentic video and audio documentaries, an audio drama, and pre-recorded audio activities – designed to be studied over eight months for approximately seven hours a week. Learner support services primarily based around the tutorial system developed by the OUUK are an important feature of the programme. The assessment component of the course includes assignments (some are computer-marked, others are marked by the tutor who provides extensive feedback) and a final examination. The language course centres on a number of contemporary themes and contemporary German life.

5.9.2 Knowledge of the learners

Baumann and Shelley point out that a knowledge of learners is an important feature of practice within the OUUK; extensive surveys are used, particularly for new courses, to develop a picture of the demographics of learners, their educational background on entry and the personal aims associated with studying at the OUUK. They wanted to develop a more detailed understanding of the kinds of learners who had chosen to study German by distance. It was important not to assume that they would be similar to the general population of learners within the OUUK – which, in line with international trends, was becoming increasingly diverse. It was also important not to assume they would be similar in background to distance learners of French and Spanish within the same institution.

One further challenge they faced relates to the scale of the course. Approximately 1,000 students were enrolled, and it was necessary to make decisions about how best to gain an understanding of this number of learners that would complement other sources of information. The tutor, who was responsible for interacting with the learners throughout the course, would have other opportunities to gain more detailed knowledge about individual learners.

After enrolment a postal questionnaire was sent to a random sample of half the learners in the course; it included items relating to demographic background, the student's experience of learning German and contacts with German-speaking countries. (Other parts of the survey, not reported here, related to knowledge and assumptions about Germany and the German way of life.) Over half of those contacted (55%) completed the survey.

Here I will focus on the significance of just three findings: age of students, prior TL experience, and reasons for studying German at a distance.

5.9.3 Age

Results indicated that the students who study German by distance are considerably older than those in the new OUUK student population. This is an important factor to understand in terms of the content and orientation of courses and also for the kinds of support that may be required, or preferred.

Baumann and Shelley then compared age-related data obtained in their questionnaire with a profile of the age range of all the students in the German course from enrolment information. The comparison revealed that learners who responded to the questionnaire were significantly older than the overall student population in the course: in the survey 62% of the respondents were over 50, while only 36% of the total population of learners in the German course were in that age group. It is likely that older learners had more time available to participate in the survey, compared to younger respondents who may have had a wider range of commitments. This highlights potential difficulties in reaching some sections of the population of distance learners, and the distorting effect of this on any profiles that are constructed of learners within the course.

5.9.4 Prior experience in the TL

Self-study was the most common means by which participants had learned German. More than half the students in the survey had experience of working in an independent context to learn German. Some had purchased commercial teach-yourself courses such as Linguaphone, or BBC German courses; others had been quite resourceful in accessing the TL through German television or radio programmes. Of course, none of these opportunities provide support services or opportunities for feedback from a tutor. This suggests that a sizeable proportion of the learners entering the German language course may already have developed some skills in self-directed learning in solo learning contexts, without many support services or opportunities for interaction. A smaller proportion of learners had studied German at school, or through adult education classes.

5.9.5 Reasons for studying German by distance

Baumann and Shelley also investigated reasons for choosing to study German through the distance mode. For this they used an open-ended question format. The learners gave wide-ranging answers but it was possible to group them into seven broad categories (see Table 5.2).

The results underline the fact that distance learning meets the need for

Table 5.2. *Reasons given for choosing to study German at a distance*

Reasons	%
The flexibility and convenience of OU study	34
Prior experience as a distance student; liked the study methods of supported distance learning	21
The good reputation of the OUUK	15
As part of study towards a degree	13
No other possibilities for learning German	12
Enjoy the discipline of distance study	9
The course goes on to higher levels of study in German	6

Source: Baumann and Shelley (2003).

learning experiences that are readily accessible, while at the same time positive experiences of distance study and the standing of the institution together account for 45 per cent of the responses. This echoes findings elsewhere in the literature about motivations for choosing and returning to distance study: while individuals may initially be attracted to distance learning for practical reasons to do with access and convenience, the reputation of the provider and a successful experience of distance study are also key influences.

Other findings broaden the picture. For example, links with Germany are strong: a third had lived in Germany for varying amounts of time, and two-thirds had friends or relatives there. More than half had learned French and a minority had learned a wide variety of other languages.

5.9.6 Commentary

The discrepancy between studying the *potential* learners for a distance course and the *actual* learners who enrol is highlighted here. While much attention had been paid to the population of potential distance learners of German – during the course proposal and course design stages – this could not be a substitute for a more detailed understanding of those who actually enrolled once the course was made available. A number of decisions had to be made about the kinds of information that would be useful, given the scale of the population as a whole and the fact that tutors had a range of opportunities to develop more detailed knowledge of individuals once the course had begun. Baumann and Shelley also wished to widen their understanding of the learners and the knowledge learners developed about the TL country as they progressed through the course; this was not the focus here, but, along with the learner background data, it provided a more complete view of the individuals within the course.

A key point to emerge is the difficulty of gaining access to some learners. It was clear that proportionately fewer of the younger students in the course, particularly those in the 30–39 age group, responded to the questionnaire. An understanding of the realities of their lives – multiple work, family and personal commitments – would suggest that this could not be a priority for them. However, it may be that they would be more willing to respond, and to share information about themselves, in another form – for example, in online discussions, which also provide opportunities to learn about others in the course. Two key points are suggested: the importance of understanding that course profiles may be distorted, and that the means used to develop a knowledge of learners may have an effect on who responds and the extent of the information they provide.

Information from this study would be useful to tutors within the course. It reveals that the population of learners within the course is too heterogeneous to provide a typical profile and that there is a need for the tutor to understand and accommodate the background and motivations of a diverse range of learners. However, a number of general points can also be drawn from the findings. The learners tend to have individual objectives for studying the course, relating more to their personal contexts and goals than to professional activities. They consider they are more proficient in reading and listening than in speaking and writing. Approximately half have experience of independent language study. The flexibility of distance study was attractive to this group, as were positive prior experiences of distance study at the OUUK. The study provides an indication of some of the dimensions along which learners are likely to vary, and thus is a useful way of orienting tutors to some of the features of the student population.

The information gathered by Baumann and Shelley was part of a larger study, and, as such, they were limited in the number of questions they could ask. The focus was not on background which could be used to inform learner support services. Had that been the case, the kinds of questions used would have related to contexts for study, access to technology, interest in study groups or online support networks, expectations of the course and of distance learning experiences, and contact with other distance learners in the course.

5.10 Summary

The strongest critics of distance education argue that it represents a depersonalisation of the learning process. This criticism has, if anything, increased as new distance education populations emerge and educational providers and institutions push to develop online course capability.

Advocates recognise, however, that an informed understanding of distance learners is a critical issue for distance education since inadequate or incomplete knowledge and awareness in this area severely compromises the quality of the learning experiences that are provided and developed. Such knowledge is required throughout the distance teaching–learning process. An important avenue of professional development for distance language teachers is to focus on extending their practical knowledge base of distance learners, in different contexts and at different stages of a distance course. It sits alongside a second key area, that of understanding the experience of adapting to and working within a distance language learning environment. This is the subject of the next chapter.

6 The initial experience of distance language learning

6.1 Introduction

This chapter focuses on the initial experience of distance language learning from two perspectives. The first perspective looks at the experience of distance language learning from the outside in. The focus is on the factors and processes involved in adjusting to the experience of distance learning. It is based principally on the observations and insights of distance educators into how individuals are socialised into a distance learning environment, and on the need to achieve congruence between individual attributes, the learning environment and personal circumstances.

The second perspective concerns learners' perceptions of the environment and their place within it. It represents an insider's perspective, that is how language learners experience distance language learning, and the knowledge and beliefs which they develop in relation to that experience. Since the initial experience of distance language learning presents a range of challenges to learners – it has been identified as a critical point in terms of a decision to persist with learning or to withdraw from the process – this period is foregrounded in the chapter. Insights are derived from quite detailed longitudinal work with language learners new to distance learning, beginning with their initial expectations of that environment.

Understanding the learners' framework of experience – that is the content and structure of the expectations, beliefs and knowledge they bring to the language learning process – is important, because until recently distance language learners have tended to be considered in more abstract terms. Consequently, the nature and impact of their framework has tended to be little understood and all too easily overlooked. A close following of the initial experience of distance language learning reveals the dynamics of learner experience and beliefs within an unfamiliar environment. Included here, too, is an account of the kinds of metacognitive experiences that individuals have identified as prompting development in their knowledge of distance language learning and of themselves as learners. A study of the initial experience of language learners in an online environment is discussed at the end of the chapter.

6.2 Participation and progression

Persistence, attrition, drop-out rates, and student progress together form a primary concern within distance language learning. Lack of persistence may be seen as a reflection of the credibility or effectiveness of particular programmes; when attrition rates become very high they call into question the viability of distance education itself (Belawati 1998). Institutions such as the Open University UK devote substantial resources and research time to investigating student retention and drop-out rates.

Harris (1995), writing about the distance ESL course developed by the AMEP in Australia, reports that tutors were perturbed by drop-out and the complex issue of persistence. The ESL learners were keen to participate in the learning experiences within the course – which aimed to transfer experiences from the materials into the communities and contexts in which they live (Candlin and Byrnes 1995) – but found it difficult to maintain the study impetus necessary to progress through the course. Tutors were all the more concerned given the high level of support they provided and the positive response of learners to the materials. In other words, two key elements within the learning context, namely the learning sources and learner support, were of high quality and well received by the adult migrant second language learners in the distance programme. In spite of high initial motivation expressed by all learners, less than half completed the course.

The issue of persistence in distance language learning is highly complex and requires attention to the contexts in which individuals pursue their learning. This is the subject of the next section, but first I would like to return to the distance ESL learners in Harris' study and their views of what is provided in a face-to-face classroom. Their view – possibly idealised but none the less very real for them – was that teacher-mediated language classes held in a particular location with learners had a number of positive factors. These related to the facilitating presence of participants (teachers, fellow learners), and to the regular structuring effect of classes on their learning.

The main inhibiting factors reported by the distance learners of English are analysed by Harris as relating to academic, practical and affective inhibition, represented in Table 6.1. The circumstances in which the inhibiting factors could arise are also given, together with extracts from the reports of learners.

6.2.1 Academic inhibition

Academic inhibition really arose from the lack of the immediate presence of the teacher to mediate learners' interactions with the materials and the

Table 6.1. *Inhibiting factors in study impetus for language learners in the AMEP distance program*

Inhibiting factors	Conditions	Comments from adult migrant learners of English
Academic inhibition	May occur when learners experience difficulties with the materials, need help, and miss the immediate face-to-face assistance of a teacher	'You need someone there like your teacher, you know, to be able to ask questions.' 'Because sometimes on the phone you can't explain very well, and in the class the teacher can use body language, or draw the picture.'
Practical inhibition	May arise as learners experience difficulty in integrating study into a busy life	'When you have to go to class, then that's easier, you know, "this is the time when I have to go to class".' 'Sometimes 12 o'clock at night-time, and then they sleep and I just can open my book . . . very tired so just cannot concentrate.'
Affective inhibition	Negative feelings arising from academic or practical problems, or from an unsatisfying emotional experience of attempting solitary study	'The only thing is that sometimes I feel a little bit lonely.' 'When you sit at home alone you can't communicate . . . and that makes it harder than when you can go to class.'

Source: Adapted from Harris (1995).

TL. It was also particularly acute in this context as learners needed to use the TL for all interactions with the teacher by distance. Learners with limited educational background and low literacy levels were particularly vulnerable to academic inhibition. Harris reports that once learners suffered academic inhibition, they were likely to become discouraged, which led to study lapse, and then attrition of language skills.

6.2.2 Practical inhibition

Practical inhibition is a problem for many distance learners. It relates to the logistics of finding study time – particularly quality study time. External factors within the wider contexts of students' lives, based around family and work commitments, have an impact on the learning environment and circumstances of distance language learners. For the migrant learners in Harris' study practical inhibition was also a reflection of the lack of support in the lives of many migrants who come to Australia, who need to work long hours to establish themselves, and who may also be isolated at home with young children.

6.2.3 Affective inhibition

Affective inhibition involves negative feelings about distance study and may be associated with academic or practical inhibition, or lack of enjoyment of individual study. The peer contact provided in face-to-face language classes was seen as providing immediate support from the teacher, opportunities for regular commitment to study that would be understood by family members, language practice in a non-threatening situation and the opportunity to make social contacts (Harris 1995).

These inhibiting factors contributed in some cases to a lack of persistence among the adult migrant learners of English. The underlying issue for these learners was the lack of support in their lives (Harris 1995: 47); most were newly arrived migrants who faced multiple settlement challenges, and who were relatively isolated from other support networks. The next section examines the processes involved in accommodating to the initial experience of distance language learning and highlights the challenges learners face as they attempt to find a measure of fit between the new learning environment, their own context (social, family, work) and their attributes as individual learners.

6.3 Learner identities

Within second language learning the situated experience of learners has been a recent focus of research. Norton and Toohey (2001: 310) observe that this involves:

> studying how learners are situated in specific social, historical and cultural contexts and how learners resist or accept the positions those contexts offer them.

This approach represents a shift towards focusing on activities, settings and participation (McKay and Wong 1996; Fay and Hill 2003). One example is a recent case study of good language learners carried out by Norton and Toohey (2001). It underlines the importance of attention to social practices in the contexts in which individuals learn L2s, and of examining how learners form their identities in those contexts.

A focus on the situated experience of students who have entered a distance learning environment for the first time is a useful approach to understanding this crucial period. It is important to give attention to the processes that learners are required to confront as they seek to develop their identities as distance language learners. This involves examining the degree of compatibility between the characteristics and circumstances of learners and their particular environments. In order to be able to participate in and benefit from the distance learning experience, learners need to be able to bring together the following:

- their own circumstances, characteristics, conditions and attributes;
- the social/work/family environment;
- the distance language learning environment.

6.3.1 Learner attributes

The characteristics of individual learners may be more or less conducive to participating successfully in distance language learning; these include demographic characteristics, orientations to study and personal characteristics. Based on his reading of research, Harrell (1998) identifies the following attitudes, dispositions and characteristics as important in adapting to distance language learning:

- the ability to meet deadlines, and to develop effective time management;
- the ability to make the psychological adjustment to learning at home;
- self-management skills to organise one's life efficiently and effectively;
- motivation and discipline;
- the ability to manage the loneliness of distance language learning;
- the ability to self-monitor for personal control over the learning process;
- the ability to assume personal responsibility for learning.

Harrell sees success in distance language learning as related to personal attributes, which will help learners to meet the challenges of what is a relatively demanding instructional context.

6.3.2 Social/family/work environment

While individual characteristics and circumstances of the learner are crucially important, integration can be enhanced or impeded by the nature of each learner's social/work/family environment. Competing family commitments, and lack of support by the employer, friends or partners may together make persistence in distance language learning much more difficult or less likely. This aspect, however, highlights the need for learners to be proactive in environmental restructuring at an early stage, as reported in the literature with regard to distance learning and self-regulated learning contexts (see, for example, Gredler and Schwartz 1997; Lyall and McNamara 2000). It is of course not always possible for students to overcome the kinds of situational barriers that may exist in their environments.

6.3.3 Distance language learning environment

Crucial, too, is the nature of the distance language learning environment and how this may impact on integration and persistence. Accessible, high-quality support services and opportunities to gain feedback early in the course are two features of the distance learning environment which have been noted as contributing to the integration process.

As part of the process of developing an identity as a distance language learner, it is necessary to reconcile the features associated with these three sets of circumstances and attributes. They are represented as three arenas in Figure 6.1.

Two of the learners in Figure 6.1 succeed in achieving partial integration between the distance learning environment and their personal attributes (learner A), or their wider environment (learner B). Students who reflect the pattern of learner A would include those who are highly motivated, who have had some experience in more self-directed learning contexts and who find they are able to match their personal learning needs with opportunities provided by the course. However, situational barriers present a considerable challenge in their case, which require the ability to resolve competing demands and priorities in the physical setting where learning takes place (usually, the home and workplace).

Students who reflect the pattern of learner B may have well-established support networks within home and work environments, and time available to study. In such cases the distance language learning environment also has many facilitating features: the course tutor has been proactive in setting up online discussion groups, and is in contact with all students working with them on establishing effective ways of managing themselves, the course and their learning context. However, the student struggles to match personal attributes with those external circumstances; this includes feelings of alienation and loneliness, and difficulty in maintaining study impetus.

Learner C has found a substantial amount of common ground between the three arenas, and has established congruence between individual factors and circumstances (including responsibilities, commitments and conditions), and the distance learning environment. It is the degree of overlap between the three arenas (individual factors, academic

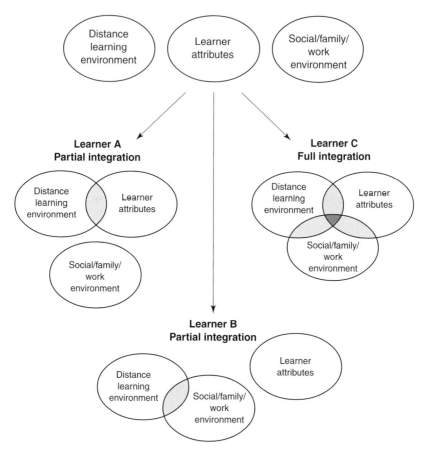

Figure 6.1 The three arenas relating to the process of integration: learner attributes, the distance learning environment and the social/family/work environment

circumstances, social/family/work circumstances) that has a bearing on the process of distance learning for each individual.

This model is useful for distance language teachers in conceptualising the process of adjusting to the new learning environment. It can be used as a means of reflecting on the concerns raised by learners, identifying facilitating factors within their contexts, a means of providing positive feedback and of identifying possible points of adjustment which can be negotiated with learners.

6.4 Integration, values and affiliation

The process of integration needs to occur early in the initial experience of distance language learning and requires students to find a measure of fit between the new learning environment, their own contexts (social, family, work) and their attributes as individual learners. Kember (1995) argues that the process of integration is enhanced by two factors which he calls *value integration* and *collective affiliation*.

6.4.1 Value integration

Integration is facilitated if there is some correspondence between the values of the course provider and those of the learners. It is the values that students hold in relation to learning experiences that influence the ways in which they perceive the course, and the extent to which they believe it can meet their learning needs. Value integration can be based on many aspects of language learning: it can be based on views of the roles of students and teachers, perceptions of what constitutes a quality learning experience, and the very fundamental question of what exactly constitutes learning a language.

A useful way of thinking about this is in terms of course epistemology and the notion of epistemological 'fit'. Epistemology means ideas about the nature of knowledge. The epistemology of language learning means ideas individuals hold about the nature of knowledge within language learning – what there is to know, how it can be known, what it entails and so on. If there is a gap between the stance taken by course designer or teacher and the stance taken by the student, then this gap will inhibit to a greater or lesser extent integration with language learning at a distance. This lack of 'fit' would be reflected in reactions such as 'I don't like the emphasis on dialogues', 'I think we are doing too much grammar', 'I feel I'm not getting enough feedback – I need a teacher there to check up on how I'm going'. Epistemological problems, then, reflect a lack of congruence between learners' ideas of what comprises language learning and the nature of language learning as presented in the course content. A further epistemological problem for learners may be that they find the content uninteresting, or lacking in personal relevance. While these issues also arise in face-to-face language learning they may have an immediate and detrimental effect on integration with the distance learning experience, and they are more difficult to detect, negotiate and resolve with distance learners.

Of course issues relating to course epistemology can be resolved in a positive way for distance learners. Many succeed in resolving and managing these problematic aspects of their environment which are at variance with what they need in order to participate and make progress in their learning. Others may develop what could be called 'epistemological flexibility' as they gain new understandings of what it means to learn a language. This brings to mind the link Candy (1991) draws between the notion of epistemological autonomy and the development of active, independent, critical learners. Others, however, may find they cannot easily accommodate to the new conventions of distance learning or to aspects of the course that they see as different from the values and visions they hold in relation to language learning. Persistence is then much less likely.

6.4.2 Collective affiliation

Affiliation to the learning group and a sense of belonging are generally a feature of face-to-face language learning systems. It is more difficult to incorporate this feature into language learning at a distance, but it is important for integration, particularly in the early stages of language learning. Generally this is established through course-related interactions, and dealings with support services, as well as through face-to-face tutorials and other opportunities for contact. The speed of response to contacts initiated by students is also important, as is the need for empathy and encouragement.

Of course, online learning environments have the potential to provide many opportunities for developing collective affiliation. A recent example comes from Christine Uber Grosse (2001) who attempted to generate feelings of community among the distance learners in her English Business Communication Course. She divided 116 students into six 'neighbourhoods' and assigned one graduate assistant to each as a 'neighbourhood manager'. The role of the managers was to facilitate online interaction among learners within the neighbourhood and to provide individualised feedback on writing. Reading Grosse's account of her course, it is evident a sense of community was first created within the neighbourhoods, and then shared with the class:

- each neighbourhood was given a place name that was important to participants, and a graphic artist created a slide for each neighbourhood;
- on the course web board a 'Meet Your Neighbours' section was created containing introductions from students and examples of their work. Students could also enter any of the other neighbourhoods to view the contributions that had been made;
- a few minutes were taken to celebrate birthdays, births and festivals in the satellite classes which took place with the whole class;

- each satellite neighbourhood manager would be invited to report about their neighbourhood, referring to students' work and aspects important to those learners.

Here, challenges associated with establishing a sense of community and collective affiliation within a large distance course were met within the small neighbourhood concept, and were judged to be effective by participants.

Relatively little is known as yet about the kinds of interactions that make the best possible contribution to a sense of collective affiliation. Part of the answer may be found in the research into the establishment of social presence and group cohesion in online distance language learning referred to in Chapter 3.

In the remainder of the chapter I continue to explore the initial experience of distance learning, but from an inside-out perspective. It is based on the beliefs learners develop in relation to their experiences in a new learning environment.

6.5 Entering the new language learning environment

Learners who undertake distance language study for the first time at the secondary or tertiary level will have had experience of learning in other settings, usually within the conventional classroom. They may have certain expectations about what it will be like to be a distance learner, or what the benefits and disadvantages of language learning in a distance programme will be. It is also likely that some of these initial expectations will not be met, or met only partially, and that new beliefs will emerge based on their experiences. As learners make their first contact with the new learning environment, they are confronted not only with a new context, but also with their own experience of learning and a new view of themselves – a new learner identity.

The initial expectations and then emergent beliefs and knowledge about distance language learning are important as a source of insight on learners' motives, goals and operations (Wenden 1999b). They are also important in that the belief systems learners hold or develop help them to define, understand and adapt to new environments, and to act in accordance with those understandings (Horwitz 1999, White 1999a). The beliefs of language learners have also been linked to affective factors such as anxiety (Oxford 1999, Horwitz 1999) and perceptions of their ability as language learners in self-directed contexts (Victori and Lockhart 1995).

Thinking about language learners who undertake distance study for the first time, a number of questions come to mind:

What do students expect when they start out on distance language learning?

About which aspects of distance language learning do they have expectations?

Are there areas in which their expectations conflict with the realities of distance language learning?

How do their expectations change as they gain experience?

What beliefs do language learners develop on the basis of their experiences?

Questions such as these about the expectations, beliefs and experiences of distance language learners point to significant aspects of the initial encounter with the distance language learning context. Here I discuss findings from a longitudinal study that traces the experiences of 'novice' distance language learners and their responses.

6.5.1 Novice distance language learners

The individuals who took part in the study had all learned a language before, but not at a distance. They could be considered 'novice' distance language learners. They were studying either Spanish or Japanese in a single semester, twelve-week course. The first part of the study took place during this period with nineteen students (see White 1999a). The following semester the research was extended to include a follow-up phase of eight weeks with those learners who continued to the next level of the language course (fifteen students). Thus what is reported here reflects the ongoing adaptations and emergent beliefs of distance language learners throughout their first 20 weeks' experience of the distance learning context.

6.5.2 Stages in entering the new learning environment

The dynamics of the experiences and emergent beliefs of novice distance language learners are related to the ongoing adaptations and adjustments they made in line with their changing perceptions of distance learning. In analysing the reports given by learners over a period of 20 weeks it was possible to identify three broad stages (Figure 6.1) starting with the anticipatory stage of deciding to become a distance language learner. Figure 6.2 is not meant to suggest that the stages are discrete and linear: learners move back and forth between the stages in response to different aspects of the course. Progressive adaptations occur throughout the experience of distance language learning. The adaptations may stem from, and result in, changes in beliefs about the language learning environment and about themselves as learners within that environment.

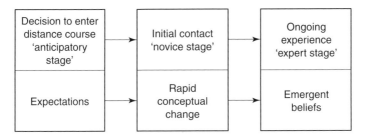

Figure 6.2 Stages in entering the new distance language learning environment

6.6 Expectations in the anticipatory phase

Of particular interest in the anticipatory stage were the domains of expectations held by students who had decided to enrol in a distance language course. Interviews with prospective distance learners took place when they had decided to enrol, well before the course had started. They were asked such questions as, 'What do you think distance language learning will be like?' and 'What expectations do you have about language learning through distance education?'

The responses were then analysed to identify the chief areas or domains in which learners held expectations:

Prior learning experiences: how distance study would be different from prior language learning experiences.
Learner role: views about what they will have to do as distance language learners.
Success: views about what would be important for them to succeed, and how they define success.
Control: views about the freedom and flexibility of distance language learning.
Context: ideas about features of the distance language learning context.
Advantages and disadvantages: ideas about positive and negative aspects of distance language learning.

The expectations represent the framework with which 'novice' distance learners are approaching the new language learning context – that is, with a view to the relative advantages or disadvantages of the environment, or with a view to their role as a learner and so on. From the responses of learners it was clear that some had based their expectations of distance language learning on their experience of classroom learning (classified as the domain of prior learning experience).

6.7 Conceptual change

The period of initial contact with distance language learning – that is when learners start working within the distance context for the first time – is a time of rapid conceptual change. The ways in which learners begin to question and re-examine their expectations and beliefs about distance language learning and about themselves as learners are shown in the extracts below. The reports come from novice distance language learners during their fourth week of experience in a distance language course at Massey University, New Zealand. The first is from a learner of Japanese:

> Well, if I am going to do well in this it's a lot harder than I thought. I was good at learning Italian, but I am struggling. I thought so long as the course is well written I won't have too much trouble. I have to set myself up a bit better I think. That's quite a nuisance – I guess I really like having someone there in person teaching you the language. I can do it all for myself, but I don't like having to think about that – well, I didn't at first.
>
> (White 1998)

This second extract is from a learner of Spanish:

> I thought I would be managing learning Spanish in the course a lot better than I seem to be doing. It's hard to be in control of a situation when you're not sure what you are doing, and what you are meant to be doing. I think I'm doing just fine, then I have lots of doubt – and I imagine everyone else is on track. I hadn't expected that it would take me so long to find my feet – but I feel I am managing things a lot better. At the start I felt like ringing the tutor at least twice in each study session. I got really anxious if things hadn't been fully explained. Sometimes I did ring the tutor – but not on every impulse.
>
> (White 1998)

At this stage it was evident that experiences in the new environment were inducing a degree of internal conflict and doubt about expectations held several weeks previously. As experience with the distance language learning context developed, three of the domains mentioned in section 6.3 were important sites for the development of new insights among learners:

- learner roles;
- what might be important for success in learning the TL;
- control in the new distance learning environment.

Previously held ideas and expectations in these areas in particular were being questioned.

6.8 Emergent beliefs: internal vs external regulation

As a result of ongoing experience in the distance language learning context, a number of new beliefs began to develop. The significance of tolerance of ambiguity and locus of control in relation to emergent beliefs is discussed in White (1999a). Here I want to discuss a third area, that is beliefs in relation to internal vs external regulation.

As language learners became more experienced in the distance context, a predominant theme in their reports was a concern with the range of things that needed to be done on a regular basis. These included:

- motivating themselves;
- making connections within the learning materials, and to their own level of knowledge;
- dealing with uncertainty;
- evaluating their learning;
- identifying problems;
- finding further examples or counter examples;
- managing the learning environment.

The term *learning functions* developed by Shuell (1988) encompasses these elements which form part of the learning process, and which can include learning strategies, affective control, and critical reflection on the learning process.

What was striking in the reports of distance language learners in the extended phase was the notion of task division and responsibility in relation to learning functions. That is, whether the regulation of learning functions is carried out by the individual learner – internal regulation – or by the teacher and the learning content – external regulation – or a combination of both. The different interpretations which language learners made of the regulation devices in the course content (see Examples 1, 2, 3), can be related to their beliefs about internal vs external regulation, and about who is responsible for carrying out learning functions.

The report in Example 1 is from a learner of Spanish. It reflects a view that learning is directed by the course content. She considers that the learning functions should arise from instruction within the materials. Clearly she feels most comfortable when learning is regulated in this way. It was evident that she did not have a strong idea of how to carry out learning functions herself when she came to parts of the course with fewer instructions. There were some elements of this point of view within six of the reports by language learners in the extended phase, but they were generally isolated comments rather than an indication of an overall belief in the importance of external regulation. The learner quoted in Example 1 was unusual in the extent of her preference for external regulation.

Example 1 External regulation: Learning functions arise from instruction

I think the best part of the Spanish course is when it is entirely clear what I need to be doing. I think the materials should state how long you need to spend on each section, just like a teacher would, and they should emphasise the most important parts of the topics. I'd like it if they were more explicit about what I need to know in terms of vocabulary and grammar. Do I need to know all the vocabulary and structures which are in the units? I'm often not clear on this.

Sometimes it's not clear what I am meant to do – for example, there may be a reading passage on one page and I am not sure where that fits in. I just read it, but I am not sure what else I should be doing with it.

(White 1998)

The extract in Example 2 from a male learner of Japanese reflects a belief in the availability of external regulation, but also in the importance of being able to choose the role it plays for each individual.

Example 2 Choice in relation to external regulation

In some of the units now I find myself skipping all the instructions and I just go to the language texts, or tasks. I find I don't often follow the directions given to me because I like to study in the order that suits me. Of course when I do the assignments I am careful to follow the directions and to do what is required, but not when I study on my own. I am really interested in learning Japanese since I have spent six months in Japan. I find the way in which they try to motivate you in the materials a bit quaint – as in the way they describe things in Japan, or about Japanese conversation. I don't need that since I have had a more direct experience, and I just want to improve my Japanese. But I can say that if you haven't been to Japan, and you aren't so motivated, those bits might be really important.

(White 1998)

In the extended phase of the study most language learners were evidently forming a view that they themselves were responsible for carrying out learning functions such as increasing their vocabulary, and that although these functions could be supported by different learning opportunities within the course, they needed to be activated primarily by themselves. Example 3 from a female learner of Japanese reflects this point of view.

Example 3 Internal regulation: Learning functions are activated by each learner

I have developed several ways to learn kanji now. I know writing out is still important for me. You are not always told that, but I have figured out that I need to do that very regularly. The exercises are good but they are not the full story. Sometimes I find I can do the exercises but I know I still don't know the kanji well enough. So I am not always very comforted by getting the answers right. Just doing that would be a minimal way to learn. I know I have to revise, revise, revise and work at bringing all the vocabulary together. For me the course is a sort of springboard – I move from there to learning in several ways. I couldn't just follow the course.

(White 1998)

The beliefs related to learning functions and the regulation of learning reported by learners revolved primarily around two interrelated questions:

a)   who was responsible for carrying out learning functions, and
b)   the degree to which learning was regulated by learners themselves or by external sources such as instruction through course materials or the teacher.

In the face-to-face language classroom many of the learning functions are initiated and overseen by the teacher, whereas in the distance context it is the learners themselves who need to assume more responsibility for fulfilling those functions. What was of interest here was the range of beliefs learners held in relation to the balance required between internal and external regulation of learning and how these beliefs fitted into their wider views of learning and of their role as learners. Individuals clearly varied in their interpretation of the regulatory devices in the distance learning texts, the importance they ascribed to them, and the place of external regulation as opposed to self-regulation in their learning.

One of the key challenges in distance language teaching is to orient learners to what may be required of them, and to assist them in having the confidence and ability to manage and pursue their learning without the ongoing, guiding presence of a teacher. Obviously individual beliefs play an important role here. The longitudinal research has shown that shifts in knowledge and beliefs take place in relation to different experiences and influences. Now an important and exciting avenue for research is to extend enquiry to include the beliefs learners hold as they enter technology-mediated distance learning environments for the first time, and the adjustments that occur.

6.9 Metacognitive experiences

Wenden (1999a: 441) in her introduction to a collection of articles on metacognitive knowledge and beliefs in language learning, raises a number of questions including:

How do learning settings shape learners' beliefs and knowledge? For example, do classroom learning and self-access learning lead to different beliefs?

How do beliefs and knowledge change over time? From one learning context to another?

To what extent do learners' active involvement in the regulation of their learning lead to changes in their beliefs and metacognitive knowledge?

Some preliminary responses to these questions have been provided for novice distance learners who are studying foreign languages. Studying the metacognitive experiences of distance language learners can also enhance our understanding of the way in which a new learning context can influence and change learners. Such experiences can occur at points when learners are confused, or uncertain, or when there is a breakdown in learning. They include the 'awarenesses, realisations, "ahas" . . .' (Garner 1987: 19) that sometimes arise from learning difficulties, and include conscious ideas and thoughts about the experience. The significance of metacognitive experiences is that they can prompt revision of the knowledge learners have developed about themselves, the learning process, particular tasks and so on.

How do metacognitive experiences manifest themselves in distance language learning? The distance language learning context calls for careful attention to the learning process and management of learning. The teacher is not always able to deal readily with every difficulty encountered by distance learners. Consideration of metacognitive experiences provides a further means of gaining insights into how learners respond to the distance language learning context – and how new knowledge or beliefs may emerge through action and interaction in that setting.

To investigate metacognitive experiences I collected data from novice distance language learners (N=31) through a verbal report procedure called the yoked subject technique. A more detailed account of the investigation of metacognitive experiences is given in White (1999b). The metacognitive experiences learners reported were numerous, and quite specific. Here I give four examples.

Example 4 is from a distance learner of Japanese. She recounts and reflects on a metacognitive experience in terms of triggers for the experience and the formative influence it has on her learning processes. Clearly this experience added to her knowledge about herself in terms of a need for confidence and the importance of focusing on current study goals.

Example 4 **Metacognitive experiences and the need for affective control**

After about the third week of study I thought I had been going quite well. I looked ahead through the rest of the units and realised there was so much more – that I'd barely scratched the surface – and I felt my confidence plummet. Lots more vocabulary, and more complex structures. I was also working on an assignment and felt increasingly unsure about things. Looking ahead had been a trigger for massive self-doubts. I contemplated giving up. Then I told myself that so long as I focused on one unit at a time I would get there. And the other thing I learned was that I had to maintain my confidence to get there.

(White 1999b: 43–4)

The comments given by the student in Example 5 identify the impact of a new learning context on her approach to learning Japanese. She does not give specific details of a single metacognitive episode, but relates how the experience as a whole served to prompt revision of metacognitive knowledge in relation to strategy use.

Example 5 **Metacognitive experiences and strategy use**

I remember when I began studying it hit me that I was into a new way of learning. I realised I had to study everything in detail – I couldn't skim over anything – so progress was very slow . . . I used to learn kanji off flash cards and then I found I couldn't really link those words with anything. I couldn't use them, I only knew them as words on cards. I felt I'd really got off on the wrong foot – and I felt quite

---

> discouraged about that. I'd wasted a lot of time and energy doing it wrong. Now I use a much better method – I learn the words together with other words, in a sentence if I can . . .
>
> (White 1999b: 44)

Metacognitive experiences frequently take place when there is a breakdown in the learning. What students can do to eliminate confusion or repair the breakdown depends in large part on the metacognitive knowledge they possess and, more importantly, are able to develop. The excerpt in Example 6 shows how metacognitive experiences are not confined to flashes of insight; this learner of Spanish has identified a problem with her learning. Finding a way through that problem involves developing metacognitive knowledge through experiences over an extended period of time.

Example 6 Metacognitive experiences and the development of metacognitive knowledge

Spanish verbs are really difficult. I was making progress with everything else but they really held me back. I tried various things: spending the first part of my study time on verbs, repeating verb forms at incidental periods during the day, having conversations with myself focusing on using verb forms that I did know . . . None of these things made a dramatic improvement so I dropped them. Eventually it occurred to me that I was having problems because verbs are hard, and that there is no single solution. From that point I returned to doing all the things I had tried out, but this time working with the verbs in lots of ways, not expecting to find a single ideal way. And, for me, this more varied approach does work.

(White 1999b: 44)

Over half the novice distance language learners in the study appeared to have complex attitudes to metacognitive experiences: they recognised them as critical points at which they moved forward as learners, but continued to express frustration about what had prompted the experience, as in Example 7. It could be that at a later stage the value rather than the frustration of these experiences comes more to the fore.

Example 7 Attitudes to metacognitive experiences

I remember I was up to Unit 5 and I had been studying regularly but putting a lot of work into the assignments. I went to the voluntary

---

> campus course and we had to work in Japanese without looking any-
> thing up. I recognised the material and I should have known it, but I
> hadn't internalised it. It was a real shock. I learned I had to revise the
> material, not just work with it and then leave it . . . I also realised I had
> to set some goals for my study – not just in hours of study – I had to
> make sure I was going to learn something and that it would be useful.
> I still feel annoyed that it took me a few weeks to work this out.
>
> (White 1999b: 44)

To return to the questions posed by Wenden (1999a) given earlier, this
part of the study suggests that the distance language learning context
contributes to the shaping of learners' beliefs and knowledge, and that
metacognitive experiences are a significant point of growth for learners.
Metacognitive experiences were not confined to specific learning difficulties, but were also strongly directed towards a concern about how best
to manage their learning within a new context. More specifically they
were concerned with how best to approach the learning units, and once
under way, how best to proceed, and to make progress as language learners. More detailed exploration of metacognitive experiences of distance
language learners – and the role they could play in reflective online text-
based interaction – is a promising avenue for future research in the field.

6.10 Environmental restructuring, internal restructuring

So far I have looked at the relationship between beliefs and experiences
during the initial experience of distance language learning, including the
shifts that may take place in learner beliefs as learners proceed along the
novice–expert continuum. These adjustments were focused on two areas
of experience:

Environmental restructuring was carried out by the learner to establish
     an optimal learning environment and circumstances.
Internal restructuring involved changes in beliefs, control of affect, and
     taking increasing responsibility for the regulation of learning.

Both environmental restructuring and internal restructuring are part of
the process of developing an effective interface with the learning context,
referred to in Chapter 4. The metacognitive experiences learners
reported, and their role in prompting revision of knowledge and beliefs,
as well as practices, adds to the perspective we have on some of the
dynamics of the experience of distance language learning.

6.11 The initial experience of learners of German in an online environment

There is a developing body of research relating to how adults in largely tertiary contexts respond to online learning in general (see, for example, Navarro and Shoemaker 2000; Nunan 1999a; Tyler, Green and Simpson 2001). However, relatively little, if any, research has focused on the experiences of online language learners at high school – or secondary school – who do not have access to face-to-face classes. The work carried out by Karin Barty in this area is a welcome contribution to the field. She traces the response of high school learners of German to an online course environment and identifies particular features of online learning that were a barrier to participation and engagement with the course for this group of learners.

6.11.1 The learners and the course

The context for the study was an online course for learners of German who were studying at the Year 11 stage in high school, aged about 17. One feature of the course was the small number of learners – eleven in total – who were scattered throughout the state of Victoria, Australia, in a number of rural schools. Each learner was relatively isolated, and the aim was to develop 'a small virtual learning community' (Barty 1999: 28).

The different learning contexts available to the individual student are presented in Figure 6.3. In developing the course environment, Barty emphasises the importance of opportunities for both synchronous and asynchronous forms of communication: these were provided by e-mail, fax, telephone, videoconferencing, and audiographics. Students were given opportunities to work on language activities with a range of others – learners in other countries, staff at their school, others on the course, and the distance language teacher. The course structure assumed that learners would spend half their time working alone on activities (two sessions a week), and for the other two sessions they would be linked with the teacher and, where possible, with other learners.

6.11.2 Learner preferences

This innovative approach to providing language learning opportunities in schools involved a relatively small number of learners who had extensive opportunities for interaction and collaboration to support their learning. Although the aim was to have 'independent learning, group work and teacher-directed learning in balance' (Barty 1999: 29), the

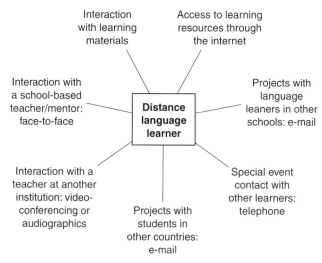

Figure 6.3 Course environment (Adapted from Barty 1999)

learners expressed strong preference for teacher-directed learning, for much of the course. While many of the participants understood the value and importance of developing skills in independent learning, they were less comfortable with these opportunities. Some had difficulty remaining on-task in independent sessions, or in staying motivated, or in concentrating. Some found it hard to make progress when they met with a difficulty or when they were unsure of what to do, while others felt paralysed in such a situation. They missed the social context of the classroom, and the ongoing guidance, structure and support it provides. As high school students all their prior learning experiences had been in such settings, and their responses indicated that they liked those traditional contexts.

Karin Barty notes that while much has been made of the attractions of moving from the conventional classroom to online environments, the learners in this study were not lured by the appeal of a state-of-the-art learning environment. On the basis of her research Barty (1999: 31) identifies three important elements in developing online language learning for secondary students:

1. regular teacher–student interaction must be retained in some form;
2. independent learning skills need to be built systematically;
3. resources that are convenient and familiar should be included in addition to newer resources.

6.11.3 *Affective response of learners*

The affective response of learners to the online learning context was prominent among the findings of the study. This is not surprising, given the degree of change for the students in ways of interacting and learning, compared to their prior learning contexts. Learning that involves significant adjustments on the part of learners – both in their ways of working and their views of the role of the teacher and of themselves – can be threatening and stressful. This is particularly acute when learners are experiencing changes, in isolation from others on the course. The teenage learners reported feeling 'overwhelmed' and 'uncertain' in the online environment when no teacher was present to offer guidance and advice. What they looked for, and expected, was the mediating presence of the teacher.

6.11.4 *The role of the teacher*

The reliance on the teacher to mediate between the individual learner and the language learning activity is a recurrent finding in the study. The learners needed support to access the TL texts, to work with the TL, and to have opportunities to reflect on their own language system and understanding. In distance learning much of the teacher's influence is indirect: she or he is not there to set up, monitor and evaluate each learning session: many of these functions are embedded within the course materials instead. For the high school learners in this study this proved to be a very real barrier in adjusting to the online environment. Barty (1999: 30) notes that the presence of the teacher appeared to have a direct influence on the level of material they could access in the TL: 'students often reported not understanding what the material was about whereas in linked sessions, with teacher guidance, the same material did not seem especially difficult'. The epistemological barriers to adapting to the online context were considerable in this context. Learners were dependent on the ways in which the classroom teacher scaffolds the learning process, and were often reluctant and/or unable to carry out these functions for themselves in the independent study sessions.

6.11.5 *Commentary*

The study does suggest that a process of adjustment, rather than outright resistance, was a feature of response to this new language learning context. For example, after about four months learners began to ask meaningful questions, and were positive about continuing on the online course for the following semester. An understanding of the process of socialisation within online learning environments is important for all participants – learners, teachers and technical support staff. The language learners had to make a considerable number of changes in adapting to the epistemology of the course, from their prior experiences of teacher-directed face-to-face classroom contexts to an online learning environment that included a substantial component of independent learning opportunities. The fact that they were presented with a rich learning environment with many opportunities for interaction went only a limited way towards easing the complex process of adjustment. These problems arose within what is generally regarded as the computer-literate generation, and online learning held fewer attractions for this group than expected.

One of the key aspects of the initial experience of a distance or online learning environment is that of learner confidence. This relates to a range of areas:

- their judgement about what is required of them;
- developing an understanding of how to proceed through the course;
- setting up their learning experiences;
- a sense of themselves as language learners, and a knowledge of their abilities;
- developing new ways of being a learner, such as being willing to proceed when things are not entirely clear.

A way of responding to the issue of learner confidence is to provide opportunities for interaction with other learners: to 'compare notes' about the course and to share experiences about how others are finding online learning – the good and the bad. Learners need to have the opportunity to have their experience validated, or challenged, by their peers. As mentioned earlier it is possible to provide a private space for this online – maybe using a chat facility – which cannot be accessed by the teacher. This is separate from the wider role the teacher may play in working with issues of learner confidence. Whether this would have been helpful in the high school context – and whether it would have been used for the purposes for which it was intended – is not entirely clear.

There has been relatively little research into online language learning in high school settings. Pivotal to the issue of adaptation to online learning environments is the influence of prior learning experiences and contexts – and the expectations and understandings which learners have developed about the learning process on the basis of those experiences. The structure of online courses needs to be developed with this understanding in mind, and to provide a link from the kinds of language learning contexts the learners have been familiar with.

6.12 Summary

A close following of the student experience reveals that learning a language within a distance environment for the first time places great demands on learners, particularly in the initial stages. It also reveals the extent to which developments take place in their knowledge of the learning environment and of themselves within that environment. From this we have a view of how distance language learners are engaged with ongoing environmental restructuring, and the internal restructuring of their expectations and beliefs in order to develop and maintain optimal learning conditions. The experience of distance language learning is influenced by a number of contextual features, only some of which lie within the control of the distance language teacher. However, the process for each learner of finding a measure of 'fit' between their own circumstances and contexts and the distance language learning environment may be facilitated by a sense of belonging to a supportive community of learners, by opportunities for interaction with teachers and peers relating to the experience of distance language learning, and by awareness of the challenges that form part of entering a new language learning environment. The processes that learners are required to confront as they seek to develop identities as distance language learners all relate to the need to integrate their characteristics and circumstances with the new learning environment. The importance of value integration and affiliation in developing an identity as a distance language learner has been underlined. The purpose of this chapter has been to chart, from different angles, the initial experience of distance learning and to focus on the way in which individuals can make the crucial step of developing a sense of congruence and affiliation with the new language learning environment.

7 Learner autonomy

7.1 Introduction

Learner autonomy has long been considered both a central and a problematic concept in distance language learning. It is closely aligned to assumptions about what constitutes an ideal learning environment and a quality distance learning experience. In some distance language courses, particularly within traditional models of distance learning, there is an emphasis on the importance of learner independence. Emerging paradigms for distance language learning place an emphasis on learner development through collaborative control of learning experiences.

Included in this chapter is an overview of the evolution of the autonomy concept – how it has been conceptualised, debated and critiqued in the field of distance learning. The components of learner autonomy identified by Tudor (2001) as learner training and learner involvement form the basis of a discussion of different approaches to helping language learners develop their capacity for autonomy with reference to two distance language programmes. The first approach is based around strategy development and learner training through materials design, while the second places emphasis on involving learners in choosing and accessing personally meaningful learning opportunities in the context of social interaction. In the second half of the chapter the central argument is that the views language teachers hold about learner autonomy need to be considered in relation to the principles and ideals associated with different paradigms of distance learning. The relationship between emerging paradigms for distance learning and opportunities to develop autonomy through collaborative control of learning experiences is an important aspect of this argument. It is linked with a discussion of research into the potential of text-based CMC for the development of reflective learning conversations among distance language learners.

7.2 Autonomy, independence and control

Learning a language in the distance mode presents learners with what may be new demands and new opportunities for self-direction. Distance language learners are involved in both self- and environment-management, and are faced with numerous decisions that may previously have been made for them by a teacher. In such a context they need to be able to assume more responsibility and control in identifying learning goals, in developing awareness of the learning process and directing their learning experiences.

While language learning at a distance may require learners to be more autonomous in the sense of having the ability to assume responsibility for their learning, it would be wrong to assume that the distance mode *per se* gives rise to learner autonomy. The distance learning environment, like any formal learning environment, may foster or limit the development of each learner's ability to understand and manage the language learning process. Much debate centres on the means by which distance language learners can be helped to develop their capacity for autonomy, both as learners and users of the TL. And this debate is closely related to different paradigms and ideals of distance language learning, and to various interpretations of learner independence, autonomy and control.

Learner   Collaborative
independence   control

Figure 7.1 Learner autonomy

The meanings ascribed to the concept of learner autonomy within distance education are related to discussions of control, self-directed learning, independence, and collaboration. It is possible to see them as ranging along a continuum with a focus on independence at one end, and collaborative control at the other (see Figure 7.1).

7.2.1 Independence

The approach to autonomy that emphasises learner independence has a long tradition in distance education. The expectation that learners can be independent and, further, that learner independence is an important goal for distance learning underlies the work of many early contributors to theory building within the field. It has been linked with discussion of self-directed learning, learner autonomy and individual responsibility. More recently, a substantial critique of the concept of independence as a key component in distance learning has been advanced (see, for example, Anderson and Garrison 1998). The conception and practice of distance education as a private form of learning based upon self-instructional texts has been challenged. It is argued that an excessive concern with independence as a desirable goal for distance education has seldom been balanced with a concern for support and recognition of the demands placed on learners.

7.2.2 Control

The concept of control has been proposed to reflect a fuller understanding of what is required of distance learners. According to this view, control is not a form of self-reliance that excludes all external interaction and resources. Instead, to exercise control learners must have freedom to explore and make choices, they must have a sufficient level of proficiency to carry out learning activities and appropriate support. Learner control is seen as developing out of a balance between three crucial elements: independence, proficiency and support (see Table 7.1).

Table 7.1. *The concept of control*

Learner control		
Independence	Proficiency	Support
The degree to which the learner is free to make choices.	The abilities and competencies of the learner to engage in a learning experience; the motivation and confidence needed to persist and succeed in a learning endeavour.	The resources available that facilitate meaningful, worthwhile learning; resources that assist the learner to participate successfully in the distance course.

Source: Adapted from Anderson and Garrison (1998).

Learner independence needs to be underpinned by the elements of learner proficiency and support which together constitute the nature of control within the learning environment. Control depends upon the opportunity (independence) and ability (proficiency) to direct the course of activities and experiences, together with the necessary resources (support).

The most recent development in the debate on autonomy and control in distance learning is that learner autonomy develops through *collaborative control* of learning experiences. According to this view, a commitment on the part of learners to responsibility for and control of the learning process can – and should – be enhanced by opportunities for sustained collaboration. The notion of collaborative control in distance language learning is based on the idea that while cognitive autonomy is largely the responsibility of each learner, this autonomy does not imply social independence. A developing view in distance language learning is that learners should have the opportunity to collaboratively control the management of learning tasks through meaningful interaction with other learners and with teachers. Collaborative control entails an emphasis on the process of negotiation in language learning, which allows learners both to develop and exercise their agency in learning (Breen and Littlejohn 2000). Possibilities for interaction and collaboration available within new learning environments now provide a context for learners to articulate and develop what Breen and Littlejohn (p. 24) refer to as 'their prior understandings, purposes and intentions as reference points for new learning'. Within emerging paradigms of distance learning, the opportunity to exercise collaborative control of learning experiences is seen as central to the development of learner autonomy. Garrison and Archer (2000) argue that, perhaps somewhat paradoxically, cognitive autonomy may best be achieved through collaboration and with external support. The notion of collaborative control will be revisited later in the chapter.

7.2.3 Related concepts

Different positions in relation to learner autonomy in distance language learning can be placed alongside discussions about control, independence, interdependence, self-directed learning and the importance of critical reflection on the learning process. Various assumptions and beliefs held in relation to these concepts are reflected in the quotations below from researchers and theorists within the field. They are presented in chronological order, and together they highlight what are seen as key issues in relation to learner autonomy in the distance context:

> *Independence, interdependence*
> We need not so much to admire the independence of learners, as we need to facilitate the interdependence of learners and the collaboration of educators. We need . . . to expand our notions of professional responsibility.
> (Burge 1988: 19)

> *Control, support, proficiency*
> In essence 'control' means having choices and making decisions as well as having the necessary contextual support and capability to successfully achieve the intended learning outcome.
> (Anderson and Garrison 1998: 99)

> *Learner autonomy and critical reflection*
> For learners with limited opportunity to interact with other target language users, the promotion of learner autonomy via

critical reflection (i.e. evaluation of one's own learning strategies) has come to be regarded as of equal importance to, say, the provision of comprehensible input and the opportunity for productive practice.

(Lamy and Goodfellow 1999a: 43)

Cognitive autonomy, collaboration and support
Although cognitive autonomy is largely the responsibility of the student, this autonomy does not imply social independence. Somewhat paradoxically, cognitive autonomy may well depend upon collaboration and external support. The issue is whether students have the opportunity to collaboratively control the management of learning tasks.

(Garrison and Archer 2000: 102)

Autonomy and course design
. . . the special situation of the distance language learner, and the inherent difficulties of providing for the needs of students one may never see and about whom little may be known. The examples . . . demonstrate how an awareness on the part of course writers of specific aspects of learner autonomy, such as the ability to organise and reflect on learning, monitor progress, identify gaps and solve problems, can be a strong basis for targeted activities designed to promote such skills, and which can be built into the course materials.

(Hurd *et al.* 2001: 354)

The extracts include examples of identification with the ideas of learner independence, control, responsibility, collaboration and critical reflection, all of which are points of discussion in this chapter.

The issue of autonomy within distance language programmes presents a range of challenges not only because of the diverse backgrounds of learners who undertake distance study, but also because adopting a more autonomous approach to learning tends to be more of an immediate imperative than in many classroom contexts. Language students new to the distance context may have had relatively little experience of assuming more responsibility for their learning, yet the ability to manage the learning process in order to meet their needs is important if they are to fully benefit from the opportunities available in distance language learning. In the next part of the chapter I discuss two approaches to helping learners develop their capacity for autonomy in distance language learning. The first reflects an approach to learner training through materials design. The second focuses on enabling learners to move beyond the prescribed subject matter to engage with language resources in their environment and, as part of this, to exercise choice as language learners. The two approaches reflect Tudor's (2001) analysis of the main components of learner autonomy as learner training and learner involvement. They can also be seen as aligned to an emphasis on learner independence on the one hand and on interaction and collaborative control on the either. Differences between the two also relate to contextual factors: in one case students are learning a foreign language, and in the other students are learning within the TL country.

7.3 A focus on learner training

One approach taken to learner autonomy within the distance context centres on strategy development and learner training through materials design. This approach falls within what Benson (2001) calls resource-based approaches to the development of autonomy which highlight the importance of independent interaction with learning materials. It is commonly adopted in large-scale distance language courses: emphasis is placed on the selection and design of learning materials for self-study that will assist learners in developing some of the skills associated with learner autonomy. Different forms of in-text support are provided within the materials which aim to facilitate independent learning and to enhance each student's repertoire of learning skills. This is the approach reported by Vanijdee (2001, 2003) at Sukhothai Thammathirat Open University in Thailand which has offered courses in general English and in English for Specific Purposes since 1980. The number of students is high: between 5,000 and 10,000 students in Foundation English each semester. The development of appropriate learning resources is seen as the key means of facilitating learner autonomy within this large-scale distance context.

The most detailed articulation of distance learner training has come from the teaching of foreign language courses in French, German and Spanish at the Open University UK. The OUUK is renowned for the high-quality courses it provides for language students, and has been seen as a model for practice in many other distance learning institutions. The emphasis is on supported distance learning, and on equal access to learning opportunities for all students. The training programme is based on a recognition and understanding of the gap between the strategic competence required for successful distance language study, and the background and skills of learners entering a distance language programme for the first time. It reflects the view of Nunan, Lai and Keobke (1999) that the sensitive teacher does not assume that learners are naturally endowed with the skills and knowledge they will need to identify what are for them optimal ways of learning a language.

Learner training within the OUUK language courses aims to help learners acquire 'a series of strategies and skills that will enable them to work individually' Hurd *et al.* (2001: 341). There is relatively little emphasis on learner choice in terms of what, how and when to learn within the course. Because of the diverse and often isolated contexts of learners, all the learning material is provided and no assumptions are made about access to native speakers, or the Internet or other learning resources. This approach is also linked to a particular philosophy of distance learning as distinct from open learning or self-access learning, expressed by Hurd *et al.* (2001: 344) as:

> Distance learning programmes have a very rigid structure in which the amount, rate and content of the learning programme is determined by the course team in charge of producing the materials, and not the student.

The response taken by course developers at the OUUK to the need to foster learner autonomy has been to develop materials that incorporate strategy development and learner training, focusing on 'the ability of learners to organise and reflect on learning, monitor progress, identify gaps and solve problems' (p. 354). Learners are encouraged to develop awareness of themselves as learners, of the techniques that work for them, and to make decisions within the structures provided by the course. According to this view, it is the clarity of the framework of the course that enables learners to make decisions and to develop awareness of their learning within the parameters that are set.

Hurd *et al.* (2001: 353) summarise the ways in which learner autonomy is promoted in the course, and these include, among others:

- Learner training that is specific enough to enable students to solve specific problems whenever and wherever they appear. Constant and varied suggestions for learning strategies so students can experiment and find those that work best for them.
- Opportunities for students to think about how they learn, in the form of a learning diary.
- Opportunities for self-evaluation and self-assessment, both through course activities and tasks, and through the formal assessment strategy.
- Opportunities for students to relate what they are learning to what they already know, in the form of language awareness activities.

The learner training approach in the distance course is adopted as a way of initiating students into a more independent form of learning. It encourages them to develop the kind of individualised self-knowledge needed for language learning within that context. It relates closely to the findings of White (1995a) that distance language learners need to be able to manage the process of language learning based on their understandings of how they learn best; they then draw on this understanding to set up learning experiences that are favourable, although not necessarily ideal.

A number of critical commentaries have been written on learner training, beginning with Rees-Miller (1993). However, in the distance context it remains one means by which learners can be encouraged to reflect on and enhance the way in which they work with the TL sources within their context. It provides opportunities for learners to grow into a more self-directive role and to overcome some of the potentially perverse effects of an isolated language learning context.

7.4 A focus on learner involvement

A different view of learner independence and autonomy underpins developments within the Adult Migrant English Program offered to distance learners in Australia. Like the OUUK, the AMEP has provided a highly successful learning environment for very large numbers of geographically dispersed learners, and the programme has been developed, modified and sustained over a number of years. A key difference is that the programme is for second language learners of English, who are living within the TL environment and who need to use English in many contexts of their daily lives. It aims to involve learners in shaping their language programme, and in making significant decisions about the content and goals of their learning, building on increased awareness of what is relevant in their own immediate conditions and lived experience. The focus is placed more directly on what Tudor (2001) calls the learner involvement rather than the learner training component of autonomy.

A seminal article by Candlin and Byrnes (1995) argued for an 'open curriculum' in distance language learning which would enable learners to develop their abilities to move beyond the prescribed subject matter and prescribed ways of studying, to engage with language resources within their environment and to exercise choice as learners. The emphasis in this approach is on 'the development of autonomy-enabling features within the curriculum materials and learning conditions' (Candlin and Byrnes 1995: 9), and a decreasing dependence on the teacher or instructional provider.

This approach is aligned to van Lier's view of the central features of autonomy as *choice* and *responsibility*. The teacher's role is to encourage and guide learners, particularly in accessing learning opportunities that are personally meaningful to them and available within their context. It is also aligned with the approach in Chapter 4 of encouraging learners to develop an effective interface with their learning context – one which enables them to continue to make significant decisions about what and how they will learn, and to identify and engage with appropriate learning experiences. The emphasis is on involving learners in developing awareness and exercising choice in learning and using the TL.

The position outlined by Candlin and Byrnes (1995) represents a significant shift in approach to learner autonomy in the distance context. It moves away from a more conventional model of materials-based distance learning – which entails a centralisation of decision-making about learning – to one based around an open curriculum. It reflects principles associated with the process syllabus (Breen and Littlejohn 2000), in that language learning content is not predefined but selected and negotiated through the course, as language learning and language use are intimately linked. The shift is reflected in the design of the materials, the roles envisaged for teachers and learners, and the formation of learning networks.

7.4.1 Open materials

The materials within this approach encourage and show learners how to access and use resources in their context, to carry their learning into the community and to develop strategies for taking greater responsibility for their learning. One way of achieving this described by Candlin and Byrnes (1995: 12) is to use a number of *Action* projects in the materials:

> These Action projects offer opportunities for learners, supported by directions in the materials and with teacher support, to transfer experiences from the materials into the community they live in, or into their workplaces. These Action projects are included in the course from the very first Unit, and form an important part of student assessments of their own learning progress.

As part of this the materials should be open enough to allow a diffusion of decision-making to learners to take place, reflecting the view that an over-explicitness in materials can increase learner dependence on the course, at the expense of developing ability and responsibility in managing learning. This approach also reflects the view that learners acquire knowledge and skills in the TL through personally meaningful activities in the context of social interaction, not by receiving knowledge in the materials.

7.4.2 Role of the teacher

It is evident that distance language learners need a substantial amount of support if they are to develop the capacity to become increasingly involved in their language learning. Candlin and Byrnes (1995: 13) see the role of the teacher as including a responsibility to:

- select learning experiences that encourage choice and expand learning options;
- provide a supportive climate for learning;
- encourage risk-taking in making efforts to change;
- provide constructive judgements and evaluations;
- involve learners actively in posing problems;
- provide opportunities for learners to communicate about learning;
- encourage learners to confirm what they know or can do by communicating with others.

One of the implications of this new range of roles is that the teacher becomes an important reference point for learners in negotiating their learning experiences. At the same time the teacher may come under great pressure from the sheer number of interactions. To counteract this possibility learners need to have access to learner networks or learning webs to support their learning.

7.4.3 Learner networks

This is the third aspect of the open curriculum: establishing and maintaining learner networks. Learners are encouraged to communicate with each other in order to learn and use the TL and to reflect on their own learning processes.

Candlin and Byrnes acknowledge that 'such networks are themselves the gradual outcome of a materials- and teacher-encouraged process of cultivating and exploiting learner autonomy' (p. 12). One assumption here is that learners will invest time and energy in learning how to participate within a learning network, and that they will find sufficient value in the experience to continue to contribute to the concerns and interests of others, and to raise problems or share learning resources. The possibilities offered by CMC have, of course, made this vision more possible, but the existence of the means does not ensure the successful realisation of the idea of learner support networks.

A detailed following of the experience of building and working within such a learning network to foster reflective interaction between distance language learners has been trialled at the OUUK. The conclusions Goodfellow, Manning and Lamy (1999: 283) draw from the pilot study relate to the feasibility of developing and maintaining networks that learners use as a resource to help direct their learning:

While the OU is committed in the long term to exactly this kind of autonomy, experience in the short term suggests that CMC by itself will not bring about an open curriculum. To get beyond the need for structured subject matter and ways of studying will require pedagogical as well as technological inspiration.

Of the three ways of fostering learner autonomy suggested by Candlin and Byrnes – through more open materials, changes in learner and teacher roles, and the development of learning networks – it is the latter that poses the most challenges in the distance context. Chapter 9 on learning sources includes further discussion on the ways in which distance language learners can be encouraged to negotiate their own paths through materials and to access and evaluate learning sources in the environment. The establishment of learning networks as a key means of developing learner involvement in the TL and the learning process is an ideal associated with emerging paradigms of distance language learning, and is the subject of the next section.

7.5 Traditional and emerging paradigms

The views that distance educators hold about learner autonomy are closely related to the distance education paradigm in which they operate and the ideals and principles associated with that paradigm. Here I place more emphasis on emerging paradigms for distance language learning, which can be related to Breen's notion of process syllabus and also to constructivist principles.

7.5.1 Traditional paradigms

Traditional paradigms of distance language learning – many of which remain the predominant model for distance learning in different parts of the world – have emphasised independent learning carried out principally through self-instructional materials. The design and delivery of high-quality, self-contained materials has been seen as the key component in fostering and maximising learner independence. And a measure of quality within this paradigm is the degree to which the course materials support the self-instruction process, and maximise self-sufficiency on the part of the learner. Interaction is to a large extent confined to learner interaction with the course materials. Separation between the teacher and the learner is a key feature of this model, with more limited opportunities for communication and feedback.

7.5.2 Emerging paradigms

As a result of new generations of communications technology, the image of distance language learners as solitary, independent individuals is changing. The development of flexible and accessible forms of two-way communication has led to a new way of thinking about distance language learning. Learners now have opportunities to manage their learning within an interactive environment, while having increased access to support and feedback from others within the learning experience, including peers and teachers. This alternative framework, referred to as an emerging paradigm, emphasises the role of collaboration in affording control to learners within the distance learning context. It draws on constructivist perspectives of learning whereby knowledge and skills are viewed as something that learners acquire by constructing new meanings through interaction with others. It places greater emphasis on the exchange of ideas and the development of abilities within collaborative learning experiences, largely through the use of CMC.

The road to autonomy within the emerging paradigm of distance education cannot be embedded exclusively in the teaching materials, since it arises from and is practised and developed in the context of sustained discourse between teacher and learner, and between learners themselves. It is concerned less with independence, self-reliance and learner training, and more with reflective interaction and collaborative control within the context of learning experiences that are meaningful and relevant to learners. The issues of meaningfulness and relevance are critically important here if learners are to want to learn, to continue learning and to take ownership of their learning. There are parallels between emerging paradigms of distance language learning and the process approach to syllabus design. Both transfer part of the responsibility for the development of the course to learners as they must make choices and decisions about their learning and their contributions within online environments. Just as the process approach to syllabus construction provides a framework to enable learners to make more effective decisions about their learning (Breen 1987), the emerging paradigms for distance learning provide learning spaces within which the course can develop based on the collaborative contributions of learners.

Learners and teachers discharge very different roles compared to those associated with more traditional syllabus types or more traditional distance learning paradigms. As Skehan (1998: 262) points out, referring to process syllabuses, 'learners need to know how to be effective learners, since they are given considerable autonomy and power . . . Similarly teachers have to *learn* how to relinquish power, as well as how to provide useful information and advice to learners for their new role'. More critically, teachers need to know how to induce learners to work in new ways within new learning environments and relationships.

Learners are also seen as developing strong identities as individual learners who are able to be effective participants in learning communities. Wilson and Lowry (2000: 82) summarise this as follows: 'learners need to develop individual competence, but within a context of effective participation in groups and communities'. The synergies between constructivism, a process-based approach to language learning and possibilities associated with emerging paradigms for distance learning are evident. A move towards the emerging paradigm for distance language learning – and associated approaches – involves new expectations about what it means to function successfully as a language learner. In terms of learner autonomy it includes the capacity to negotiate and develop control of learning experiences while interacting with others in the learning community. It also involves the ability to critically reflect on those learning experiences, in private and in reflective conversations. It is based on the development of individual competence as learners and the development of the capacity to participate in and contribute to learning communities. These ideals should be balanced against the well-attested research findings in distance education that learners are not uniform in their needs and preferences for interaction, nor in the roles they perceive for interaction in their individual learning environment.

In the next section I discuss tandem learning partnerships as one example of opportunities to develop collaborative control of learning experiences.

7.6 Towards collaborative control

Kötter (2002: 32) identifies 'the promotion of a balanced combination of individual and collaborative learning' as a key ingredient of learner autonomy in language learning. Interaction and collaboration are seen as crucial in enabling learners to develop and maintain control of their learning experiences, and to the development of learner autonomy. This view is close to the work of Little (2001) who argues that autonomy in language learning develops through interaction – and that independence for the learner develops from *interdependence*.

The kinds of experiences available through tandem learning partnerships via the Internet (Kötter 2001; Little, 2001) are examples of how learners may develop and exercise autonomy in language learning through interaction. Although there are no published accounts of how tandem learning has been integrated into language learning in distance education, it offers the kinds of opportunities for collaboration and the development of interactive competence that are often lacking in more traditional approaches to distance language learning. And while tandem learning is not described as an example of collaborative control in action, it shares many of the key features associated with a collaborative control approach to learner autonomy.

Tandem learning involves two students with different mother tongues working together in a text-based online environment in order to learn each other's language. Learners can benefit from their partner's expert knowledge about language and cultural issues, and they are able to improve their communicative competence by conversing with native speakers in a non-threatening environment, as well as by receiving feedback (Kötter 2001). Little and Brammerts (1996) argue that tandem learning is governed by principles of reciprocity and learner autonomy. Both partners are required to contribute equally to collaboration, that is reciprocity, and they are responsible for their own learning and the learning within the partnership. Each partner enacts the roles of learner and of native speaker, and the growth in autonomy that emerges in the relationship is the product of an interdependent, collaborative process.

Of course it is not envisaged that tandem learning partnerships proceed without support, but that support and advice should be 'mediated through exploration, reflection and negotiation' (Little 2001: 32). The aim should be to maximise the opportunity for the development of participants as learners and users of their respective TLs through the reciprocal dynamic of the partnership.

Collaborative control of the learning experience is negotiated through interactions between the teacher and the learners, and between the learners themselves. Students have the freedom to work together in tandem, and to set their personal agendas for learning (independence); they are able to use and extend their competencies in interaction (proficiency); and they have recourse to support through their partner, and also through the teacher (support). The three elements of control: independence, proficiency and support are negotiated and exercised in the course of online exchanges.

Learner tandems have much to offer distance language learners in terms of opportunities to develop collaborative control of learning experiences. A key challenge is how to integrate tandem learning opportunities into a distance language programme. Experience tells us that simply providing opportunities for text-based interaction online, even with adequate support, still raises issues of access, participation, involvement and so on. These issues become all the more complex in the kind of tandem learning environment explored by Kötter (2002). The students in his study interacted in realtime in a text-based environment, but they were not part of a distance learning programme. A key aspect raised by

Kötter is that of teacher involvement, and he suggests that in order to provide support teachers should ideally be in the same physical location as their students. This is of course a key constraint for distance language learning. Little also outlines a number of organisational problems that may impact on the frequency and nature of interaction, including ease of access to e-mail, the reliability of computer networks, and scheduling issues.

There are many constraints in bringing the concept of collaborative control into practice in distance language learning. It involves learning new roles for both learners and teachers. More specifically it involves a new learning context, comprising an interconnected community of learners rather than an isolated series of individual learners. It involves exploring and working within a new medium, that is different kinds of text-based online environments. And it involves developing new ways of going about learning, with higher levels of interaction and collaboration. At the same time it presents exciting possibilities for the development of learner control and interactive competence, which were not possible in more traditional paradigms for distance language learning.

The next section discusses an important avenue for research into learner autonomy in online environments. The focal point for the study is an evaluation of the potential for more fluid course elements (text-based CMC) to develop reflective learning conversations. Critical reflection as a means of fostering learner autonomy is part of ongoing research with distance language learners at the Open University UK.

7.7 Reflective interaction in an online learning environment

Marie-Noëlle Lamy and Robin Goodfellow have explored the role of reflection and reflective conversation in the learning of French at the Open University UK. As background to their research, they draw on two main areas covered in the literature – critical reflection and contingent interaction.

7.7.1 Critical reflection

Lamy and Goodfellow argue that in the distance learning context, learner autonomy is best developed through opportunities for reflection on, and evaluation of learning strategies and experiences. This position informs their research and is reflected in their statement about pedagogical aspects of learner autonomy at the start of this chapter (Lamy and Goodfellow 1999a: 43). They situate their work alongside that of Little (1996, 1997), and the arguments that have been advanced about the contribution of reflective processes to the autonomy of individuals as language learners and language users. The work of Broady and Kenning (1996) and Little (1997) forms the basis of the following definition of reflection: 'by reflection, we mean having a critical internal conversation about our own understanding of linguistic structures and the processes of our own language learning' (Lamy and Goodfellow 1999b: 458). Lamy and Goodfellow are concerned with the use of asynchronous conferencing to encourage reflection, and argue that this kind of 'slow-motion' conversation may be particularly advantageous in encouraging reflective practice.

7.7.2 Contingent interaction

A number of recent studies have explored the ways in which reflection can be combined optimally with interaction in text-based computer conferencing (Goodfellow *et al.* 1999; Lamy and Goodfellow 1999a, 1999b). Interaction is seen as important, not only for the negotiation of meaning, but also as the means by which the educational experience is constructed in a contingent manner. The notion of 'contingent interaction' is based on the work of Van Lier (1996), which explores power relations in the classroom and the kinds of interactions that take place between teacher and learner. He identifies contingent interaction as contributing to high-quality learning since the agenda and participation is shared by both or all parties. This contingent interaction is characterised not only by equality among participants, but also by communicative symmetry (in terms of distribution of turns and roles), and a balance of familiar and unpredictable subject matter. Contingency in interaction facilitates reflective practice and learning. This view is congruent with Garrison's views of collaborative control of learning transactions.

7.7.3 The Lexica Online project

Reflection was an integral part of the Lexica Online project, which had as a focus the management and sharing of vocabulary learning strategies through group discussion via CMC. The study process is described as 'a cyclical one, involving both private study and public sharing within the group' (Lamy and Goodfellow 1999b: 462). Ten adult learners in the second-level French course (higher intermediate) at the OUUK participated in the study. The computer conferencing system was moderated by two tutors who were native speakers of French. The aim of the research was to explore the nature of reflective interaction among learners participating in reflective conversations as part of Lexica Online.

Table 7.2. *Message types within CMC discourse*

Message type	Features
'Monologue'	Text containing no invitation to interaction; generally narrative in structure; may contain evidence of reflection; texts do not generate further exchanges; at the closed rather than contingent end of the continuum.
'Reflective conversation'	Interaction where the content is 'talk about language'; contingency is central to the conversation; meets the learning goals of reflectiveness and interaction.
'Social conversation'	Exchanges of a social nature; short messages, conversations keep going for some time; at the contingent rather than closed end of the continuum.

Source: Adapted from Lamy and Goodfellow (1999a, 1999b).

7.7.4 Findings

Messages from six weeks of conferencing were analysed and used to develop the framework in Table 7.2.

This framework reflects two key points of interest in the analysis of the CMC of distance language learners: interactivity and reflectiveness. Neither monologue-type texts nor social conversation-type texts were seen as contributing significantly to language learning. However, reflective-conversation messages displayed both reflectiveness and contingency. In addition they were interactional 'in both information-processing and social-interactional senses' (1999a: 52). In such an exchange:

1. understanding is negotiated;
2. there is explicit reference to knowledge about language and language learning;
3. the control dimension is present.

7.7.5 The issue of control

The control dimension is seen as important in that 'learner engagement is rooted in a social context in which participants are able to negotiate the dimension of control in the interaction, that is to be both learner and teacher or expert, setting the agenda for each other' (Lamy and Goodfellow 1999a: 52). The issue of control is one of balance. If control remains in the hands of the teacher, this militates against 'both reflection and facilitative interaction' (van Lier 1996: 180–1). Lamy and Goodfellow suggest that a beneficial way in which the tutor can exert control in a CMC environment, is as a language expert, modelling appropriate ways of using language. Ideally, reflective conversations enable learners to assume control of the interaction, by nominating the topic, raising questions and negotiating meaning, for example. The tutor may exercise control by modelling features of the language they wish learners to use.

7.7.6 Tutor styles

Lamy and Goodfellow are also concerned with fostering 'more sustained conversations leading to autonomous peer-exchanges' (1999b: 458), rather than the teacher–student dialogue variety of exchange. To investigate how this might be achieved, they looked inside the facilitation process. They compared tutor interaction in terms of the pattern and content of tutor intervention. What they identified are two quite distinct tutor styles: one placed emphasis on the socio-affective needs of the students, and the other on syllabus content. The former group was socially cohesive but had relatively little form-focused discussion, while the more cognitive group were less able to manage the interaction and create 'autonomous peer exchanges'. They identify the most advantageous approach as a combination of tutorial styles of both the social and the cognitive tutor. Lamy and Goodfellow (1999b: 476) suggest that online tutors need to have exemplars of reflective interaction in the context of a series of exchanges:

> one way of approaching this is through modelling, by which we mean extracting exchanges from successful conferences, to serve as examples of tutoring strategies for the benefit of teachers, and encouraging the teachers to model styles of participation for the benefit of students.

7.7.7 Commentary

The work of Lamy and Goodfellow concerning the development of reflective conversation within a text-based CMC environment reflects an important concern with how best to develop learner autonomy within the emerging paradigm of distance education. One of the challenges within this paradigm is that learners' response to, and participation within, text-based CMC has turned out to be less straightforward than may have been assumed, as has been confirmed in many other studies (see, for example, Vrasidas and McIsaac 2000). None the less, one of the rewards in reading the work of Lamy and Goodfellow is the way in which they move the field forward in identifying optimal features of message types which are associated with both reflection on language and learning, and contingent interaction. They identify the redefinition of the role of the teacher in an online language learning environment, as one which involves combining a concern with affect and social cohesion, with a focus on language and language learning. As a definition this may not appear so different from that of the face-to-face language teacher, but we still know relatively little about how to achieve these aims in online environments. In an extension of the Lexica Online research, Lamy and Hassan (2003) investigate the impact of socio-cultural factors and task design on reflective interaction online among distance learners of French. The work of Lamy and her co-researchers is salient to one of the espoused goals and responsibilities of distance learning in the 21st century, namely to provide a means of developing not only subject matter expertise, but also the ability to co-create learning, to provoke enquiry and to establish and participate in learning networks (Latchem and Hanna 2001).

7.8 Summary

In this chapter I have traced the range of perspectives and concepts associated with learner autonomy in distance language learning. Interpretations of the concept itself stem from different paradigms of distance learning, and their associated assumptions and goals.

One of the representations of learner autonomy emphasises learner *independence*, that is the capacity of learners to proceed without direct assistance from teacher or peers. This position has been criticised as reflecting an exclusive, narrow and unrealistic approach to the learner and learning processes. It is often juxtaposed with the notion of interdependence and *collaborative control* as a key feature of autonomy – that is interdependence and collaboration between learners, the teacher and the learning environment. Interaction and support are central to this conception of learner autonomy. According to this view, interactions function not only as a means of providing practice in the TL, but are a means by which learners can negotiate and collaborate with others to develop and enhance the learning environment and their capability and competence as language learners within that environment.

In current practice learner autonomy often presents a mixture of the independence and collaborative control views. In any particular context, the weight and importance ascribed to these two aspects, and the particular balance that may be achieved between them reflect wider philosophies and assumptions about the learning–teaching relationship in distance education. It is also influenced by features of the context of delivery such as the number of learners within a course, access to technology and, most crucially, the participants themselves.

8 Learner support

8.1 Introduction

A common view of distance language learning has been that it presents learners with an essentially limited experience of learning the TL, and provides fewer of the benefits and support structures than those that are available in classroom settings. In fact a clearly articulated philosophy of learner support is considered fundamental to good practice in distance language learning, together with a range of support services appropriate to different stages of distance study. To underline this point providers sometimes use the term *supported distance language learning/teaching* to refer to what they do.

Richards (2001), writing about face-to-face language classes, also argues that support mechanisms for learners are a component of course delivery: feedback to learners, opportunities provided for faster or slower learners, and the provision of self-access components to address specific learning needs and interests are identified as part of the support process. Further support needs of distance language learners arise as part of the process of adjusting to a new learning environment in which interactions with the TL are not mediated by a teacher. Some of these may also relate to self-access contexts, and to some learner advisory centres. Learner support within the distance context includes a number of additional issues relating to the affective aspects of language learning and administrative and technical support.

In this chapter I outline the meaning and importance of learner support in distance language learning. The range of concerns and requests for support made by language students are examined including how they relate to features of the distance learning context and experience. Following on from this the primary functions of learner support – cognitive, affective, systemic – are outlined and illustrated with reference to two distance language programmes. Key sources of support for distance language learners include teachers, other students and native speakers as well as other social networks. Examples of the ways in which they may contribute to aspects of the support process are discussed. The latter part of the chapter focuses on the means by which support is made available to learners, including online support. Consistent with a learner-centred view of support the argument is developed that decisions about the mode and form of learner support should be informed by attention to the issues of access, added value and congruence for individual learners. A small but important section of the chapter considers the situated nature of learner support, that is the way in which contextual factors influence how teachers and learners may respond to the philosophy and associated practices of learner support developed mostly in Western contexts.

8.2 Definition: Learner support as response

Learner support involves interaction with learners about their interests and concerns on an individual basis usually through a range of support systems. The learner support model, in Figure 8.1, represents two processes: the production and delivery of courses, and learner support. This broad representation of learner support includes *all* activities which take place over and above the development and dissemination of learning materials. It incorporates a range of academic and non-academic activities that assist learners in developing an effective learning environment, and in making progress as distance language learners.

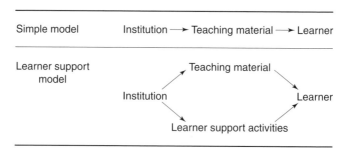

*Figure 8.1 Two models of distance language learning (*Adapted from *Simpson 2000)*

While distance language learning is sometimes conceptualised as a simple transfer of teaching material from the institution to the learner with minimal interaction between the student and the teacher/institution (the simple model in Figure 8.1), such a limited view reflects a misunderstanding of the process. Planning for learner support is a critical component in course design, and is integral to the delivery of a language course at a distance. Learner support does not simply consist of the production and distribution of, for example, learning guides, which would be little different from the design and delivery of course content. A key conceptual component in any definition is that support is *a response to the individual learner*, rather than a standard or uniform product. Learner support involves acknowledging the identity of each learner and responding to his or her needs. This is, of course, complex and demanding in distance language learning and there is an enormous variation in the degree to which institutions and teachers are responsive to individual learners.

8.3 The case for learner support

8.3.1 The contribution of learner support

As increasing numbers of institutions move to offering online courses, books and manuals have been published that offer templates of how to implement distance courses, e-courses, online courses, and so on (see, for example, Bélanger and Jordan 2000; Mantyla and Gividen 1997; Oblinger 1999). The emphasis in these publications is on the 'successful' implementation of distance courses, with an almost exclusive focus on course development and delivery. The crucial element of learner support is just about entirely absent. Yet our understanding of the realities of distance language learning is that support services are vital if the experience is not to be akin to what Simpson (2000) calls 'educational Passchendaelism' – that is throwing students at courses in the hope that some will make it.

There is, of course, a resourcing issue in all of this. Attention is often placed on course design as a means of improving provision of language learning opportunities. In this more singular focus on the development of materials, the need to reflect on the role of learner support activities, and how these may be enhanced, can be overlooked. Yet it is the *quality of student learning* within the course that should be the primary focus, and this requires response to each individual student. What is highlighted here are the tensions that can arise when a balance is being struck between the resources that need to be allocated to course development on the one hand, and ongoing learner support activities on the other.

8.3.2 Quality provision

The provision of learner support is central to quality provision of distance learning opportunities, as discussed in Chapter 3. The UK

Guidelines in the Quality Assurance of Distance Learning published by the Quality Assurance Agency for Higher Education also give prominence to student support and the communication aspects of distance provision, rather than a more singular focus on the development of materials.

Epstein (2001) describes how features of two distance programmes for language teachers were examined according to a number of quality indicators. One of the quality indicators was *supporting the needs of learners*. Here I will focus on the Thai Teaching English as a Foreign Language (TEFL) Program, developed by York University in Toronto, Canada, in collaboration with the Regional English Language Centre, Singapore. Most support was provided by a number of tutors who worked in teachers' colleges in local regions. Tutor workload, however, emerged as a key issue in terms of the quality of support available: turnaround time for assignments tended to be slow, so feedback was delayed, and the slow mail system exacerbated this. Tutors were not always available by phone, and participants were reluctant to disturb tutors with their questions. Epstein notes that additional support took the form of:

• two face-to-face weekend seminars (an orientation seminar and a mid-course seminar);
• potential peer contact in some schools;
• audio- and videocassettes.

The most successful support systems were face-to-face seminars: participants rated them highly in terms of helping them maintain motivation, meet course expectations and improve assignments. The peer support aspect of the programme was generally not successful: it was constrained by lack of time, work and home responsibilities, programme demands, cost and distance. While audio- and videocassettes do not fall within the view of support as response to individual learners, they were provided as additional materials in response to requests from participants.

Epstein (2001: 137) concludes her study with a number of suggestions as to how the needs of distance learners could be supported including:

• ensure adequate orientation to distance education for learners;
• ensure the commitment of tutors to learners (i.e. availability, responsiveness, thorough feedback on assignments);
• develop a system to facilitate reliable, frequent contact between tutors and learners;
• minimise learner isolation (e.g. through on-site workshops; pairing with peers; and advanced communications technology such as

computer-mediated communication, if accessible to learners and financially feasible);
- ensure administrative, academic and personal support.

These could, broadly speaking, also function as further quality indicators for distance learner support.

8.3.3 Student retention

Another argument in the case for enhanced learner support relates to the issue of drop-out or the converse of this, student retention. While lack of persistence is an issue in a range of language learning contexts, it is a key source of concern in distance programmes as discussed in Chapter 6.

A difficulty faced by distance language teachers is that evidence of the contribution of elements of learner support is not always tangible, or readily identifiable. There are no hard findings that indicate that investment in a particular level or type of support will reduce drop-out by a certain amount. Within some institutional contexts, this lack of hard evidence may make learner support vulnerable to cuts.

8.4 Concerns expressed by learners

8.4.1 Learner requests

Distance learners may be affected by a range of concerns, doubts, difficulties, uncertainties, misunderstandings, and so on, at different points of their study. The examples in the Reflections and experiences section show that the concerns expressed by learners arise from three broad areas:

- the impact of circumstances on their language learning;
- their perception of their ability and sense of progress (from self-evaluation or feedback they have received);
- course content and their learning of the TL.

In putting forward a request or framing a concern, learners are asking for a response that will provide support or guidance and assist them in working more effectively as distance language learners. It is well documented that some learners are initially nervous or reluctant to contact the tutor, since they think their concerns may be trivial, or outside the scope of responsibility of the tutor. This should be borne in mind by teachers in developing a response to the request.

Reflections and experiences

Requests for support

The following are examples of requests for help from distance language learners over a period of six weeks. The requests were selected from communications received on three distance language courses at Massey University and the University of South Africa, and were chosen to give some indication of the range of questions to which a distance teacher may be asked to respond.

I need more focus on grammar in this course. How can I get this? It's the grammar I really need since I can already speak quite well. Can you recommend something?

I am having problems accessing WebCT. I am not sure whether it is a problem with my computer, or my skills, or WebCT itself. I seem to be wasting a lot of time on this.

When I started the course I could learn everything in the materials. Lately I find I am meeting words I don't know. Am I falling behind?

I got a 'B' for the last assignment. Does that mean I am only just making enough progress? I have been an 'A' student in my other courses.

I tried to contact you by phone but I got the answer phone. I am not sure about how to approach the writing task in unit 5. Can I speak to you some time soon? I want to complete the unit this weekend because of other commitments.

I am having a very difficult time at work since we are in the middle of restructuring. I can't devote as much time to study as I would like. I am thinking of withdrawing but thought that I would discuss my options with you first.

8.4.2 Teacher response

Distance language learners attach a lot of weight to the response they receive from teachers. A recurrent theme in the reports of distance foreign language learners of French and Japanese (White 1993, 1995c) – in a study of their use of language learning strategies – was that while they were able to develop a range of affective and social strategies to deal with adverse circumstances, the support available from the teacher, their student liaison advisor or other services in the institution played a key role. Given the critically vulnerable nature of morale in the distance language learning environment, it is essential that the response given by teachers be prompt and empathetic, and that it provides a basis for further interaction, should learners wish that.

The ways in which teachers respond to learners is an important avenue for research. The following observations of Candlin and Byrnes (1995: 17) still hold for research into distance language learning:

> . . . very little research has been done on how *distance learning teachers* actually manage the learning, much less research, for example, than has been done into how *classroom teachers* manage the learning. What is it that distance learning teachers do and how do they do it? What characterises teacher talk in distance learning? Such questions would provide the basis for focussed and action-research based professional development of distance learning teachers.

This gap is a further reflection of the primary focus within distance language learning on course development and materials design.

Research carried out into advising for self-directed language learning in face-to-face contexts (Gremmo and Riley 1995; Kelly 1996; Pemberton, Toogood, Ho and Lam 2001) could inform research and practice into learner–teacher interaction in distance language learning. Pemberton *et al.* (2001) provide what they describe as a preliminary listing of advising strategies based on their analysis of advising discourse. This is given in Table 8.1.

Of the major features of advising discourse – asking questions, clarifying, advising and motivating – it is motivating that comes to the fore as a critical feature of learner support interactions in the distance context. Whatever the request, the response of the teacher needs to be at once encouraging, interested, empathetic and validating of the experience of students. A further point is the impact of the context on the strategies used for learner support. In distance language learning only a small proportion of support is enacted in face-to-face contexts. Most commonly it is carried out by telephone, chat, e-mail or asynchronous discussion. In synchronous contexts – such as telephone or chat conversations – it is possible to apportion time to asking questions in combination with other advising functions. When support is mediated by e-mail or asynchronous discussion there is less room for asking questions, which could be interpreted as calling into question the aptness of the request itself. Instead, the teacher is more likely to combine clarifying functions with advising and motivating strategies.

Future research is needed on the influence of different environments and modes of support on the nature of teacher–learner interaction in distance language learning. Findings from this research would contribute to decisions about the forms of support made available to learners.

Table 8.1. *Strategies used in learner advisory sessions*

Asking questions	• eliciting (information, goals, progress, beliefs, feelings); • probing; • passing the learner's question back to them.
Clarifying	• requesting clarification; • restating; • summarising; • interpreting; • checking comprehension; • highlighting contradictions in what the learner has said/planned.
Advising	• helping analyse needs; • helping focus goals; • identifying possible problems in the learner's plan/learning method; • reminding the learner of their original goals/plan; • offering suggestions re: planning; record-keeping (writing of plan, diaries, portfolio report); time allocation; materials and activities; (alternative) learning strategies; evaluation; • providing feedback; • evaluating progress and/or performance; • providing information on language features and/or terminology (e.g. accents, contraction).
Motivating	• encouraging/praising; • empathising; • mentioning experiences of other learners (including the adviser).

Source: Pemberton *et al.* (2001: 22).

8.5 Functions and scope

Support in distance language learning generally aims to contribute to:

- maintaining or increasing learner motivation;
- promoting effective learning skills;
- generating a feeling of 'belonging' to the institution, or course, through contact with tutors and learners;
- providing access to resources;
- providing administrative advice.

Broadly speaking, there are three primary functions of learner support – cognitive, affective, systemic – as identified in Tait (2000). Table 8.2 shows the range of support services to fulfil different functions.

Table 8.2. *Functions and scope of learner support*

Functions of Learner Support	Scope of Learner Support Services
Cognitive	• tutoring • study groups and centres, actual and virtual • feedback on assessment and progress • learning support (including study and exam skills seminars, 1:1 assistance)
Affective	• guidance and advisory services (including motivational counselling) • residential schools • peer contact
Systemic	• enquiry and admission services • course/academic information and guidance

I will discuss the functions of learner support with reference to two distance language programmes. The first is a technology mediated distance language course developed by Fox (1997, 1998), as part of the Language Learning Network project, funded by the Higher Education Funding Council in England. The second is a computer-mediated distance language course, *Parliamo italiano*, developed by Radic (2000, 2001) at the University of Auckland, New Zealand. In both courses learners were able to obtain advice, feedback and support by phone, private e-mail or on the class discussion list. While Fox's course had one tutor for the six students in the programme, in Radic's course there were 35 students supported by one tutor and an online testing assistant.

8.5.1 Cognitive functions

The *cognitive* functions of learner support relate to the need to enhance and assist the learning process, and the teaching–learning relationship. The regular course materials can be mediated by a range of interactive opportunities: interaction with the tutor, or with the tutor and/or peers (face-to-face, via telephone, or electronically), study groups (actual or virtual), feedback concerning progress, and more general learning support services (involving, for example, exam preparation, time management, study skills).

In the Language Learning Network Project, ongoing support for the learning process was given in weekly one-to-one telephone tutorials scheduled between the tutor and each student. The support during these tutorials included:

- negotiating learning targets for the week;
- identifying further materials for each learner based on individual needs;
- advice on learning routes and language learning strategies;
- feedback on performance – simple error correction offered instantaneously; evaluation and correction of pronunciation and intonation; summary of errors and correction of structures at the end of interchanges; evaluation of progress as a whole.

(Fox 1998: 64)

In the Italian distance language course, the cognitive functions of learner support were addressed through:

- the asynchronous discussion list in which learners were encouraged to ask course-related questions or to seek further explanation;
- personalised feedback on submitted work provided by e-mail;
- oral practice provided by phone sessions with the tutor.

(Radic 2000, 2001)

8.5.2 Affective functions

Affective functions of learner support are critical for distance language learners to help them develop a comfortable, effective learning environment, and to ameliorate as far as possible any difficulties that arise. Tait (2000: 289) describes the affective functions of support as 'providing an environment which supports students, creates commitment, and enhances self-esteem'. These last two elements, relating to commitment and self-esteem, are key dimensions in developing persistence and a sense of high morale and agency on the part of learners.

Affective support was provided in the Language Learning Network largely by a proactive approach on the part of the tutor. In one-to-one sessions with learners this included:

- a process of reassurance and praise which was undertaken intensively by the tutor, communicated via e-mail or phone;
- paying attention to the level of motivation of individual learners;
- paying attention to social exchange at the start and end of tutorials, to be conducted in the TL.

A proactive approach to the affective dimension of learning was also considered to be a critical enabler in the distance Italian course. Establishing a personal interest in the students and a comfortable learning environment at the outset were considered priorities, described by Radic (2000) as:

> The single most successful strategy was a personalised ('I want to know what your interests are!') and individualised (one-to-

one) approach to students. I tried (and was successful in) establishing personal contact with students from their first e-mails, through the enrolment procedure and then through the course itself. This contact helped me give a 'human face' to our joint effort to learn a language . . . This approach helped established contacts among students, unveil common interests, express views and offer comments, establishing a healthy study atmosphere.

8.5.3 Systemic functions

The *systemic* functions of support may easily be overlooked, but they are necessary for learners to relate easily and effectively with the institution. Learners need to feel that the administrative services are helpful, efficient, transparent and reliable. Technical support is important here too.

Fox used letters and e-mail in the Language Learning Network project to communicate important issues to do with the course, and the one-to-one tutorials were used for reminders to students about deadlines and administrative matters. Technical support was given in the form of Information Technology induction at the start of the course, then subsequently by phone on an *ad hoc* basis. Fox notes that tutors should not be expected to get involved in technical issues, because of demands on their time and expertise.

Radic (2000) had a technical help desk set up for the students and himself, which he judged to be central to the effectiveness of the course:

> Such assistance proved to be a great asset not only in terms of solving technical problems but . . . in establishing students' confidence in the institution, the mode of delivery, method of teaching and ultimately the tutor/moderator.

The three core functions of learner support are interconnected, and can work together to provide a much enhanced experience for learners. Attention to affective aspects of learner support, in particular, plays a key role in developing not only the confidence and motivation of learners, but in providing a basis for the course as a whole. While the two courses discussed here made provision for all the main functions of learner support, other programmes may value or fulfil only some of the functions, resulting in a less satisfactory learning environment for many distance language learners.

8.6 Sources of support

Distance learning is generally characterised as a solitary pursuit. A closer following of the experience of distance language learners, however, reveals that they gain support from a range of sources from within the various contexts in which they operate.

8.6.1 The teacher and the institution

The teacher and the institution have key roles to play in addressing the whole range of support needs of distance language learners. An understanding of student expectations of support is useful here. The prominence given by learners to the interpersonal and communication skills of the tutor was an important finding in a report of a European Union Project of tutor support in distance learning programmes (Stevenson *et al.* 2000). The project included a substantial proportion of language programmes in Hungary, Spain, Sweden and the UK. While learners expected a tutor to be a subject expert they also expected a friendly and approachable response. Qualities associated with responsiveness were rated more highly than the provision of quality feedback on assignments. These findings draw attention to the need to bear in mind the quality of empathy as an essential attribute of the distance learning–teaching relationship, including all forms of support. The importance of the affective domain in distance language learning is evident here too.

It is equally important for teachers and institutions to relate to learners as individuals and to respond promptly and cordially to their concerns. In some programmes limits are set for the turnaround time of assessments, and there may be a requirement that student concerns are responded to within 48 hours. While these measures improve response time, they should not be at the expense of the quality of the response or feedback.

8.6.2 Peer support

Peer support may play an important role in the support network of distance language learners. Online facilities for student–student interaction in the form of chat rooms or discussion groups have reduced the isolation of learners, and vastly increased the possibility of the peer group as a form of support. Interactions that learners initiate and manage for themselves, and which are not moderated by the institution, can be the means for learners to provide a frank exchange of reactions to the experience of distance learning, and also to identify further sources of support. In my experience this is one of the most useful and sustainable forms of learner–learner support. Other forms of peer support systems, such as face-to-face study groups, may be difficult to establish or maintain largely due to the range of personal and professional commitments of students.

Mentoring is another form of peer support. It generally implies support from learners who have more experience with distance learning, or who have taken the language course before. Novice distance learners may benefit from a mentoring programme since they are particularly vulnerable to periods of low confidence and uncertainty, which may be intensified by a sense of isolation. Hau Yoon (1994) uses mentors or 'peer proctors' in face-to-face study groups in her distance Chinese language programme at the University of South Africa. The peer proctors are students who have already completed the course and who themselves are supported by the course tutor. Important roles for the peer proctors are to help learners to gain increasing independence but also to encourage interaction with the tutor in relation to specific needs.

As with certain other aspects of learner support, there are some difficulties in the development of mentoring services. Simpson (2000: 112), in a discussion of the positive aspects of mentoring in distance learning, notes that there are also problems in 'scaling it up to be an effective element in an institution's student support armoury'. Looking ahead, it may well be that mentoring could emerge in distance language learning as a feature of learner support, but that it remains a relatively small scale undertaking to be underpinned by the ongoing expertise and the interest of a course tutor.

8.6.3 Native speakers

Opportunities to practise the TL with native speakers are an important development in support for distance language learners. The most promising of these has been with the development of e-mail partnerships in which learners of different languages are paired, one of whom is a native speaker of the language the other wishes to learn. The partnerships allow learners to practise their TL with native speakers, to exchange points of view and to give and obtain feedback on the language used. Learners can get advice on their TL use, and can also gain affective support, both directly and indirectly from their e-mail partner, the tutor and the learning group.

While interactions with native speakers can provide important support for distance learners, these interactions themselves need to take place within a network of support. An example of the context of support that can be developed is given in an account of the use of e-mail partnerships as an optional element in an extension course by Labour (2000). A range of types of collaboration provide support for the partnerships:

- access to native speakers online on a one-to-one basis referred to as *horizontal collaboration* or *peer teaching*;

- interaction with the teacher referred to as *teacher–learner dialogue* or *vertical collaboration*;
- *peer support* in face-to-face sessions at the University of Valenciennes in which learners discuss how they communicated with their e-mail partners to iron out problems and to encourage each other.

Key aspects in the teacher–learner dialogue are identified by Labour as:

- assisting learners to negotiate help within the learning partnership;
- enquiring, advising and giving general feedback, including boosting confidence and providing alternative ways of thinking about things;
- positive reinforcement through praising achievements;
- involving students in the decision-making process.

Technical support is provided at the start of the process in the form of a training session in how to use the Internet, e-mail and a word processor, and ongoing support is provided throughout the partnerships by the teacher. A well-developed network of support underpins the further support learners get from their interactions with native speakers. This is a promising area for future research and development within distance language learning environments.

8.6.4 Partners, family and friends

The support available within social networks and relationships is considered by learners to be crucial to a successful outcome with distance learning (see, for example, White 1993). They are dependent upon the backing, encouragement and positive attitude of other people who are important in their lives, as they need to integrate the demands of study with a range of other commitments. Belawati (1998: 87), writing from the Indonesian situation, adds that 'if their studies do not fit well with the agenda of those significant others, it is likely that study would become a lower priority on their agenda also.' In responding to the needs and concerns expressed by distance language learners, teachers need to be sensitive to the ways, often unexpressed, in which individual circumstances impact positively or negatively on learning.

8.7 Online learner support: access, value and congruence

8.7.1 New forms of learner support

In the past mail, telephone and fax were the main means available to distance language learners to contact the institution and access support services. There were also, in all likelihood, some limited face-to-face opportunities. The telephone remains extremely important in distance language learning. It offers interactive opportunities relating to speaking and listening, and is an important means of providing help with pronunciation, and for immediate feedback on performance.

E-mail has, however, revolutionised the ease with which students can get in touch with their tutor, other support staff and administrative services. The feelings of trepidation and inhibition that students have reported in relation to making that initial phone contact are not reported in relation to e-mail. The asynchronous nature of the medium means that students can compose their messages when they are ready, can review what they send, and have time to reflect on the answer they receive. The teacher, too, has time to reflect on both the question and his or her response, and to document a number of alternatives or options.

Online environments offer many new advantages in terms of addressing learner support needs. I think one of the most important is that these new environments allow more of the individual learner to come into view. Not only do they provide an additional number of ways in which learners can raise issues or concerns, but in computer conferencing, for example, the teacher and other learners become aware of how others are responding to the course. This provides an excellent forum for interaction and feedback, which can be tailored to the expressed interests and needs of individuals. When we consider again the idea of learner support as response to the individual learner, online environments provide more opportunities to respond to both individuals and groups of learners, and to gain a sense of the kinds of concerns that arise throughout the course.

There are several other features of online environments that support the learning process. The possibility to send regular messages to learners can be used as a means of structuring the learning process – they can be reminded of upcoming assignments, of alternative resources, and of what is important at a particular point in the course, for example. Timely feedback has also been identified as an important component in student motivation, and assignment turnaround time can be speeded up in online environments.

Online learner support brings into focus again the fundamental distinction between communication and information referred to in Chapter 1. Frequently asked questions (FAQs) and online information guides can provide important support, particularly for administrative and some technical issues. However, it should be remembered that many students want communication, not just information, in relation to the issues and questions they raise and are not necessarily happy just to be directed to information on the course website. This aspect is particularly important in pre-enrolment support services where students want to discuss their individual circumstances and needs as language learners as part of making decisions about entering the course. Such conversations provide valuable information to the teacher about students on a course. Learner support at all stages of the course is labour-intensive, but FAQs and other sources of information should be used *in addition to* a personal response rather than as a substitute for interaction.

8.7.2 *Maintaining a learner-centred approach*

If learner support is viewed solely from the perspective of a paradigm of institutional concerns, then the focus tends to be on what is economical, feasible, and – possibly – innovative. However, the forms of support chosen on this basis may be less adequate or appropriate when placed within a paradigm that is informed by learner needs, concerns and experiences. It is essential to distinguish between those forms of support that the institution finds desirable, or has access to, and those forms that learners can readily access and use. This is particularly pertinent as institutions may feel impelled to deliver support through ICT, and it is important to be aware of who will be included and excluded by particular choices.

A learner-centred approach recognises that different media can be particularly right and fitting at different stages of learner experience. Thus, in the beginning stages, face-to-face support with a local course adviser may be highly valued by some learners, but may not be necessary at later stages when telephone or e-mail contact can suffice. Ideally, perhaps, learner support would be available and delivered entirely according to the means and preferences of the learner, thus including the possibility for face-to-face, telephone, print and virtual communication. Financial constraints generally make this less likely.

Blanchfield, Patrick and Simpson (1999), in considering computer conferencing for guidance and support, argue that if a particular medium of support is to be judged useful by students, it must be appropriate in terms of access, added value and congruence.

Access   The *access* issue means that the support must be to hand, or easy to get to, efficient, and economical in terms of time and money. Students cannot be expected to invest a lot of time and energy in attempting to access a service, or in gaining the support they need.

Value   The *value* feature means that the medium of support must add 'study value', and must be perceived by learners as adding study value to their core concerns of learning the TL. In other words, learners must feel that there are clear personal benefits that will enhance their studies.

Congruence   The medium of support needs to be *congruent* – at least to some degree – with the preferred approaches and study methods of distance language learners. Given the time constraints many distance language learners face, they tend to prefer the ways of learning and getting support which they have established for themselves, or methods which are closely aligned to and congruent with their own methods.

Of course, sometimes dramatic shifts take place in terms of familiarity with new forms of learner support such as computer conferencing. And the role of the individual distance teacher is crucial in terms of the ways in which a medium of support is made available, used and maintained. A further key point is that the circumstances and experiences of learners can change quite markedly at times within a single course and one would hope this was recognised as an important aspect of the learning experience. At such points different support media become valuable or even essential.

While the potential of the new technologies to enhance the quality of the learning experience is exciting, there has been no systematic research into the efficacy of online support services. At present the very newness of these services, and their patchy implementation, has prevented the definitive research that is needed (Ryan 2001). Tait (2000: 288) makes the crucial point that such monitoring is essential if *provision* is not to replace *service*, and elaborates as follows:

> ICT presents enormous opportunities to rethink student support in ways that are not yet fully understood, in particular with regard to time and place, and the social dimension of learning which can be enhanced or diminished through CMC . . . It may be in due course that ICT will lead to more uniformity in global terms in the ways in which services to students are delivered in the future. However, it also remains true that for some audiences and in many societies the new technologies are having a limited impact on the delivery of ODL.

Tait's final sentence draws attention again to the importance of considering the individual and the wider society in the selection of different media and delivery mechanisms for learner support.

The issues surrounding online support services are such that most providers who use online support will need to maintain dual systems (traditional and virtual) for some time to come. At the same time there is an urgent need to provide ongoing professional development for language teachers in relation to the kinds of interpersonal and communication skills that are needed to provide appropriate support for learners in different environments.

8.8 The situated nature of learner support

The social contexts encountered in different educational environments shape the process of language learning and teaching in significant ways. An important contribution to our understanding of the extent to which social contexts are more than simply a backdrop to English language teaching has come from the work of Adrian Holliday (1994: 9) who investigates how learning may be affected by:

> the attitudes and expectations that people bring to the learning situation, which are influenced by social forces both within the institution and the wider community outside the classroom, and which in turn influence the ways in which people deal with each other.

This approach is also useful in understanding the range of attitudes that may exist to learner support, and which influence how distance language learners and teachers may respond to the idea of supported distance language learning.

The learner support practices associated with distance learning have, for the most part, been developed in Western contexts, most notably by the Open University UK. A number of descriptive studies have documented the response of various cultures to such practices. Here I refer to two contexts that together illustrate a common theme within reports of practice, namely that learner support is heavily contingent on local circumstances.

Koul (1995) explores the response of distance learners within India to learner counselling – a response which he claims would also apply, at least in part, to other non-Western nations. He is interested in the ethos of learner counselling, the role of the counsellor, and the realities of counselling sessions. Three of the many observations he makes are:

- At the philosophical level, the notion of counselling generally remains alien to the average student in developing countries, where the extended family has mechanisms for solving problems, psychological or otherwise, and problems are not for outsiders to explore.
- The expressly appointed learning counsellors are seen as teachers, and what a teacher does is to teach, not deal with the learner's problems, however intimately they may be related to their studies.
- Having come from the same cultural base, counsellors are not able to see themselves as able to look into the problems of the students. Thus academic counselling sessions become (i) note-giving/note-taking sessions, (ii) sessions for the simplification and interpretation of the materials, often in the mother tongue, (iii) sessions for providing clarification on assignments.

As one might expect, the philosophy and practices of learner counselling in this context have become overlaid with the cultural practices of the host society.

Attitudes concerning the value of learner support are also diverse. While the tradition of individual support for students is extensive in the UK, as in the United States, Canada and Australia, it does not exist to the same extent in other countries, such as Germany and Spain or even Israel (Guri-Rosenblit 1999). Peters (1992), for example, argues that in Germany 'the active support of students to reduce the drop-out rate has no tradition in German universities . . .' (p. 258). In such a culture of practice, the expectation is that concessions are not made to the different starting positions of learners, and *how* students acquire knowledge is on the whole left to them, at both the FernUniversität – the major distance-teaching university in Germany – as well as in more traditional universities. Furthermore, learner-oriented teaching and support services are not really part of the practice of distance education provision in Germany since, as Peters (1998: 14) notes, 'most of the university's teachers would regard this as an undesirable school-like structuring of university teaching and would be greatly concerned with their academic dignity'.

Most of the research into learner support has been carried out on a fairly narrow research base. Once researchers move outside these settings, much greater diversity is encountered, not only in terms of the characteristics of the learners, and their expectations, but in terms of the cultures of practice which infuse educational contexts and the relationships within them. As many distance education providers seek to enter global markets, issues relating to learner support – the extent of support provided, appropriate forms of support, the ways in which support services are delivered – become infinitely more complex. This is a crucial area for future research.

8.9 Feedback as support for learners of English

Feedback plays a critical role for distance language learners, not only as a response to their performance, but also as a means of providing support, encouragement and motivation to continue. Within a classroom environment, language learners can make some judgements about their progress as they have access to the responses of others, to classroom interactions and to ongoing monitoring and feedback from the teacher. These elements are not so readily available in distance learning so students look to written feedback to gain a sense of their overall competence. Feedback is also an important part of the ongoing teacher–learner relationship; it contributes to how the learner sees the role of the teacher and indicates the extent to which the teacher is prepared to provide individual support.

Fiona Hyland (2001) provides the first published study of feedback in the context of a distance language learning programme. She focuses on the nature, perceptions and use of feedback provided to distance learners of English at the Open University of Hong Kong. Here I will review and discuss part of the study relating to the kinds of feedback that are provided, the ways in which they were considered beneficial or effective, and practical issues surrounding the issues of feedback to distance language learners.

8.9.1 The learners and the course

The distance learners were enrolled on a general English proficiency course, *EL100*, open to all learners at the Open University of Hong Kong. The course ran for 10 months and at the time of the study comprised a wide range of self-instructional materials (print and audio-visual), and optional face-to-face tutorials (32 hours of tutorial time in total). Feedback for submitted work was provided in the form of in-text interventions and written comments, notes and corrections on a summary sheet. Other opportunities for feedback, and to discuss work were provided – by phone, at allocated times, or during face-to-face tutorials – but those discussions needed to be initiated by the learner.

8.9.2 Issues

A number of issues relating to feedback can be identified as part of the background to the study by Hyland. Those that arise from the particular nature of the distance context include:

- the wider teaching and support role of feedback in the distance context;
- the possibility of a mismatch in expectations of feedback between learners and tutors;
- the possibility for feedback to be misunderstood or misinterpreted due to the constraints of distance;
- the need to provide feedback that focuses on the learning process as well as on the product;
- the need to examine the kinds of information, support and training given to distance tutors that would guide them in providing more appropriate, effective feedback;
- the relationship between feedback and the development of effective language learning strategies.

A further issue is the gap between the aims identified in distance education theories and research, and realities of current practice. One of the aims is that feedback should be the basis of, and should encourage, dialogue between the teacher and the learner (e.g. Carnwell 1999), although in current provision this is seldom the case.

8.9.3 The study

Feedback in this context was investigated in terms of what feedback was provided, tutors' and learners' expectations and perceptions of feedback, and how learners made use of that feedback. Data was gathered through 108 completed questionnaires, interviews with 10 learners and 4 tutors and from the feedback given on assignments. Here I will focus on the nature of feedback provided in relation to the learning process, including a discussion of perceptions of feedback on the part of learners and tutors.

8.9.4 Feedback relating to the learning process

The feedback given to distance learners in this study was seen as relating to two broad categories:

- *the product* (i.e. the strengths and weaknesses of the assignment itself); or
- *the learning process* (i.e. the strategies and actions the students should take to improve their language)

Hyland (2001: 237)

Given the wider teaching and support functions of feedback in the distance context, and the need for distance learners to establish effective ways of working to develop TL skills for themselves, the second category of feedback is an important part of this study, and is the focus here.

Less than 17% of teacher comments on submitted work focused on the learning process; the vast majority of comments were concerned with learning products, that is content, organisation, language accuracy and presentation. Feedback that focused on the learning process fell into one of three categories:

1. **Encouragement:** These comments tended to be generalised but were valued by learners. Tutors were aware that, in some cases, they provided the main form of contact between teachers and learners, particularly for those who did not attend tutorials. Tutors also felt competent in providing encouragement and felt positively about this aspect of their work (see extracts in *Reflections and experiences* in

section 8.9.5). This was the most frequently used category of comments that focused on aspects of the learning process.

2. **Reinforcement of learning materials:** This category was the least used by tutors. In prior training sessions for tutors, the course co-ordinator had underlined the importance of linking comments to other learning sources within the course so students could work further on the points that were made. One explanation for the lack of linkages to the course material is that the tutors were relatively new and may not have developed detailed knowledge of the course content. Time may also have been operating as a constraint for the tutors, or they may have felt the linkages should be obvious enough to the learners. None the less, this is an important aspect of feedback to consider since Hyland found elsewhere in the study that learners spent much time consulting course materials and other learning sources when they had difficulty in understanding or using the feedback they had been given. Since distance learners frequently consult other learning sources in response to uncertainty (see, for example, White 1995c, 1997), it would seem appropriate for distance tutors to suggest where learners could follow up on the points made. How they might follow up on the points made is the third category of feedback relating to the learning process.

3. **Suggesting learning strategies:** This category of response was frequently used, almost as much as encouragement. The tutors were aware of the actions that learners could take to improve their learning. In some cases this involved suggesting that learners attend the face-to-face tutorials, in other cases more specific learning strategies were suggested.

8.9.5 Commentary

One aspect of the study, not discussed above, is that on the whole students wanted feedback concerning accuracy, and detailed feedback on problems identified within their assignments. That is, they were focused almost exclusively on feedback related to products. This is somewhat at odds with the view of researchers and theorists advanced in the literature. Feedback according to those sources is a means of establishing dialogue with learners, providing support, and enhancing the distance language learning experience for individuals, as well as responding to the performance of individuals.

These functions may well be important to learners, but it appears that attaching them to assessment exercises may be less effective. The advent of CMC provides an opportunity to carry out many of the support and teaching functions through text-based discussions. They may then be linked to course work rather than assessment. At the same time it is important to remember that assessment exercises frequently drive learning within distance contexts, and therefore the dialogue surrounding these aspects of the course may be more salient to learners than dialogue in other parts of the course.

The tutors in the study were relatively new to distance learning contexts and took time to gain an appreciation of the different functions and prominence attached to feedback in the distance context. The challenge, of course, is to establish two-way communication in relation to feedback – that is, dialogue. My own impression is that this dialogue happens more easily, and more frequently, when learners are invited to respond, and when feedback is given through a medium that readily supports two-way communication, such as e-mail.

Hyland does not mention electronic feedback, but she approaches the issue of dialogue from another angle, which is that it can be initiated by learners. The suggestion is that opportunities be provided for learners to indicate requirements for feedback, which can then open the dialogue with the tutor. A cover sheet is included with their assignment where students can raise questions and indicate areas for feedback that they would find useful. Hyland goes on to suggest that students could also be asked to reflect on their needs in relation to feedback, and how they will use it, and to attach this with submitted work. In terms of my knowledge of distance language learners, these two suggestions are promising. I think it would also be a useful area in which to provide one or two extracts from the reflections of former students, to act as a prompt for distance learners who may not have had experience of such a process.

Learner–learner feedback is now an important option possible in a number of electronic learning environments. It is mentioned, as in Raskin (2001), but remains relatively unexplored in terms of its viability and contribution to distance language courses. Many of the issues that are raised in this study concerning the negotiation of feedback, dialogue, and the functions of feedback can be applied to peer feedback. This is a promising area for future research.

Reflections and experiences

Tutor perspectives on feedback

Tutors within the distance English language programme at the Open University of Hong Kong were asked about their views of the feedback they gave to the learners. They were relatively unsure about the extent to which their feedback helped to improve the actual proficiency of learners in English, but felt confident that the affective support they provided was important and effective. The comments below are from four tutors in the course, and the interviewer.

I see my main role as supporter because I realise how vulnerable a lot of them are; if I am not careful they would drop and then they would lose hope. So encouragement is the most important thing.

I hope the encouragement I put in the feedback sheet will be very helpful to them. Because just some grammar points may not be very helpful to improve the language, because they cannot improve the language overnight.

I have got to be more understanding and should be more compassionate when I understand that the adults have got such a hard job.

Interviewer: Do you think you have changed the way you give feedback compared with other teaching situations?

Tutor: Yes definitely, more detailed and more encouragement . . . In the first year I was less sympathetic. I was treating it as a regular assignment where I was seeing the students regularly.

(Source: Hyland 2001: 244)

8.10 Summary

Since learner support essentially comprises response to the individual learner as a means of enhancing the language learning process, it may be viewed as both *ad hoc* and ephemeral compared with the course development aspect of distance language learning and teaching. The limitations of this perspective and the importance of learner support have been highlighted in this chapter. Emphasis has been placed on the kinds of sources of support which may be available to distance language learners, together with the functions of learner support. In practice however, learner support is most often a pragmatic activity carried out in a particular context, strongly influenced by a range of institutional and cultural factors, as well as by the experiences and resources of participants. There is a need to document the processes of learner–teacher interactions in distance language learning, the better to understand them, and to provide the basis for professional development for distance language teachers. Such an approach would also serve to counter the perception that learner support is a minority concern or peripheral issue. The approach taken by Hyland (2001) in analysing feedback given to distance learners of English is one example of such an approach, and research carried out in face-to-face advisory centres for language learners is an important related area. The way learner support functions in online environments, particularly in terms of the social and affective dimensions of learning, is a significant – and much needed – direction for research. While attention in distance language learning is often focused on course development and delivery, the diverse and complex nature of learner support cannot be overlooked, neither can the crucial role it plays in the development of quality learning experiences in both hi-tech and low-tech environments.

9 Learning sources

9.1 Introduction

The focus in this chapter is on the learning sources available within a distance language course. It follows two avenues of enquiry. I begin with the more traditional notion of course content, which is linked to course design and course delivery. As part of this I focus on how content has been conceptualised in distance learning and teaching, and consider some of the mechanisms and stages in course production, and the role of course production teams, which are a distinctive feature of distance education. This has been an influential approach in distance education and reflects a concern with how content can best be developed, constructed and delivered to learners to provide optimal learning experiences. The emphasis is generally on the development of predetermined, pre-packaged content.

The second half of the chapter moves away from the idea of static content to consider the role of fluid course elements – such as CMC discussions – as important learning sources within a course. This is also congruent with a move away from a linear course model towards using multiple sources for learning. The idea of learning sources reflects a view of course content from the perspective of the learners rather than the course designer or the teacher. As part of this I draw a key distinction between *potential* texts and *actual* texts, in relation to the multiple learning sources that are available to learners. An extension of this approach is a view of each distance language learner as a course producer who actively selects and constructs content from a range of sources. It is these sources which contribute to his or her learning environment and experience of the TL, and become, in effect, the course. At the end of the chapter I discuss a study of the kinds of judgements and decisions that distance language learners make when they first begin to work with multiple learning sources and incorporate them into their language learning environment. It provides some preliminary insights into how distance learners select and construct the content of their language courses.

9.2 Conceptualising content

The centrality of learning resources to distance language learning has meant that much effort has been directed towards the development of courses consisting of carefully constructed pre-determined content. In more traditional course models it is this content that functions almost exclusively as the main source of instruction. Emphasis is placed on developing materials that foster learner engagement with the content. Benson (2001: 133) notes that distance learning materials often address the isolation of learners 'in highly directive ways, and some of the best-known general guides in writing distance materials emphasise the need to direct the learner explicitly'. Developments include the use of access devices, the 'tutorial-in-print', the 'reflective action guide' and self-assessment questions (see, for example, Rowntree 1997). Emphasis has also been placed on planning and evaluation processes and on good practice in relation to the development of self-instructional texts. Developments in the last decade have centred on enhancing instructional design with different technological tools and media (Bates 1997, 2000), although not explicitly for language learning. Implicit within this approach is the view that the course is something that is developed by a teacher or course team and is then delivered to the learners. This orthodox way of conceptualising content which emphasises course development, production and delivery is represented in Figure 9.1.

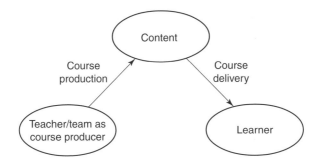

Figure 9.1 Orthodox approach: the teacher/team as course producer

It is possible, however, to view course content from a more learner-centred perspective. The content of the course then consists of a number of what I call learning sources, some of which learners select and engage with, according to their needs, preferences, abilities and resources. What arises out of this process is 'the course' from each learner's perspective. This alternative approach, represented in Figure 9.2, foregrounds the learners as agents in developing the course. They make decisions in

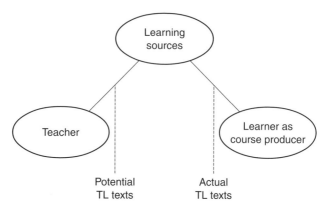

Figure 9.2 Multiple learning sources: learner as course producer

relation to the range of potential TL texts which have been developed by the teacher or course team. As they engage meaningfully with their selection these potential texts become the actual TL texts that form part of their learning environment.

The approach I take here has a number of equivalent themes in the second language teaching literature based on face-to-face teaching contexts. It reflects the distinction drawn by Nunan (1989: 9) between the curriculum as a 'statement of intent' and what actually occurs in the language classroom. The work of Clarke (1989) is relevant here too concerning the ways in which language classes can involve learners in the processes of materials adaptation and materials development. Different forms of these processes play an important role in distance language learning as learners select and integrate materials into their individual learning environments. And the more learner-centred approach to the idea of what constitutes a distance language course is related to an ecological perspective on language teaching proposed by van Lier (2002). He argues that language within the learning environment 'is not seen as input directed at the learner for the purposes of intake and eventual output, but rather as potential affordances, that is, as signs that acquire meaning and relevance as a result of purposeful activity and participation by the learner' (p. 783).

The ideas associated with Figure 9.2 represent a shift in emphasis from the distance language teacher as someone who develops and delivers the course, to one that also includes learners who are actively involved in creating their course as they select from and interact meaningfully with a range of learning sources. In this view it is not the learners who are remote, but the teacher who is remote from the different learning sites and from the course as produced by each learner. This approach will be revisited later in the chapter. It should not be interpreted as undervaluing attention to the processes of planning and development in relation to course content, which is the subject of the next section.

9.3 Development of course content

The process of developing course content in distance education has a number of distinctive features. It includes, for example, making decisions about the shelf life of courses or course components, making explicit what is often implicit in the mind of the teacher, paying attention to compatibility between different course elements, ensuring the clarity – and succinctness – of instructions, and securing copyright clearances. A detailed examination of the development of course content for language programmes is beyond the scope of this chapter. However, I will focus on four features of the process:

- the need for extensive planning at the initial stages;
- complex choices in relation to media and delivery options;
- working within a team environment;
- a consideration of static and fluid content alongside variant and invariant content.

9.3.1 Stages in course production

The time commitment involved in producing distance language courses is substantial. It may take up to three years to develop a course. Course coordinators usually work within the framework of tight deadlines required by their institution. Similarly, revising and updating course materials is time-consuming, particularly if they involve quite fundamental changes to the structure, orientation, emphasis, content or mode of delivery of a course. And work in multimedia-based teams is inevitably more complicated. The key point here is that course developers must necessarily invest a great deal of time, energy and effort in producing a course in which the production quality is generally to a very high standard. The construction–trial–rewrite–trial cycle has a central place in distance language teaching. One illustration of the intense, complex nature of the course production cycle is given by Hurd, Beaven and Ortega (2001), based on the OUUK language courses. Course production takes three years, and comprises a number of stages, set out in Table 9.1.

Of course the stages are neither entirely linear nor discrete. However, it is useful to map out the stages, to reflect on them and to consider them as a guide to the range of processes that are involved in course

Table 9.1. *Stages in course production*

Stage 1	Writing a preliminary draft syllabus, with functions, topics and linguistic elements to be studied.
Stage 2	Drawing up the specifications of audio-visual materials, prepared by the academic team and closely discussed with the editorial team in charge of the technical part of the project at the BBC.
Stage 3	Gathering of authentic audio-visual resources in the target countries.
Stage 4	Editing the video resources and the preselection of suitable audio resources.
Stage 5	Producing a refined version of the syllabus, based on the linguistic exponents present in the audio-visual materials gathered.
Stage 6	Writing the course books, and reviewing drafts by the course team.
Stage 7	Producing activities on CDs (which include extracts of authentic audio and scripted activities recorded in the studio).
Stage 8	Editing the written materials (involves editorial queries to academic team, production of artwork, book design and printing).
Stage 9	Producing an assessment strategy and assessment materials for the course.

Source: Adapted from Hurd *et al.* (2001).

production. This is particularly important given the tendency for course developers to severely underestimate the time involved in the processes, especially during their first experience of developing a distance course (see, for example, Harland *et al.* 1997).

9.3.2 Course production team

A further key feature of distance education is that course development usually involves a team of people who contribute expertise at different stages of the process; this has become the standard method for producing distance learning materials. Since the content of distance courses is public and open to scrutiny, use of the services of a team may be compulsory in some institutions where the team is considered to have a quality control role. The point at which the design team becomes involved with the process may also vary: some are involved from the initial conception phase, whereas others become involved more as editors during the physical production phase. An example of the roles and responsibilities of people involved in course production is given in Table 9.2.

Course development teams may only include three or four of the people shown in Table 9.2, depending on resources, subject area, and the

Table 9.2. *Roles and responsibilities within a course production team*

Role	Responsibility
Subject expert	An expert in the subject area who is responsible for curriculum design, selection and development of course content and assessment. Responsibility for learner support.
Course tutor	May contribute to the functions outlined for the subject expert and may trial the materials with individual students. May also be responsible for providing support during the course.
Teaching consultants and editors	Provide advice on and critique course development. Responsibility for ensuring the quality of the layout, design and editing of courses, and compliance with copyright.
Production team	Experts in word processing, layout, graphics, and relatively routine procedures in course production.
Online consultant	Provides advice and support for online aspects of course delivery including web-based instruction and use of e-mail.
Media specialist	Provides assistance with audio and video components.
Resource specialist	Compilation of further resources for individual courses.

expressed needs of the course co-ordinator, or teacher, who will be responsible for the ongoing delivery of the course. A potentially difficult problem can be conflict within the course team: the underlying teaching philosophy of the subject expert may differ markedly from that of the teaching consultant, for example. Given that course production is a lengthy process in the distance context, and that course teams have to work together for protracted periods, often under time pressure, it is important to be aware of the need to manage conflict and disagreement, and to have ways of resolving this at an early stage.

9.3.3 Media and delivery options

Most distance language learning formats conform to combinations of the following media and delivery options:

Print: study guides, workbooks, textbooks, course guides;
Audio: radio, telephone, audiocassette, audioconferencing and voice-mail;
Video: videocassette, instructional TV, videoconferencing, satellite TV, desktop video (video available on a personal computer);
Computing: computer conferencing, e-mail, chat, multimedia, bulletin boards;
Face-to-face: contact courses, study groups, regional tutorials.

Printed text is still an important medium of instruction for distance language learning. This usually takes the form of specially prepared materials in the form of work books, study guides, course guides and so on. However, as we have seen the significant shifts in distance language learning opportunities over the last two decades have been in relation to the increasing range of teaching elements and media that are available to course developers. Technologies that are most commonly used, in addition to print, now include:

- television;
- radio;
- telephone;
- audiocassettes;
- videocassettes;
- CD-ROM;
- e-mail;
- computer conferencing;
- videoconferencing;
- Internet;
- computer-based multimedia;
- World Wide Web;
- VLE.

In such an environment, there is no longer a single, primary mode of delivery; clearly technology has changed the variety, amount, sources and media of the information available to the teacher and the learners. Course developers may incorporate a range of delivery media into distance learning packages, which include varying forms of print-based texts, audiocassettes, videocassettes, CD-ROMs, and online communications, and which may be supplemented by opportunities for face-to-face instruction. In practice many institutions may use only two or three of these.

One of the major challenges in designing a distance course is to provide high-quality, pre-prepared materials using delivery options that are available to all learners, while at the same time providing possibilities for interactive learning opportunities and two-way communication between learners and teachers. This challenge encompasses the important issues of feedback, interaction, and the need for flexible course design which enable learners to develop TL skills by various means. As Bourdeau and Bates (1997: 376) emphasise:

> . . . Because DL is media based, the instructional design process must be completed with constant thought to being flexible or

adaptable enough to respond to all students with their differences. For instance, wherever possible students should be offered the option of *self-directed learning* versus frequent interaction with a tutor or with peers, the option of audiovisual versus printed material, and so forth.

The distinction between one-way and two-way technologies is important here. Two-way technologies allow for more interaction and more extended interpersonal communication between learner and teacher and sometimes between learners themselves. The distinction between the two, and their applications, is given in Table 9.3, based on the work of Bates (1995, 2000).

Table 9.3. *One-way and two-way technology applications*

Media	One-way technology applications	Two-way technology applications
Text	course units; supplementary materials	'correspondence' tutoring
Audio	radio programmes; cassette programmes	telephone tutoring; audio conferencing
Television	broadcast programmes; cassette programmes	interactive television (ITV); video conferencing
Computing	computer assisted learning; multimedia	e-mail; interactive databases; computer conferencing

For a detailed treatment of technology and technology options in distance education, see Bates (1995, 2000), Bourdeau and Bates (1997), Laurillard (2002) and Mason (1994, 1998b), all of which are relevant to current contexts and practices.

While course content for distance language learning has generally been based on the use of one-way technology to compile materials well in advance of the start of the course, the limitations inherent in this approach have been recognised. The next two sections take an alternative approach by contrasting pre-determined content with content that is derived from the contributions of participants within the course.

9.3.4 Static and fluid content

The contribution of fluid course elements to distance language learning environments is often overlooked. The most obvious means of developing fluid course elements is CMC discussion, although videoconferencing,

ITV, and audioconferencing are other technology-mediated options. Fluid course elements are those that develop through the contributions and interactions of learners and teachers. They also include the use of language texts (spoken and written) produced by the learners, which are incorporated into the course.

It is important to be aware of the tendency in theory and practice to over-emphasise the accessibility of the static course content that can be made available to large numbers of students, particularly on the web. The danger of this approach is that it can diminish the importance of more fluid course content and dynamics in the distance learning environment. Issues relating to the balance between static and fluid content within a course are not confined to the distance context as Irujo (2000: 220) emphasises in a discussion of implementing a process syllabus:

> When the content of a course is pre-determined by the teacher, learners view the content as coming from the teacher and/or textbooks. They do not view either themselves or their fellow students as sources of knowledge, which limits the amount of interaction that they engage in. If we share the belief that social interaction facilitates the construction of new knowledge, we should be fostering interaction among our students and helping them see each other as resources.

The more fluid elements within distance language courses are most easily provided by CMC. They are now the focus of attention because of their presence in the new learning spaces and because of the possibilities they provide for interaction in the TL, and for developing social presence within a course. Language learners, however, may prefer to focus on static content within a course, and may ascribe less value to fluid course elements. They may be reluctant to participate in opportunities to contribute to the content of the course through discussion, collaboration and reflection. These issues will be discussed further in the next chapter. Certainly both teachers and learners need to give attention to balancing the emphasis they give to the static and fluid elements within a course, and both need to be prepared to encounter different views on the role of these elements within the learning environment.

There are, of course, particular economic imperatives and economies of scale that can be more easily met when the philosophy of distance education focuses on the course as a fixed entity that can be made available to learners and that may be seen as the means through which they develop independent learning skills. At many points in this book I have pointed to the criticisms that have been raised in relation to such an approach.

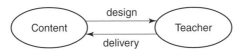

Figure 9.3 Teacher–content interactions at both the design and delivery stages

9.3.5 Variant and invariant content

Traditionally, distance education has been predicated on the finalisation of teaching material in advance of its use (Thorpe 1995). Until recently, once distance courses were developed and produced, teachers were generally wedded to that particular content, at least for that study year. It was not possible to adjust the content as learners gave feedback about the appropriateness of particular materials and as gaps and unforeseen needs emerged in a particular group of learners. However, it is now possible to counteract these limitations as online learning environments offer the possibility of presenting new or modified content related to learner needs. It is possible, for example, to change instructional materials within a VLE such as *WebCT* or *FirstClass*. Interactions between the teacher and the content may now take place during course development and course delivery, as shown in Figure 9.3.

Tuovinen (2000) suggests that a useful distinction can now be drawn between:

- *invariant content*, which represents stable aspects of the course; and
- *changing content*, which represents parts of the course that may be modified.

If staff can interact with the content during the course, the learning material can be made more appropriate and more responsive to the expressed or emerging needs of learners. However, as Tuovinen points out, the educational benefits of instructor–content interaction during the course have not yet been thoroughly researched, so any conclusions or recommendations can only be tentative.

More fundamental questions may be raised about the role and responsibility of the teacher in selecting and adapting material for individual distance learners. That is, to what extent can the distance language teacher be responsible for ensuring the maximum degree of 'fit' between individual learners and course content? Distance teachers are acutely aware of some of the limitations that exist in this regard, and propose instead the inclusion of multiple learning sources as a fundamental principle of course design. It provides a mechanism for meeting the differing needs of students within the same overall structure.

9.4 Multiple sources for learning

There has been a shift away from a course model in which students move in a linear fashion from one teaching text to the next in a printed guide – the linear model – to the development of a learning environment that consists of multiple sources for learning.

9.4.1 A linear course model

Earlier models of distance education consisted mostly of print-based materials and were strongly influenced by an approach to teaching through text that was heavily teacher-directed. Marland and Store (1993: 138) note that typically:

> specific goals are defined for students; content and resources are presented by the teacher; interactive processes and patterns are largely initiated, guided and controlled by the teacher; obligatory assessment activities are set by the teacher; feedback is provided by the teacher.

It is possible to discuss the relative merits of a more structured, prescriptive learning environment as opposed to a more 'open' learning environment. For example, students who have experienced only teacher-fronted language classes, or students who are less confident about their independent learning skills are two groups who may benefit from a course structure in which processes and paths are highly specified, particularly in the initial stages of the course.

Certain features of more highly structured distance language learning may also mitigate against the development of independent learning. There are, in my view, a number of potentially negative outcomes from relying on highly structured course materials with a linear format. These include:

- specially packaged materials, with a set learning path, may mean that learners follow what they perceive to be the 'authority route' through the materials;
- in following the 'authority route' learners may be less responsive to their own learning needs, preferences and skills;
- more highly structured procedures and materials may suggest that there is a single, right way to learn;
- pre-packaged materials may shift the focus of curriculum decision-making away from the learners;
- learners may be reluctant to go beyond the course materials to explore other sources, which have not been endorsed by the tutor;

- packaged materials may lead learners to the view that the object of learning is full mastery of those 'texts' in the course.

A common thread running through this is that in *over-specifying* everything, experience and learning is confined, and learners have less capacity to move beyond the detailed texts provided for the course. A further limitation is that learners may become deskilled, and may not develop the ability to select materials that are relevant to their background, needs, and learning preferences. This is a particular concern in distance language learning, since students must be encouraged and enabled to engage with the TL beyond the carefully tailored sources provided by the course. This problem remains a key issue, though a number of ways out of the difficulty have been suggested. What is prominent in such solutions is the need for tangible signs of our belief in the value of student independence, starting with the way the course is structured.

9.4.2 An enhanced course model

A more recent trend is towards using multiple sources for learning, which provide learners with the possibility of selecting and accessing material in a textual form which accords with their own learning preferences. This is sometimes called an *enhanced course model*. Learners are encouraged to navigate their own learning paths through the sources. Such an approach gives learners scope to make decisions about:

- which texts are to be learning sources;
- the order in which they are deployed;
- how the texts will contribute to their learning environment;
- whether such texts become primary or secondary learning sources;
- how they are used in combination with other texts.

In other words learners are able to choose how and the degree to which they interact with, interpret and derive meaning from a range of texts. When a course comprises multiple learning sources, students are able to exert a level of control that is greater than that which is offered by linear media.

The use of multiple sources is also aligned to a wider view of learning sources, namely that people generally learn languages through a mixed means learning route, including teach-yourself courses, interactions with native speakers, some classroom-based learning, and accessing TL sources on the web. In other words, the distance course is likely to be only *one* learning context among many in the experience (past, current, future) of learners. This approach reflects what actually happens as learners attempt to operate within the TL environment beyond the distance learning course. In the real world they need to be able to interact with the TL, and to derive meaning from different sources.

However, it is also important to remember that the multiple sources approach presents learners with a more complex course structure, which may take more time to navigate and construct. For some learners it may substantially increase their workload, which in turn can act as a barrier to successful completion of the course. Of course, working within an environment of multiple sources does not mean confronting learners with an infinite variety of sources, and it needs to be underpinned by understanding on the part of learners of the importance of making choices in relation to their learning experiences.

9.5 Learners as course producers

A key role for distance language learners is the ability to seek, identify and engage with appropriate TL sources. In a course based around multiple sources for learning they have the opportunity to select their own path through the material according to their preferences, progress and need for further practice and revision. In this way they are able to exert a level of control that is greater than that which is offered by the linear structure that characterised early, correspondence forms of distance education. The inclusion of a range of textual forms as vehicles for course content ensures that flexibility is built into the course, and that learners have the possibility of personalising their learning path. In such an approach there is an emphasis on understanding that learning sources are not the course: rather the course is something that is unique to each learner as they find their learning path through multiple sources. They can be seen as course producers who select and work with texts which can become an effective part of their language learning environment. There is also a recognition that the course will be experienced quite differently by different students. The following observation by Nunan (1989: 176) is equally pertinent to classroom and distance language learning:

> The effectiveness of a language programme will be dictated as much by the attitudes and expectations of the learners as by the specifications of the official curriculum . . . Learners have their own agendas in the language lessons they attend. These agendas, as much as the teacher's objectives, determine what learners take from any given teaching/learning encounter.

Of course learners may differ in their ability to identify and evaluate the usefulness of different learning sources. In addition some may be less able to identify how they could contribute to their language learning needs and goals. The investigation of how students actually use distance learning materials may present some unexpected feedback to the teacher, and challenge their beliefs about the role of particular aspects of the course. Teachers may be offended by the reactions of learners, particularly when they find the course is not being used as they envisaged and intended. But such messages are important and should be incorporated into our understanding of how learners engage with and learn from different TL sources. An understanding of how students react to particular course components provides the teacher with a sense of how the course works from the student's point of view. This is the subject of the next section.

9.6 Learner response to multiple sources in a distance Spanish course

In a face-to-face classroom the teacher is there to select, set up, monitor and adjust the learning sources, and the ways in which they are used. How learners manage and use different sources for language learning within a course is a central question for our understanding of distance language learning. In the period 1998–1999 I carried out research into how language learners responded to the different learning sources within a distance Spanish course (White 2000; White, Easton and Anderson 2000). One part of the research dealt with the decisions and judgements learners made about how to select and work with the range of learning sources available to them. The main emphasis here was on how learners operated in the early part of the course – at a time at which they need to confront a range of questions and choices about how best to construct their learning environment from the available sources.

Here I will focus on the views learners develop early on in relation to the place, value and contribution of the different learning sources. Two aspects of the findings are reported:

- the perceived role of different sources;
- the contribution of print vs video sources.

9.6.1 The learners and learning sources

Participants in the study were tertiary learners of Spanish enrolled in the first semester of a distance language programme at Massey University, New Zealand. Thirty-one students took part in the first part of the research reported here, which relates to the first four weeks of study in a

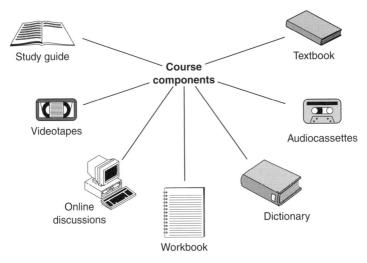

Figure 9.4 Course components in a distance Spanish course

twelve-week semester. The learners were studying an introductory Spanish course. The course was built around seven key sources for learning given in Figure 9.4. The video was not an ancillary media, but an integral part of the programme. There was a face-to-face component, held later in the semester, so it did not figure in this part of the study. Not all learners were able to access the WebCT learning space to participate in online discussions, so this component was only investigated in part of the study with a small number of learners.

9.6.2 Research focus

The kinds of questions that prompted this research included:

- How do language learners operate on a range of learning sources within a distance language learning environment?
- How do learners perceive and respond to the opportunity to use multiple sources for language learning?
- What are the affordances of the different sources according to the learners?
- Are the different sources viewed as alternative delivery devices, or do they each afford particular learning opportunities?
- How do learners evaluate the different learning sources in terms of the usefulness for their learning environment?

9.6.3 The role of different sources

Results showed that by week four of a twelve-week course learners had made decisions about the role of sources relative to each other and in relation to:

Primary vs secondary sources: Findings revealed that at about three weeks into the course students were able to identify sources as either primary or secondary texts in terms of their learning needs. The distance learners reported that for them:

- the principal sources for learning were the videotape, the study guide and the textbook;
- the secondary sources were usually the audiotape and the workbook, but for a small number of learners they were the videotape and the textbook;
- the online discussions were checked by students who could access them, but time prevented them from contributing on a regular basis;
- some learners made use of resources outside the course materials: CD-ROMs, a vocabulary textbook, music tapes, the Internet, conversation classes, family members, and another introductory published course;
- other learners mentioned using Spanish speakers, a Spanish grammar, and Spanish verb tables which they had located for themselves.

Preferred sources for initial input: In addition they had developed patterns for providing initial input at the start of each learning session ('getting started' and establishing a dynamic with the TL materials was nominated as a key issue/concern). There was a marked difference between learners who preferred audio-visual initial input (in the form of the video), and those who preferred to work with the permanent written word (in the study guide).

The demands of different sources: Learners reported that each source required a different type of interaction and a different level of engagement, with the most marked contrast being between the visual forms and the print forms. The diverse demands of the texts were seen as providing variety, and different challenges, and as enhancing motivation and interest.

A further way in which learners made judgements about the learning sources was in terms of how these different sources contributed to their learning.

9.6.4 *The contribution of print vs video sources*

By week four learners were able to report how they used each source, either by itself or in conjunction with other sources, as in:

> I start each unit using the video. It's a good way to get a sense of what lies ahead – and how much you know. I watch it several times, and then turn to the study guide. In my mind I try to link that with what I saw and heard. I do this as much as I can over several days. I use the textbook too in much the same way – to check more things out. Only then do I go back to the video – I am usually pleased by how much I've learnt.

The learners had made judgments about how to use the different sources, and how they could contribute to the process of language learning. They saw a key distinction between the contribution of print sources (study guide, textbook, workbook, dictionary) and the video. The audiocassette was considered ancillary in this context. The value learners ascribed to print sources is shown in Figure 9.5.

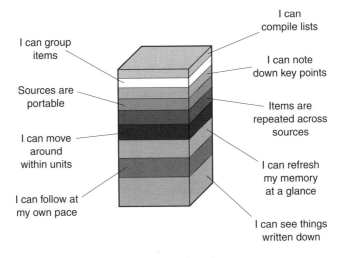

Figure 9.5 Learner response concerning printed sources

Print sources were seen as allowing learners to have ready access to the TL, to make connections between different parts of the course and to make comparisons between TL forms in different sources. Print sources were also useful in that learners felt they could easily work with and manipulate the TL, by making lists, noting down points, grouping items and so on. Learners were able to exert some control over the TL input – since print is an asynchronous medium – and this was seen as contributing to understanding and memorisation. Seeing the language written down also helped understanding and memorisation; this was the preferred mode of input for many of the learners. The flexibility of the print sources was experienced by learners in terms of pace of input and possibilities to select, combine, repeat, and manipulate input. Print-based sources were a highly valued part of the language learning environment.

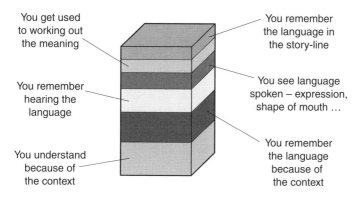

You get used to working out the meaning

You remember hearing the language

You understand because of the context

You remember the language in the story-line

You see language spoken – expression, shape of mouth ...

You remember the language because of the context

Figure 9.6 Learner response concerning video sources

The video was also valued, but it was seen as contributing in quite a different way to print sources (see Figure 9.6). It helped the learners to both understand and remember the language, mainly through the richness of the medium. It allowed learners to both hear the language, and to see the language spoken – together with facial expression and gestures – in a meaningful context, and as part of an extended narrative context. A finding from other parts of the study – of particular importance in the distance context – is the affective contribution of the video. For distance learners the video was enjoyable and interesting, and involved them in the language. It provided them with 'relief' and a 'break from studying books'. It also provided a level of engagement that was different from what they experienced using written sources. For distance learning students in particular, the opportunity to witness the dynamics of interaction in the cultural context was highly valued (White 2000).

Reflections and experiences

Working with multiple sources: learners' perspectives

Learners of Spanish reported their perspectives on learning a language within an environment which allows them to work with multiple sources of TL input.

> *All the sources work best for me because essentially they help me study Spanish in pronunciation, writing, the structures, in conversation . . . The sources complement one another.*
>
> *I find it annoying that the material is spread over a wide variety of materials as it takes a long time to find things.*
>
> *The videotape and the other parts of the course support each other and reinforce each other.*
>
> *I have had to spend time working out how I am going to work with different parts of the course. It also takes confidence to realise that you have learnt enough, that you don't have to cover everything because it is time to go on. Later on I will go back and use other material to revise and check up on how much I understand – to see if I have any gaps.*
>
> *Using the course is like layering my knowledge – I begin learning one way, then build on this using the video, then go back to the written part. I build up what I know. You can't learn a language using just one set of materials. It's much better this way.*

9.6.5 Commentary

The distance language learners in this study on the whole valued the choice and learning opportunities provided by a multiple learning sources environment. In such an environment they made decisions about which sources they would work with, how they would co-ordinate them, and how the sources may contribute to their language learning experience. In other words, learners monitored and evaluated not only their own learning, but the appropriateness and potential of the learning sources available to them.

Clearly, working with multiple sources can be a complex endeavour, particularly at the initial stages of a course. Learners have many ways in which to access and work with the TL, and many opportunities for further practice, recycling TL forms in other tasks, and in using the language in a range of contexts and modes. Most learners appreciated these opportunities, as is evident in the *Reflections and experiences* section included earlier. They appreciated the complementary nature of the sources and variety they provided. Some noted that they felt more confident as they became used to learning the language through a variety of sources.

Clearly a few learners would have preferred a linear course model where their route through the language was laid out, and where they would not have so many choices. For these learners, the more open course environment added to the uncertainty they were experiencing, and detracted from the more positive aspects of the course. Studying the response of learners to different sources within a course is a form of evaluation that is not generally used in distance learning. It provides the teacher with a view into the kinds of decisions and judgements learners make when they begin to interact with a range of sources. It is evident that learners are highly selective in terms of what they import into their language learning environment and into how they construct the course for themselves. It provides a broad view of the strategies learners use in relation to particular sources. Further, more detailed studies of this kind would allow us to see the extent of the gap or overlap between the intended use and the actual use of learning sources.

9.7 Summary

Issues relating to the way we conceptualise content remain central to the field of distance language learning. It is quite proper that distance language teachers are concerned with principles and practicalities of course design. A number of distinctive features of course design in distance education have been reviewed such as the protracted nature of the process, the stages which it may entail, the course team environment and media and delivery options. It is, however, important to examine critically the notion of course content as part of adopting a learner-centred perspective on distance language learning. The view put forward in this chapter moves well beyond a concern for the compilation and packaging of content. It includes an understanding of the role of multiple sources within distance language learning, of the need to differentiate between potential and actual texts for distance language learners and to view distance language learners as central to the construction of their course and their learning environment. It presents an alternative view that is based on the actions of learners as deliberately incorporating learning sources into their environment and engaging with them in personally meaningfully ways according to their own learning agendas. This, for learners, is the essential nature of the course.

10 New learning spaces and the way ahead

10.1 Introduction

The major shift now under way in distance language learning is the creation of new spaces in which learning can occur, in large part a result of developments in information and communication technologies. In this chapter I introduce the notion of learning spaces, and how it relates to the emerging paradigms for distance language learning. The pressures that are prompting the development of new learning spaces are explored and are related to concerns about the limitations of existing distance learning environments, as well as to a drive to reach new audiences and new markets. A number of interpretations and frameworks relating to the new learning spaces have emerged, and I discuss these, together with some examples. This is followed by an outline of integrated electronic learning environments, and the ways in which they seek to meet the learning, administrative and support needs of distance learners. The final sections of the chapter, and of the book, examine the process of innovation in distance education – its relationship to practice and to the aims and needs of key participants and stakeholders within the field. The central argument is that the way ahead for distance language learning and teaching can best be discerned if attention is paid not simply to the path of innovation, but also to the immediate context and to the learners along the way.

10.2 The notion of learning spaces

We have developed a picture of distance language learners interacting with the learning context – however it is configured – to set up an optimal learning environment for themselves. The learning environment is seen as being constructed by learners from available learning sources which – within the dominant paradigms for distance language learning – comprise mostly preprepared content, with some more fluid course elements.

There now exists the possibility of new kinds of learning architecture for distance language learning as part of emerging paradigms of distance education. They offer a greater range of presentation options compared to more traditional forms of access to distance learning opportunities. More important, according to the different affordances of each learning space, different kinds of interaction and collaboration among remote participants are possible, as well as different kinds of support.

The term *learning spaces* was used by Selinger (2000) in a discussion of the ways in which new learning and teaching spaces have been opened up by electronic communications within distance education. Learning spaces refers to online environments for learning, with an emphasis on the emerging paradigms of distance learning, in which part of the content of the course is constructed and developed by participants as they interact and collaborate on particular topics or tasks. The word *spaces* is appealing because it contains the idea of openness, of an open space – it suggests an area in which events may take place. The course is then created within the new learning spaces, as individuals take advantage of the opportunities they provide, and make their contribution to the content of the course.

Commentaries on distance learning opportunities now include reference to virtual classrooms, to virtual communities, virtual learning environments and virtual interaction. Virtual in this sense means computer-mediated or computer-generated. Distance learners can now meet in different learning spaces within virtual environments, which provide contexts for the development of virtual learning communities.

10.3 The development of new learning spaces

The new learning spaces are associated with such approaches as networked learning, e-education, virtual learning environments, and cyber-learning. They are part of the move away from print as the dominant medium, to the virtual environment, largely through the web and CMC. The emphasis is on possibilities for communication, interaction and collaboration among remote participants.

Opportunities to take part in synchronous and asynchronous learning events with others online have transcended both American and European models of distance education (Rumble 2001), as shown in Figure 10.1. Traditionally the American model of distance learning was based on synchronous audio or video presentations and conferences, sometimes including videotaped courses, while the European model centred on print-based independent learning opportunities, supplemented by the use of the telephone, face-to-face opportunities, audio, video and CD-ROM.

The first, important facility made available by the Internet was e-mail: students in print-based courses could use e-mail to contact the institution

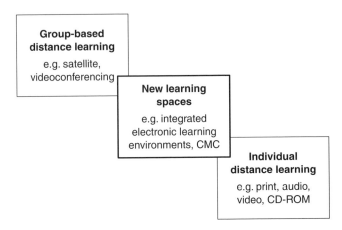

Figure 10.1 New learning spaces and distance learning contexts

or the tutor, and later, other learners on the course. Other options that also opened up with the Internet included different uses of CMC and Internet-based audioconferencing as elements within distance language courses.

A major catalyst for change in the field of distance education came with the World Wide Web. Distance education providers are making increasing use of the web as the medium of course provision. Web-based distance courses would normally have at least one of the following facilities:

- access to course resources;
- student interaction with tutor or fellow students;
- access to or submission of assignments;
- activities/simulations/exercises;
- assessments.

There tend to be two different orientations to the use of the web. One is associated with interactivity and dialogue, the other with putting materials on the web. Some providers tend to focus on the web as a means of getting materials into electronic format, and tend to view the new learning spaces as something to be filled by their printed study materials, with perhaps some links to other sites. This is a very typical approach. In this view the new spaces are used as a means of course dissemination, rather than as a new, rich learning context in themselves. Others extend this approach, developing spaces for interaction and discussion, which may be integrated with the printed content to varying degrees. They see the possibilities for enhanced communication through the use of CMC – which includes e-mail, computer conferencing, electronic bulletin boards and chat.

In my view it is these possibilities for interaction that are making the greatest impact in terms of the development of new learning spaces for the distance learner. The functionalities of CMC are a major addition to the distance learning experience, whatever the attendant disadvantages, shortcomings and challenges. What is attractive in the new learning spaces is the level of immediacy and the range of interactions that were not available in traditional formats, or available only intermittently through study groups or audioconferencing. The response capabilities for comments and discussion in the online context mean that learning can be supported in 'an incremental, tailored and iterative way so that learners develop and build upon their own tangible and continuing successes' (Morgan and O'Reilly 1999, p. 34).

Of course, the value of these advantages is totally dependent on the congruence between different course elements, the kinds of activities that are devised, the skills of the teacher and, most importantly, the overall quality of support within the context of delivery.

The focus in developing new learning spaces should not be confined to a concern with courseware over course delivery. One of the concerns discussed earlier in the book is that the actual delivery of a course is less open to scrutiny, beyond that of the immediate participants. This has often resulted in a tendency to commit greater resources to courseware development than to course delivery – more than is optimal. Given that the new learning spaces represent a shift in focus towards more fluid course elements, which merge both content and support functions, it is crucial that an appropriate balance is struck between the development of new learning spaces, and the construction of the course within these spaces by participants.

10.4 A taxonomy of online courses

Opportunities for language learning in distance education are diverse, and include various permutations of media use, interaction and support. Examples of current diversity include:

- satellite-delivered classes to several sites with medium-sized numbers, augmented by print materials and weekly computer conferences;
- print-based courses with CD-ROM and real-time chat systems;
- multimedia courses, combining a range of synchronous and asynchronous media;
- broadcast TV, supplemented by print and audio materials, and some chat facilities;

- print-based courses with electronic support systems to relatively large numbers;
- web-based courses.

Obviously each of the courses outlined above represents a very different learning space for the participants. Within these permutations, it is none the less possible to identify different interpretations and models which reveal more clearly the actual focus of a course in terms of such elements as content, interaction and support.

One taxonomy of online courses was developed by McGreal of TeleEducation New Brunswick. He makes a distinction between:

Online correspondence courses: make use of print, audio and video tapes and e-mail and probably some computer-based training courseware.

CMC courses: may have a similar element to online courses, including written texts and possibly audio/video tapes and computer software. Enhanced communication is possible through discussion packages, listservs (an e-mail discussion list) or bulletin boards.

World Wide Web courses: can be followed on the World Wide Web and can take advantage of links to other relevant sites. These courses can be either text-based, or can include graphics and animation. This grouping includes synchronous communication.

From the frameworks presented here it will be evident that the term *online course* has been used to apply to nearly any course that makes even passing use of the Internet, as well as to those where every aspect of the course is only accessible electronically (Mason 1998b). For example, many online courses only have a component of the course that is followed online: print materials, CD-ROMs, audio and video materials may be sent to the learners, and there may also be face-to-face components available. The online component may include access online to the teacher with some computer conferencing.

10.5 Online course models

A different framework, put forward by Mason (1998b), also represents three models of online courses: the content + support model, the wrap-around model and the integrated model. This framework permits insights into some of the key differences that exist in practice between online courses.

10.5.1 Content + Support Model

This model consists of the two main elements in Figure 10.2.

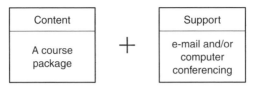

Figure 10.2 The Content + Support model of an online course

The course package may consist mostly of print with some audio or video. The package itself may be accessible on the web. For the most part this type of course is based around pre-determined content – that is fixed course elements, which we discussed in the previous chapter. There may be some interaction between learners to support the learning process, as in giving peer feedback on writing, or participating in online discussions, but these activities represent only a small proportion of study time. Students in such courses quite often report experiencing some conflict between learning within the course package and using the online support elements (Mason 1998b). In other words there may be a substantial epistemological gap between the two learning spaces. In the cases where the course content is on the web, and where it involves the use of websites, the gap between learning the content and participating in discussions may be somewhat less. This model is the most widespread model for online courses with a small proportion of online working based on e-mail only (Salmon 2000).

Example: The University of South Africa – Chinese distance language course

The University of South Africa (UNISA) has offered a distance course in Mandarin Chinese since 1993. The course has been modified and refined since that time, particularly with regard to learner support functions. It retains the features of a traditional approach, and fits within the Content + Support Model where the online component is provided via e-mail support opportunities (see Figure 10.3). This model reflects the way in which the original online courses were generally structured. The boxes on the left represent the content aspects of the course, which are based around independent study, while the boxes on the right represent the support functions.

Some of the features of this course are:

- opportunities for individual study working with a range of learning sources;

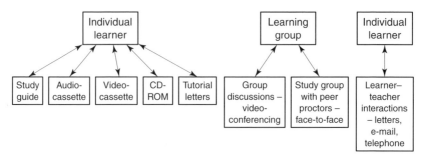

Figure 10.3 Distance Chinese course at UNISA

- orientation is provided through a videotape;
- learner support functions are for the most part optional and group-based;
- individual support is available from the tutor via e-mail;
- group discussions using teleconferencing are scheduled to coincide with assignment submission times;
- the use of mentors, or 'peer proctors' in face-to-face study groups;
- the tutor initiates some interactions with learners, and provides a range of opportunities for contact with her;
- teaching functions and support functions are largely separated, except for tutorial letters which offer encouragement and guidance about the learning process.

10.5.2 Wrap-around model

The core of this model is existing material, such as textbooks, CD-ROM resources and commercial videos. Specially designed materials are then 'wrapped around' the existing materials, usually in the form of a study guide, activities and discussion. In this model much of the learning takes place through online interactions and discussions, while working with the predetermined content takes up the remainder of the study time. This type of course is more demanding on teachers who must invest substantial time, skills and commitment in creating the course through interactions with the learners. Certainly more of the responsibility for the content of the course rests with the teacher each time the course is offered. Mason (1998b) makes a number of observations about this course model:

- learners are given more freedom and responsibility to interpret the course for themselves;
- the teacher's role is more extensive: less of the course is predetermined,

and more emerges through discussion and activities as the course develops;
• this model is congruent with a resource-based approach to learning.

This type of course requires a higher ratio of tutors to students. It tends to be used in those courses that have a relatively small number of students.

Example: The University of Auckland – Italian distance language course

The distance Italian for Beginners course offered at the University of Auckland, New Zealand, is a prime example of the wrap around model of an online course (see Figure 10.4). The existing materials were a commercially produced text book – *Adesso* – and dictionary, while the tailor-made materials consist of CD-ROMs, the web page and the hand-out with real-time communication exercises (Radic 2001).

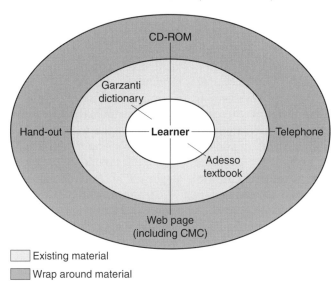

Figure 10.4 Italian distance language course: the wrap-around model

Learners have the opportunity to:

• access the TL through video and audio clips, and other examples of authentic language, through the specially prepared CD-ROM;
• interact with the multimedia software as well as with peers via the asynchronous discussion board;
• interact with the facilitator via e-mail, the discussion board and by telephone;

- participate in the online activities and online tests;
- contribute to the content of the course by posting writing and using this as the basis for communication with others;
- select a time to contact the tutor by phone for oral practice;
- make use of the audio dictionary;
- access all the material on the web page or through the hard-copy handout;
- develop skills in lifelong language learning via the web.

10.5.3 Integrated model

In the integrated model there is even less emphasis on predetermined content. The course itself develops online through various discussions and activities, as learners participate in collaborative activities, as they work on assignments together and as they evaluate and share learning resources. Although some resources are provided, the content of the course is determined to a substantial degree by what learners bring to it. Real-time communication is used to support many of the collaborative activities. In this model, the content and support aspects of the course are merged, and take place within the context of an online learning community.

In practice this type of course is rare indeed. Reports of working within this model have mostly come from courses with small numbers of select learners who have an interest in online learning. Reported studies have been at the MA level in papers devoted to such topics as teaching and learning online (Mason 2001; Gibson 2000). The model itself has many promising aspects for distance language learners including the use of real-time events and an emphasis on the collaborative, task-oriented and discussion-based activities, along with opportunities for critical reflection within an online learning community. However, it presents considerable challenges in terms of what we know about orienting learners and teachers to working within the new learning spaces.

10.6 Integrated electronic learning environments

Many of those who are working in distance education for the first time tend to conceive of this mode of delivery in terms of the development of web-based courseware or in terms of the creation of virtual classroom environments. However, the delivery of a distance course does not stop with the launching of courseware or the provision of online conferences. Many support functions are required, including appropriate assessment, tutorial and administrative support and the dispatch and receipt of assignments. A system for supporting online learning therefore involves

Table 10.1. *Functions of integrated electronic learning environments*

Functions	Consisting of
Course information	background information on the course, a timetable of major events and deadlines, what the learner can expect from the course, what the course requires of the learner, aims of the course, and a syllabus.
Course orientation	orientation to working within the learning spaces that are provided in the course, and accessing help services.
Course content	this may include text, audio, video, graphics, simulations, and should be integrated with assignment work and the interactive elements of the course.
Interactivity	this can be synchronous or asynchronous. It is usually in the form of: *e-mail*: for learner-to-institution interaction; *chat*: for one-to-one real-time meetings, and also for student interactions in private chat rooms; *discussion groups*: for learners and tutors to interact asynchronously, to collaborate on tasks and activities; *bulletin board*: useful for posting notices from the institution to the learners.
Testing	this includes self-assessment questions and computer-marked quizzes and tests.
Assignments	these can be submitted electronically – notification of receipt of the assignment, group feedback and individual feedback can all be provided electronically.
Course management	this would include maintenance of student records, course evaluation processes, management of student progress details.
Support services	this includes access to library resources and to technical, academic, personal and administrative support.

the creation of spaces in which the learning, administrative and support needs of learners are all met (see Table 10.1).

This list is not exhaustive, and particular combinations of these elements are present in the learning spaces provided by a distance course.

Inglis (2001) uses the term *integrated electronic learning environment* to refer both to the software and to the learning context provided by the software. A key feature of integrated electronic learning environments is that they support and integrate disparate functions, such as delivery of course materials, provision of chat facilities, and computer-marked testing. From the learner's point of view this integration offers the convenience of a single environment for access to teaching, interaction and administrative support. The various forms of discussion, conferencing and chat are the most extensively used of the system features.

The term *Virtual Learning Environment* (VLE) is also sometimes used. Course developers need to decide whether to adopt a virtual learning environment or create their own. The benefits of a standard supported platform may need to be balanced against the learning and teaching restrictions they impose. A number of criteria are available which allow distance educators to weigh up which VLE, or integrated electronic learning environment, is likely to be most appropriate for them (see for example Inglis *et al.* 1999; Inglis 2001).

At the same time commercial companies are working hard for market share for integrated electronic learning environments. Examples include WebCT, Blackboard, Lotus Learning Space, First Class, CU Online, TopClass, Web Course in a Box, The Learning Manager, Courseinfo and Virtual-U. Here I will refer to two of these: Virtual-U and WebCT.

Virtual-U is an integrated electronic learning environment designed by academics at Simon Fraser University. It uses a visual metaphor of the physical campus to help students to navigate through the key facilities offered, with buildings entitled library, admin., courses, café, gallery etc. This is a common device in many of the products referred to above. It offers the teacher a template for preparing the syllabus and another for designing the conference structure for online collaboration and communication.

Another integrated electronic learning environment also widely used in distance education institutions is *WebCT – World Wide Web Course Tools*. Developed by Goldberg at the University of British Columbia it provides a range of ongoing support and professional development opportunities. My institution uses WebCT for distance language learners as a supplement to the other course materials; print, audio and video materials are retained. The WebCT learning spaces are used for discussion and chat, for course information, quizzes and access to administration and support services. The following are examples of the kinds of activities that take place within a study session which includes use of the learning spaces created by WebCT:

- the learner logs on for the first time that week and gets the weekly timetable which has been posted on the bulletin board;
- she goes to the relevant sections in the contents section, and then finds them in the hard copy study guides;
- she watches the video for unit 5 a couple of times, and then begins to work on the related sections in the study guide;

- she puts the unit 5 audiocassette in the car for listening practice the next day;
- she has a go at completing a quick quiz in WebCT, and decides she'll sit it again at the end of the week before going on to the next one;
- she begins to prepare the upcoming assignment and visits the FAQ space in WebCT to check if there are any relevant questions there;
- she goes to the discussion list and posts a question about the listening task for the assignment which she is not quite sure about;
- finding just one person in the chat room she has a quick talk and then logs off.

WebCT has a student progress tracking facility which registers every hit for students within each WebCT area. Thus it is possible to see how often and when students make use of different learning spaces. Catterick (2001) in a class of eight learners used the tracking facility to see which learners may need encouragement to keep up with the weekly postings. There are, as he notes, Big Brother overtones to all of this. Careful protocols need to be set up in relation to the use of the tracking device, and students need to be informed if and how it will be used. For more on ethical issues relating to anonymity, privacy and confidentiality in online distance learning environments see Holt (1998).

10.7 Innovation and uptake

The innovations reported in the literature owe much to the work of early adopters, who pursue those innovations, find ways through the barriers that emerge and report their findings. However, early adopters tend to highlight the advantages of innovation and to downplay disadvantages or limitations (Inglis *et al.* 1999). Perhaps it would be fairer to say that they may not be aware of the limitations that might arise were the innovation to be adopted within mainstream practices, especially considering the wide range of learners who choose to participate in distance language courses. So it is important to acknowledge that while a particular technology, or a particular learning space, may be ripe for exploration by early adopters – usually with a small group of learners who may have access to extensive assistance and encouragement – this does not mean that it is ready to be incorporated into the more prevalent contexts of provision. To date, most large-scale distance teaching institutions have tended to look for technology that is reliable and can be applied with confidence. Institutions have been wary of locking themselves in to a single technology, and experienced distance teachers tend to endorse the position that variety can in itself be a powerful teaching tool.

To some, the extent of the gap between innovation and practice in distance education may be a source of concern. To others it may reflect a recognition of the fact that there is still much to be gained from lower-tech systems, particularly when the crucial issues of contexts, costs, access and flexibility are taken into account. There will continue to be an important place for lower-tech systems such as e-mail and basic computer conferencing, as well as for audio- and video-cassettes. And when the actual contexts of practice are acknowledged, there will continue to be a place for distance language learning courses that do not use any of the new ICTs.

There are a number of important tensions within the field, some of which have been identified by Keegan (2000). They exist between those who promote the web as the way forward, and those who continue to place more value in other technologies for learning at a distance. They exist between innovators and practitioners. But, most crucially, tensions exist between those who emphasise technological innovation in tertiary environments as the route to take, and those who focus on the learners and ways of enhancing the quality of their learning experiences, given such issues as access, resources, and learner preferences. In my view the ideal position is one that accommodates both concerns: a concern for innovation, and enhanced learning experiences informed by an understanding of the realities of distance study for the many different learners who enter distance language programmes. Research has a crucial role to play in the viability of this position.

Innovation is of course crucially important to the field. However, here I have placed less emphasis on innovations relating to small-scale contexts or pilot studies, and more on developing insights into the particular circumstances and challenges of distance language learners, which need to be accommodated in any form of distance learning. As distance language learning generally takes place at a site remote from the teacher, the crucial issue for learners is to establish an effective interface between themselves and the learning context. In my view, the success and sustainability of distance learning opportunities depends much less on any single innovation, and more on the extent to which attention is paid to learners in relation to those opportunities.

10.8 Participants

There are many stakeholders with an interest in the new learning spaces: the commercial companies that have developed Blackboard, CU Online, Virtual-U and similar products; the institutions that are pushing further into e-education; administrative and technical support staff; and then of course teachers and learners. The main participants in the new learning spaces are the latter groups – the learners, the teachers, and support staff. For these participants the new learning spaces present enormous opportunities to rethink distance language learning in ways that are not, as yet, fully understood. Not all teachers are willing participants in these changes. Anyone who is currently working within the field of distance education will acknowledge that there are very definite imperatives on practitioners to move to working within the new learning spaces. This pressure has come largely from an enduring sense of the limitations of traditional forms of distance education, relating to limited opportunities for dialogue, interaction and a social context for learning.

Only a limited amount of expertise in working within the new learning spaces can be developed before a course is launched – since much depends on how the learners respond. This expertise needs to be augmented once the course is running, alongside the other functions of learner support, advice, assessment, interaction and so on. The intensity associated with this type of learning is exciting, but also very demanding and usually underestimated. Distance language teaching professionals will need to pay attention to this issue, which goes beyond that of workload and other time pressures, if they are to sustain their involvement, and continue to develop their expertise over many courses. This is at a time when distance language teaching professionals in many contexts are struggling with higher teacher: student ratios, concerns about outsourcing, and shrinking budgets.

However, this pressure for change is timely, and useful, in that it requires sustained critical reflection on our beliefs, knowledge and practices in relation to language learning in distance education. It involves a new understanding of the learning context, of the roles of the participants – including learners, teachers, and a range of support staff – and the development of new practices that involve more of a constructivist approach to learning. Equally importantly at present, it has to involve assisting learners to work effectively in the new learning spaces. This is a tall order, especially for distance language teachers involved in large-scale distance education contexts, with diverse groups of learners.

While many students have embraced language learning within the new learning spaces, they perhaps need to be seen as 'early adopters' within the overall population of distance language learners. The vast majority of learners will want to know what exactly it is that we are offering that makes all the effort worthwhile. For language learners this questioning is particularly acute since one of the recurrent themes developed in this book is that learners expend a lot of energy dealing with their own learning processes, and working out how they learn best in more traditional course formats, and do not readily acknowledge the value of developing independent skills in language learning. If we add another border crossing to this – related to unfamiliar technology – there will be learners who feel it is not worth the trouble. Distance language learners need both technical orientation and help in establishing new communication protocols so that they feel comfortable interacting in online environments. In the new learning spaces both teachers and learners are bound up in parallel processes. Both are concerned to familiarise themselves with the spaces, with other participants, to learn how they themselves, and others, are responding to the opportunities, to work with snags and hitches and more complex demands and difficulties and, most importantly, to identify the affordances, and deficits of the learning spaces. Schrum (1998) argues that the new learning spaces are restructuring the lines of status and control that have defined more traditional learning contexts. This is seen as occurring principally through the move away from static content that we noted earlier to a focus on the shared process of constructing meaning which then creates 'the course'. One of the exciting things about distance language teaching at present is that all participants are learners, and face a range of challenges and prospects that could not have been envisaged a decade ago.

While the needs and responses of learners may not have been as evident in previous generations of distance language provision – or may have been more easily discounted – the new learning spaces foreground the ways in which learners use opportunities that are available, and what works and does not work for them. The visibility of learners, and evidence about their involvement, may be disconcerting but it provides the teacher with a reality check about what the whole experience means to the main participants. It is important to go with the grain of the learners' responses and to build on what we know. The distance language teacher can be an important voice in terms of equity of access to learning spaces, and also an important advocate for the needs and concerns of learners.

10.9 The way ahead

The whole context for distance language learning is in transition, and the ultimate destination is not entirely clear. The way ahead is often seen in terms of single technological innovations. According to this view distance learning will be transformed by wireless technologies, or by voice synthesis, by improvements in the telecommunications industry or by the extension of synchronous electronic delivery systems. Others see the way ahead as an issue of access: free Internet access, the cost of personal computers and the development of electronic literacy. Still others see the way ahead in terms of relationships, in particular the development of communities of learners or virtual communities. And still others look to emerging providers, university consortia and global online education as the way of the future.

Looking ahead to what might be around the corner, there are a number of sure things. One of these is that each innovation creates both new opportunities and new demands, and these must be considered carefully, and realistically, before they displace tried and tested practices. A move towards the new teaching and learning spaces involves a complete rethinking of all aspects of practice, for all participants. It means working with an interconnected community of learners, using a number of new media such as text-based online conferencing, and it means higher levels of interaction and collaboration, which in turn require particular kinds of skills, motivation and commitment. This suits some learners far less well than others and it will be some time before such forms of learning and participation are second nature to a significant proportion of people who enter distance language learning programmes. In all of this it is important to avoid the automatic equation of technological advances with progress. The new paradigms involve many unresolved questions relating to access, learning styles, flexibility and participation, added value for learners, and issues of scale, sustainability and costs.

It is not at all clear what would be the net loss or gain from a wholesale move to the new learning spaces. Most of the major providers of distance learning are taking time to think about the ways in which and the extent to which they introduce such changes, largely because of a range of issues affecting the response of learners to the new opportunities. One of these is access. That distance learning opportunities should be available to all individuals is still axiomatic for many of the more established providers of distance education. Access may be denied to learners without an Internet connection, or to those who cannot afford to invest in computing faculties, or to those who are not computer-literate and lack the confidence to develop the requisite skills. Furthermore, the flexibility and independence that are important to many distance learners may be compromised. Once courses include synchronous learning opportunities, learners are likely to have more paced and structured encounters, analogous to scheduled weekly classes. We also now know that interactive and collaborative opportunities are likely to be resisted if they are experienced as tangential to the needs and individual aims of learners, or to the overall aims of the course.

Imagining the future is far easier in terms of technological developments, than in terms of the social changes that might take place alongside and in response to those developments. Ultimately, the ways in which and the extent to which learners make use of the new learning spaces are at least as likely to be shaped by social and economic forces as by the efforts of researchers, innovators and teachers. One of the issues that I developed early on in this book related to concerns about a two-tier system of provision in distance language learning contexts: that there may be small providers as well as mass providers. In itself this would be no bad thing, were it not for concerns about the quality of provision. In all likelihood the small providers could rapidly become the elite providers who work in small-scale contexts with select groups who have access to well-developed support systems. Providing high-quality distance language learning opportunities for all learners is still a key challenge for the field, and whether providers meet this challenge successfully, particularly in the global context, remains to be seen. New providers and learners will continue to be drawn to the promise of technology-mediated distance education, even in the face of cautions about the overselling of technology and of the relatively slow learner acceptance of some of the new learning spaces. This is a fundamental paradox related to emerging paradigms for distance learning which is likely in time to become even more acute.

Imagining the future also perhaps involves looking back to the past, particularly as far as technological revolutions are concerned. The vast overselling of language laboratories in the 1960s and 1970s can serve as a warning of what could be around the corner. Language laboratories were embraced as 'the answer' to providing a language learning environment, and were installed around the globe, to be used to greater or lesser effect. The hype ran its course, and a decade later language laboratories came to be seen as just one of a range of options for enhancing language learning environments. We should be aware of possible parallels in the present. Mason (1998a), for example, cautions that while the current revolutionary possibility centres on the web – and that while it is a phenomenally successful medium – it will soon be seen to have been oversold, and just one tool among many.

My view is that much of the way ahead is uncertain. However, I am optimistic about the future of distance language learning. Distance language teachers have worked hard to improve the quality of the learning environments that were available to them at different periods, and to encourage learners to adjust to those environments. Distance language learners have also worked hard to understand and overcome some of the limitations of their learning context, to assume more responsibility for their learning, and to manage the context in ways that are optimal for themselves. One of the great advantages of the new learning spaces is that the way learners respond, contribute and raise questions is suddenly centre stage. As more aspects of the learners come into view, we can see the process as more challenging, more interesting, and with more inherent limitations than has perhaps been envisaged or acknowledged up to now. Ultimately it is the participants themselves, and the attention that is paid to the participants within each context of delivery, that will determine the future of language learning in distance education, far more than any single innovation. Equally importantly, there is a need to match the new possibilities that lie ahead with our knowledge of distance language learners, and with the crucial role played by learner support and the wider context of delivery. Alongside the development of new practices and roles for participants within the new learning spaces, there is an urgent need for further research into how these learning spaces function from the point of view of learners. This would extend our present understanding of language learning in distance education, and would allow us to focus on what really matters in the way ahead.

Appendix

The resources listed below provide further information about many of the themes explored in this book. The sites are updated regularly and provide links to information about conferences, current issues, trends and other sources of information. The list is by no means exhaustive.

Websites

International Centre for Distance Learning
http://www-icdl.open.ac.uk/
The ICDL is based in the Open University UK. It has a searchable database of literature of over 12,000 items relating to all aspects of the theory and practice of distance education.

Distance Education Clearinghouse
http://www.uwex.edu/disted/home.html
Distance Education Clearinghouse is managed and produced by the University of Wisconsin-Extension. It has many links including case studies, bibliographies, current news, policy, guidelines, journals and newsletters.

Distance-Educator.com
http://www.distance-educator.com/
This is a comprehensive and well established database of resources for distance education topics. It is continually maintained and updated. Users may also sign up for daily news updates.

ACSDE Resource Links
http://www.ed.psu.edu/acsde/resources.asp
The American Centre for the Study of Distance Education (ACSDE) provides this list of links to major organisations, associations and journals.

Journals

The list of journals below is by no means exclusive but covers the main publications in the field. Further details about journals and newsletters can be found on the websites listed earlier.

The American Journal of Distance Education
http://www.ajde.com/index.htm
The American Journal of Distance Education was established at the Pennsylvania State University in 1987. Contents and abstracts are provided free online.

Distance Education: An International Journal
http://www.odlaa.org/publications.htm
This journal publishes research in distance education, open learning and flexible learning systems. It is published twice a year, in May and October, by the Open and Distance Learning Association of Australia (ODLAA).

Journal of Distance Education
http://www.cade-aced.ca
The Journal of Distance Education is an international publication of the Canadian Association for Distance Education (CADE).

Open Learning: The Journal of Open and Distance Learning
http://www.tandf.co.uk/journals/carfax/02680513.html
Open Learning is an international journal for those involved in open and flexible learning and training, and in distance education throughout the world. It is published three times a year. You can browse the contents pages of online issues free of charge.

International Review of Research in Open and Distance Learning
http://www.irrodl.org/
IRRODL is a refereed electronic journal concerning research, theory and practice of ODL worldwide. Subscription is free.

The European Journal of Open and Distance Learning
http://www.1nks.no/eurodl/
EURODL is an electronic journal with free subscription. It presents a forum for discussion of ODL issues at all educational levels and in all training contexts.

ReCALL Journal
http://uk.cambridge.org/journals/
ReCALL is the journal of the European Association for Computer Assisted Language Learning. It focuses primarily on the use of technologies for language learning and teaching, including all aspects of research and development.

Resources

Journal of Asynchronous Learning Networks
http://www.aln.org/alnweb/journal/jaln.htm
The Journal of Asynchronous Learning Networks (JALN) contains research articles that describe original work in ALN, including experimental results, as well as major reviews and articles that outline current thinking. Access is free.

Newsgroups

The Distance Education Online Symposium (DEOS)
The Distance Education Online Symposium (DEOS) is run by ACSDE. The symposium is comprised of DEOSNEWS and DEOS-L. Details relating to the online symposium can be found at:
http://www.ed.psu.edu/acsde/deos/deos.asp

References

Almeda, M. and K. Rose. 2000. Instructor satisfaction in University of California Extension's on-line writing curriculum. *Journal of Asynchronous Learning Networks* 4 (3).
http://www.aln.org/alnweb/journal/Vol4_issue3/fs/almeda/fs-almeda.htm

Anderson, T. D. and D. R. Garrison. 1998. Learning in a networked world: new roles and responsibilities. In C. C. Gibson (ed.) *Distance Learners in Higher Education: Institutional responses for quality outcomes.* Madison, Wisconsin: Atwood Publishing.

Anderton, M. and A. Nicholson. 1995. *New Technology and Curriculum design. A Research Project with NESB Distance Learning Students.* Sydney: Macquarie University NCELTR.

Arnold, J. (ed.). 1999. *Affect in Language Learning.* Cambridge: Cambridge University Press.

Arnold, J. and H. Douglas Brown. 1999. A map of the terrain. In J. Arnold (ed.) *Affect in Language Learning.* Cambridge: Cambridge University Press.

Ayers, R. and P. Brown. 2002. IELTS Writing Online: An example of flexible learning in practice. Paper presented at CLESOL 2002 Conference, 5–8 July. Wellington, New Zealand.

Barnes, S. 2000. What does electronic conferencing afford distance education? *Distance Education* 21 (2) 236–247.

Barty, K. 1999. Developing an understanding of on-line course provision for secondary students. *Open, Flexible and Distance Learning: Challenges of the New Millennium. 14th Biennial Forum of the Open and Distance Learning Association of Australia, Deakin University, 27–30 September 1999.* 28–33.

Bates, A. W. 1995. *Technology, Open Learning and Distance Education.* New York: Routledge.

Bates, A. W. 1997. The impact of technological change in open and distance learning. *Distance Education* 18 (1) 93–109.

Bates, A. W. 2000. *Managing Technological Change. Strategies for college and university leaders.* San Francisco: Jossey-Bass.

Baumann, U. and M. A. Shelley. 2003. The experience of learning German at a distance. *Open Learning* 18 (1) 61–74.

Belanger, F. and D. H. Jordan. 2000. *Evaluation and Implementation of Distance Learning: Technologies, Tools and Techniques.* London: Idea Publishing Group.

Belawati, T. 1998. Increasing student persistence in Indonesian post-secondary distance education. *Distance Education* 19 (1) 81–108.

References

Benson, P. 2001. *Teaching and Researching Autonomy in Language Learning.* London: Longman.

Blanchfield, L., I. Patrick and O. Simpson. 1999. Computer conferencing for guidance and support. *British Journal of Educational Technology* 31 (4) 295–306.

Bourdeau, J. and A. Bates. 1997. Instructional design for distance learning. In S. Djikstra, N. Seel, F. Schott, and R. D. Tennyson (eds) *Instructional Design: International perspectives. Vol 2. Solving Instructional Design Problems.* New Jersey: Lawrence Erlbaum.

Boyle, R. 1994. ESP and distance learning. *English for Specific Purposes* 13 (2) 115–128.

Boyle, R. 1995. Language teaching at a distance: From the first generation model to the third. *System* 23 (3) 283–294.

Breen, M. P. 1987. Contemporary paradigms in syllabus design. *Language Teaching* 20 (3) 157–174.

Breen, M. P. (ed.). 2001. *Learner Contributions to Language Learning: New directions in research.* Harlow, England: Longman.

Breen, M. P. and A. Littlejohn (eds). 2000. *The Process Syllabus: Negotiation in the Language Classroom.* Cambridge: Cambridge University Press.

Broady, E. and M.-M. Kenning (eds). 1996. *Promoting learner autonomy in university language teaching.* AFLS/CILT.

Brumfit, C. 1984. *Communicative Methodology in Language Teaching: The roles of fluency and accuracy.* Cambridge: Cambridge University Press.

Burge, E. 1988. Beyond andragogy: Some explorations for distance learning design. *Journal of Distance Education* 3 (1) 5–23.

Burge, E. (ed.). 2000. *The Strategic Use of Learning Technologies.* San Francisco: Jossey-Bass.

Burge, E. and M. Haughey (eds). 2001. *Using Learning Technologies: International perspectives on practice.* London: Routledge.

Calder, J. 2000. Beauty lies in the eye of the beholder. *International Review of Research in Open and Distance Learning* 1 (1). http://www.icaap.org149.1.1.10.

Candlin, C. and F. Byrnes. 1995. Designing for open language learning: Teaching roles and learning strategies. In S. Gollin (ed.) *Language in Distance Education: How far can we go?* Proceedings of the NCELTR Conference. Sydney: NCELTR.

Candy, P. C. 1991. *Self-direction for Lifelong Learning.* San Francisco: Jossey-Bass.

Carnwell, R. 1999. Distance education and the need for dialogue. *Open Learning* 14 (1) 50–55.

Castro, A. and C. Wong. 1996. Policy and practices in Hong Kong. In T. Evans and D. Nation (eds) *Opening Education. Policies and practices from open and distance education.* London: Routledge.

Catterick, D. 2001. An academic writing course in cyberspace. In Henrichsen, L. E. (ed.) *Distance-learning programs.* Alexandria, Virginia: TESOL.

Clarke, D. 1989. Materials adaptation. Why leave it all to the teacher? *ELT Journal* 43 (2) 133–141.

Collis, B. and J. Moonen. 2001. *Flexible Learning in a Digital World: Experiences and expectations.* London: Kogan Page.

Cunningham, E. 1994. *Language Learner Strategies of Off-Campus Students of Japanese.* Unpublished MA thesis, Monash University, Melbourne, Australia.

Curtis, S. A., J. Duchastel and N. Radic. 1999. Proposal for an online language course. *ReCALL* 11 (2) 38–45.

Cusinato, G. 1996. *Distance Education. Learning and Teaching a Language at a Distance through the Internet.* Unpublished MA thesis, University of Venice, Italy.

Daniel, J. S. 1999. Distance learning in the era of networks. *The ACU Bulletin of Current Documentation* 138 (April) 7–9.

De Kline, E. 1999. Testing technology for tele-education: Pilot projects at KPN in The Netherlands. In Mitter, S. and M.-I. Bastos (eds) *Europe and Developing Countries in the Globalised Information Economy.* London: Routledge.

Dickey, R. J. 2001. Make it a conference call: An English conversation course by telephone in South Korea. In Henrichsen, L. E. (ed.) *Distance-learning programs.* Alexandria, Virginia: TESOL.

Donaldson, R. P. and M. Kötter. 1999. Language learning in cyberspace: Teleporting the classroom into the target culture. *CALICO Journal* 16 (4) 531–557.

Dörnyei, Z. and A. Maldarez. 1997. Group dynamics and foreign language teaching. *System* 25 65–81.

Doughty, C. and M. H. Long. 2002. Optimal psycholinguistic environments for distance foreign language learning. Paper presented at *Distance Learning of the Less Commonly Taught Languages Conference.* 1–3 February, Washington. http://langinnovate.msu.edu/commpapers.html#doughty

Duggleby, J. 2000. *How to be an Online Tutor.* Aldershot: Gower.

Eastmond, D. V. 1993. *Alone But Together: Adult distance study by computer conferencing* (Unpublished doctoral dissertation). Syracuse, NY: Adult Education, Syracuse Univ.

Ehrman, M. and Z. Dörnyei. 1998. *Interpersonal Dynamics in Second Language Education: The Visible and Invisible Classroom.* Thousand Oaks, CA: Sage Publications.

Epstein, R. 2001. Teacher education at a distance in Canada and Thailand: How two cases measure up to quality distance education indicators. In Henrichsen, L. E. (ed.) *Distance-learning Programs.* Alexandria, Virginia: TESOL.

Esch, E. and C. Zähner. 2000. The contribution of information and communication technology (ICT) to language learning environments or the mystery of the secret agent. *ReCALL* 12 (1) 5–18.

Evans, T., E. Stacey and K. Tregenza. 1999. Interactive television in primary schools: Children's experiences of learning with SOFNet. Australian Association of Research in Education conference, Melbourne.

Evans, T., E. Stacey and K. Tregenza. 2000. Close encounters in distance education: Research issues from case-study research on interactive television in schools. Paper presented at the Research in Distance Education Conference, Deakin University, Geelong.

Evans, T., E. Stacey and K. Tregenza. 2001. Interactive television in schools: An Australian study of the tensions of educational technology and change. *International Review of Research in Open and Distance Learning* 2 (1). http://www.irrodl.org.

Fay, R. and M. Hill 2003. Educating language teachers through distance learning: The need for culturally appropriate DL methodology. *Open Learning* 18 (1) 9–19.

Fox, M. 1997. Beyond the technocentric – developing and evaluating content-driven, Internet-based language acquisition courses. *Computer Assisted Language Learning* 10 (5) 443–453.

Fox, M. 1998. Breaking down the barriers: Perceptions and practice in technology-mediated distance language acquisition. *ReCALL* 10 (1) 59–67.

Fulford, C. P. and S. Zhang. 1993. Perceptions of interaction: the critical predictor in distance education. *American Journal of Distance Education* 7 (3) 8–21.

Gardner, D. and L. Miller 1999. *Establishing Self-Access: From theory to practice*. Cambridge: Cambridge University Press.

Garing, P. 2002. Adapting and developing e-learning courses: The challenge of keeping the quality. Conference Proceedings DEANZ April 2002, Evolving e-learning. Wellington, New Zealand.

Garner, R. 1987. *Metacognition and reading comprehension*. Norwood, NJ: Ablex.

Garrison, R. 2000. Theoretical challenges for distance education in the 21st century: a shift from structural to transactional issues. *International Review of Research in Open and Distance Learning* 1 (1). http://www.irrodl.org.

Garrison, R. and T. Anderson. 2000. Transforming and enhancing university teaching: Stronger and weaker technological influences. In T. Evans and D. Nation (eds) *Changing University Teaching: Reflections on creating educational technologies*. London: Kogan Page.

Garrison, D. R. T. Anderson and W. Archer. 2000. Critical inquiry in a text-based environment: Computer conferencing in higher education. *The Internet and Higher Education* 2 (2–3) 1–19.

Garrison, D. R., and W. Archer. 2000. *A Transactional Perspective on Teaching and Learning: A framework for adult and higher education*. Oxford: Pergamon.

Gibson, C. 1992. Changing perceptions of learners and learning at a distance: a review of selected recent research. *Distance Education Symposium: Selected papers, Part 1* (ACSDE Research Monograph No. 4), 34–42. University Park, PA: American Center for the Study of Distance Education, Pennsylvania State University.

Gibson, C. 1996. Towards an understanding of academic self-concept in distance education. *The American Journal of Distance Education* 10 (3) 60–74.

Gibson, C. 1998. The distance learner in context. In C. Gibson (ed.) *Distance Learners in Higher Education: Institutional responses for quality outcomes*. Madison Wisconsin: Atwood Publishing. pp 113–125.

Gibson, C. 2000. The ultimate disorienting dilemma: the online learning community. In T. Evans and D. Nation (eds) *Changing University Teaching. Reflections on Creating Educational Technologies.* London: Kogan Page.

Gibson, J. J. 1986. *The Ecological Approach to Visual Perception.* Hillsdale, NJ: Erlbaum.

Glisan, E. W., K. P. Dudt and M. S. Howe. 1998. Teaching Spanish through distance education: implications of a pilot study. *Foreign Language Annals* 31 (1) 48–66.

Goodfellow, R., P. Manning, and M.-N. Lamy. 1999. Building an online open and distance language learning environment. In R. Debski and M. Levy. (eds) *Worldcall: Global perspectives on computer-assisted language learning.* Exton, PA: Swets and Zeitlinger.

Gredler, M. and L. Schwartz. 1997. Factorial structure of the self-efficacy for self-regulated learning scale. *Psychological Reports* 81 51–57.

Greeno, J. G. 1994. Gibson's affordances. *Psychological Review* 101 (2) 236–342.

Gremmo, M.-J. and P. Riley. 1995. Autonomy, self-direction and self-access in language teaching and learning: The history of an idea. *System* 23 (2)151–164.

Grosse, C. U. 2001. 'Show the Baby,' the Wave, and 1,000 thanks: three reasons to teach via satellite television and the Internet. In Henrichsen, L. E. (ed.) *Distance-learning Programs.* Alexandria, Virginia: TESOL.

Gunawardena, C. N. and R. H. Zittle. 1998. Faculty development programmes in distance education in American higher education. In Latchem and Lockwood (eds.) *Staff Development in Open and Flexible Learning.* London: Routledge.

Guri-Rosenblit, S. 1999. *Distance and Campus Universities: Tensions and interactions. A comparative study of five countries.* Oxford: Pergamon.

Harasim, L. 1989. On-line education: A new domain. In R. Mason and A. Kaye (eds) *Mindweave: Communications, computers, and distance education.* Elmsford, New York: Pergamon Press.

Harland, M., E. McAteer and N. Sclater. 1997. Integrated courseware in language learning. In S. Brown (Ed.) *Open and Distance Learning: Case studies from industry and education.* London: Kogan Page.

Harrell, W. 1998. Language learning at a distance via computer. *Indian Journal of Open Learning* 7 (2) 179–90.

Harris, C. 1995. 'What do the learners think?': A study of how *It's Over to You* learners define successful learning at a distance. In S. Gollin (ed.) *Language in Distance Education: How far can we go?* Proceedings of the NCELTR Conference. Sydney: NCELTR.

Hau Yoon, L. 1994. The development of a self-study Mandarin Chinese language course for distance learners at the University of South Africa. *Progressio* 16 (1) 70–80.

Hauck, M. and B. Haezewindt. 1999. Adding a new perspective to distance (language) learning and teaching – the tutor's perspective. *ReCALL* 11 (2) 46–54.

Holliday, A. 1994. *Appropriate Methodology and Social Context.* Cambridge: Cambridge University Press.

Holmberg, B. 1986. *Growth and Structure of Distance Education.* London: Croom Helm.

Holmberg, B. 1995. *Theory and Practice of Distance Education* (second revised edition). London: Routledge.

Holt, M. E. 1998. Ethical Considerations in Internet-Based Adult Education. In B. Cahoon (ed.) *Adult Learning and the Internet.* San Francisco: Jossey-Bass Publishers.

Horwitz, E. 1999. Cultural and situational influences on foreign language learners' beliefs about language learning: a review of BALLI studies, *System* 27 557–576.

Hurd, S., T. Beaven and A. Ortega. 2001. Developing autonomy in a distance language learning context: issues and dilemmas for course writers. *System* 29 (3) 341–355.

Hyland, F. 2001. Providing effective support: Investigating feedback to distance language learners. *Open Learning* 16 (3) 233–247.

Inglis, A., P. Ling, and V. Joosten. 1999. *Delivering Digitally: Managing the transition to the knowledge media.* London: Kogan Page.

Inglis, A. 2001. Selecting an integrated electronic learning environment. In F. Lockwood and A. Gooley (eds) *Innovation in Open and Distance Learning: Successful development of online and web-based learning.* London: Kogan Page.

Irujo, S. 2000. A process syllabus in a methodology course: Experiences, beliefs, challenges. In Breen, M. P. and A. Littlejohn (eds) *The Process Syllabus: Negotiation in the language classroom.* Cambridge: Cambridge University Press.

Jaffee, D. 1998. Institutionalised resistance to asynchronous learning networks. *Journal of Asynchronous Learning Networks* 2 (2).

Jegede, O. 2000. The wedlock between technology and open and distance education. In T. Evans, and D. Nation (eds) *Changing University Teaching: Reflections on creating educational technologies.* London: Kogan Page.

Kearsley, G. 2000. *Online Education: Learning and teaching in cyberspace.* Belmont, CA: Wadsworth.

Keegan, D. 1990. *Foundations of Distance Education.* London and New York: Routledge.

Keegan D. (ed.). 1993. *Theoretical Principles of Distance Education.* London and New York: Routledge.

Keegan, D. 2000. *Distance Training. Taking stock at a time of change.* London: Routledge Falmer.

Kelly, R. 1996. Language counselling for learner autonomy: the skilled helper in self-access language learning. In R. Pemberton *et al.* (eds) *Taking Control: Autonomy in language learning.* Hong Kong: Hong Kong University Press.

Kelsey, K. D. 2000. Participant interaction in a course delivered by interactive compressed video technology. *The American Journal of Distance Education* 14 (3) 63–74.

Kember, D. 1995. *Open Learning Courses for Adults: A model of student progress*. Educational Technology Publications: New Jersey.

Kern, R. and M. Warschauer. 2000. Theory and practice of network-based language teaching. In M. Warschauer and R. Kern (eds) *Network-based Language Teaching: Concepts and practice*. Cambridge: Cambridge University Press.

King, B. 2001. Making a virtue of a necessity: A low-cost comprehensive online teaching and learning environment. In F. Lockwood and A. Gooley (eds) *Innovation in Open and Distance Learning: Successful development of online and web-based learning*. London: Kogan Page.

Kirkwood, A. 1998. New media mania: Can information and communication technologies enhance the quality of open and distance learning? *Distance Education* 19 (2) 228–241.

Kopij, S. 1989. Personal support and assistance in distance learning. *Prospect* 4 63–67.

Kötter, M., L. Shield and A. Stevens 1999. Real-time audio and email for fluency: promoting distance language learners' aural and oral skills via the internet. *ReCALL* 11 (2) 55–60.

Kötter, M., L. Shield and C. Rodine. 1999. Voice conferencing on the Internet: creating richer online communities for distance learning. In *Proceedings of Ed-Media*, Seattle, 1057–60.

Kötter, M. 2001. Developing distance learners' interactive competence: Can synchronous audio do the trick? *International Journal of Educational Telecommunications* 7 (4) 327–353.

Kötter, M. 2002. *Tandem Learning on the Internet*. Frankfurt am Main: Peter Lang.

Koul, B. N. 1995. Trends, directions and needs: a view from developing countries. In F. Lockwood (ed.) *Open and Distance Learning Today*. London: Routledge.

Koumi, J. 1995. Building good quality in rather than inspecting bad quality out. In F. Lockwood (ed.) *Open and Distance Learning Today*. London: Routledge.

Labour, M. 2000. Online tutoring: Communicating in a foreign language via email. OTIS e-workshop. 8–12 May 2000. http://otis.scotcit.ac.uk/case-study/labour.doc

Lamy, M.-N. and R. Goodfellow. 1999a. 'Reflective conversation' in the virtual language classroom. *Language Learning and Technology* 2 (2) 43–61.

Lamy, M.-N. and R. Goodfellow. 1999b. Supporting language students' interactions in web-based conferencing. *Computer Assisted Language Learning* 12 (5) 457–477.

Lamy, M.-N. and X. Hassan. 2003. What influences reflective interaction in distance peer learning? A longitudinal study of four online learners of French. *Open Learning* 18 (1) 397–60.

Laouénan, M. and S. Stacey. 1999. A brief experiment in distance teaching and learning of French. *British Journal of Educational Technology* 30 (2) 177–180.

Latchem. C. and F. Lockwood (eds). 1998. *Staff Development in Open and Flexible Learning*. London: Routledge.

Latchem, C. and D. Hanna (eds.) 2001. *Leadership for 21st Century Learning: Global perspectives from educational innovators.* London: Kogan Page.

Laurillard, D. 2002. *Rethinking University Teaching. A conversational framework for the effective use of learning technologies.* 2nd ed. London: Routledge.

Leung Y.-B. 1999. The achievement of language students in distance learning in Hong Kong. *Pan-Commonwealth Forum on Open Learning: Empowerment through knowledge and technology.* 1–5 March Brunei Darussalam.

Little, D. 1996. Freedom to learn and compulsion to interact: Promoting learner autonomy through the use of information systems and information technologies. In R. Pemberton, E. S. L. Li, W. W. F. Or and H. D. Pierson (eds) *Taking Control: Autonomy in language learning.* Hong Kong: Hong Kong University Press.

Little, D. 1997. Linguistic awareness and writing: Exploring the relationship with language awareness. *Language Awareness* 6 (2–3).

Little, D. 2001. Learner autonomy and the challenge of tandem language learning via the Internet. In Chambers, A. and Davies, G. (eds) *ICT and Language Learning: a European perspective.* Lisse: Swets and Zeitlinger.

Little, D. and H. Brammerts (eds). 1996. A guide to language learning in tandem via the Internet. CLCS Occasional Paper No. 46. Dublin: Trinity College, Centre for Language and Communication Studies.

Lyall, R. and S. McNamara. 2000. Influences on the orientations to learning of distance education students in Australia. *Open Learning* 15 (2) 107–121.

Mantyla, K. and J. R. Gividen. 1997. *Distance Education: A step-by-step guide for trainers.* American Society for Training and Development Alexandria, VA.

Marland, P. 1997. *Towards More Effective Open and Distance Teaching.* London: Kogan Page.

Marland, P. and R. Store. 1993. Some instructional strategies for improved learning from distance teaching materials in Harry, K., L. M. John and D. Keegan (eds) *Distance Education: New perspectives.* London/New York: Routledge.

Mason, R. 1994. *Using Communications Media in Open and Flexible Learning.* Kogan Page, London.

Mason, R. 1998a. *Globalising Education: Trends and applications.* London: Routledge.

Mason, R. 1998b. Models of online courses. *Journal of Asynchronous Learning Networks* 2 (2). http://www.aln.org/alnweb/magazine/vol2_issue2/Masonfinal.htm

Mason, R. 2001. IET's Masters in open and distance education: What have we learned? http://iet.open.ac.uk/pp/r.d.mason/downloads/maeval.pdf

McIsaac, M. S., J. M. Blocher, V. Mahes and C. Vraisdas. 1999. Student and teacher perceptions of interaction in computer-mediated communication. *EMI* 36 (2) 121–131.

McKay, S. and S. Wong (eds). 1996. *New Immigrants in the United States: Readings for second language education.* Cambridge: Cambridge University Press.

McVay Lynch, M. 2002. *The Online Educator: a guide to creating the virtual classroom.* London; New York: Routledge Falmer.

Miller, W. and J. K. Webster. 1997. A comparison of interaction needs and performance of distance learners in synchronous and asynchronous classes. Paper presented at the Conference of the American Vocational Association, Las Vegas, December 1997.

Mitchell, R. and F. Myles. 1998. Chapter 7. Sociological perspectives on second language learning. *Second Language Learning Theories.* New York: Arnold.

Mitter, S. and M.-I. Bastos (eds). 1999. *Europe and Developing Countries in the Globalised Information Economy.* London: Routledge.

Möllering, M. 2000. Computer mediated communication: learning German online in Australia. *ReCALL* 12 (1) 27–34.

Moore, G. S., K. Winograd and D. Lange. 2001. *You Can Teach Online: Building a creative learning environment.* Boston, Mass.: McGraw-Hill.

Moore, M. G. 1993. Theory of transactional distance. In D. Keegan (ed.) *Theoretical Principles of Distance Education.* London/New York: Routledge.

Moore, M. G. and G. Kearsley. 1996. *Distance Education: a systems view.* Wadsworth: California.

Moore, N. A. J. 2002. Review of e-moderating: The key to teaching and learning online. *Language Learning & Technology* 6 (3) 21–24.

Morgan, C. and M. O'Reilly. 1999. *Assessing Open and Distance Learners.* London, Kogan Page.

Morgan, C. and M. O'Reilly. 2001. Innovations in online assessment. In F. Lockwood and A. Gooley (eds) *Innovation in Open and Distance Learning: Successful development of online and web-based learning.* London: Kogan Page.

Murray, D. 2000. Protean communication: The language of computer-mediated communication. *TESOL Quarterly* 34 (3) 397–421.

Navarro, P. and J. Shoemaker. 2000. Performance and perceptions of distance learners in cyberspace. In M. G. Moore and G. T. Cozine (eds) *Web-based Communications, the Internet and Distance Education.* Pennsylvania, The American Centre for the Study of Distance Education. pp. 1–15.

Norton, B. and K. Toohey. 2001. Changing perspectives on good language learners. *TESOL Quarterly* 35 (2) 307–322.

Nunan, D. 1989. Toward a collaborative approach to curriculum development: A case study. *TESOL Quarterly* 23 9–25.

Nunan, D. 1999a. A foot in the world of ideas: Graduate study through the Internet. *Language Learning & Technology* 3 (1) 52–74.

Nunan, D. 1999b. *Second Language Teaching and Learning.* Boston, Massachusetts: Heinle and Heinle.

Nunan, D. and C. Lamb. 1996. *The self-directed Teacher: Managing the learning process.* Cambridge/New York: Cambridge University Press.

Nunan, D., J. Lai and K. Keobke. 1999. Towards autonomous language learning: strategies, reflection and navigation. In S. Cotterall and D. Crabbe (eds) *Learner Autonomy in Language Learning: Defining the field and effecting change*. Bayreuth Contributions to Glottodidactics, Vol 8. Frankfurt am Main: Lang.

Oblinger, D. 1999. *Putting Students At The Center: a planning guide to distributed learning*. Boulder, CO: Educause.

Ortega, L. 1997. Processes and outcomes in networked classroom interaction: Defining the research agenda for L2 computer-assisted classroom discussion. *Language Learning & Technology*, 1 (1) 82–93.

Oxford, R., Y. Rivera-Castillo, C. Feyten and J. Nutta. 1998. Computers and more: Creative uses of technology for learning a second or foreign language. In V. Darleguy, Ding, A. and Svensson, M. (eds) *Les Nouvelles Technologies Educatives dans l'apprentissage des langues vivantes: Réflexion théorique et applications pratiques (Educational Technology in language learning: Theoretical considerations and practical applications)*. http://www.insalyon.fr/Departements/CDRL/computers.html

Oxford, R. 1999. Anxiety and the language learner: New insights. In J. Arnold (ed.) *Affect in Language Learning*. Cambridge: Cambridge University Press.

Palloff, R. and K. Pratt. 1999. *Building Learning Communities in Cyberspace: Effective strategies for the online classroom*. San Francisco: Jossey-Bass.

Palloff, R. and K. Pratt. 2001. *Lessons from the Cyberspace Classroom: the Realities of Online Teaching*. San Francisco: Jossey-Bass.

Pemberton, R., S. Toogood, S. Ho, and J. Lam. 2001. Approaches to advising for self-directed language learning. In L. Dam (ed.) *Learner Autonomy: New insights*. AILA Review 15. Association Internationale de Linguistique Appliquée.

Peters, O. 1992. Some observations on dropping out in distance education. *Distance Education*, 13 (2) 234–269.

Peters, O. 1998. *Learning and Teaching In Distance Education: Analyses and interpretations from an international perspective*. London: Kogan Page

Radic, N. 2000. Parliamo italiano: A computer-mediated course of Italian for beginners delivered at a distance. OTIS e-workshop. 8–12 May 2000. http://otis.scotcit.ac.uk/casestudy/radic.doc

Radic, N. 2001. Classroom vs. virtual language learning environment. AAIS 2001 Conference University of Pennsylvania, Philadelphia.

Ramirez, S. and K. L. Savage. 2001. Closing the distance in adult ESL: Two approaches to video-based learning. In Henrichsen, L. E. (ed.) *Distance-learning Programs*. Alexandria, Virginia: TESOL.

Raskin, J. 2001. Using the World Wide Web as a resource for models and interaction in a writing course. In Henrichsen, L. E. (ed.) *Distance-learning Programs*. Alexandria, Virginia: TESOL.

Rees-Miller, J. 1993. A critical appraisal of learner training: Theoretical bases and teaching implications. *TESOL Quarterly* 27: 4 679–689.

Richards, J. C. 2001. *Curriculum Development in Language Teaching*. Cambridge: Cambridge University Press.

Richards, J. C. and W. A. Renandya (eds). 2002. *Methodology in Language Teaching: An anthology of current practice*. Cambridge: Cambridge University Press.

Richards, K. and P. Roe (eds). 1994. *Distance Learning in ELT*. London: MEP/The British Council.

Robinson, B. 1992. Applying quality standards in distance and open learning. *EADTU News* 11 11–17.

Robinson, B. 2001. Innovation in open and distance learning: some Lessons from experience and research. In F. Lockwood and A. Gooley (eds) *Innovation in Open and Distance Learning: Successful development of online and web-based learning*. London: Kogan Page.

Rogers, D. and A. B. Wolff. 2000. *El español . . . ¡a distancia!*: Developing a technology-based distance education intermediate Spanish course. *Journal of General Education* 49 (1) (2000): 44–52.

Rothenberg, M. 1998. The new face of distance learning in language instruction. In W. Gewehr (ed.) *Aspects of Modern Language Teaching in Europe*. London: Routledge.

Rourke, L., T. Anderson, D. R. Garrison and W. Archer. 2001. Assessing social presence in asynchronous text-based computer conferencing. *Journal of Distance Education* 14 (2).

Rowntree, D. 1997 *Making Materials-based Learning Work*. London: Kogan Page.

Rumble, G. 2000. Student support in distance education in the 21st century: Learning from service management. *Distance Education* 21 (2) 216–235.

Rumble, G. 2001. E-Education: Whose benefits, whose costs? Inaugural lecture, OUUK, 28 February 2001.

Ryan, Y. 2001. The provision of learner support services online. In Farrell, G. (ed.) *The Changing Faces of Virtual Education*. Vancouver, Canada: The Commonwealth of Learning.

Salmon, G. 2000. *E-moderating: The key to teaching and learning online*. London: Kogan Page.

Schrum, L. 1998. On-line education: a study of emerging pedagogy. In B. Cahoon (ed.) *Adult Learning and the Internet*. San Francisco: Jossey-Bass Publishers.

Selinger, M. 2000. Opening up new teaching and learning spaces. In T. Evans and D. Nation (eds) *Changing University Teaching: Reflections on creating educational technologies*. London: Kogan Page.

Shelley, M. A. 2000. Distance education. In M. S. Byram (ed.) *Encyclopedia of Language Teaching and Learning*. London: Routledge.

Sherry, A. C., C. P. Fulford and S. Zhang. 1998. Assessing distance learners' satisfaction with instruction: a quantitative and qualitative measure. *American Journal of Distance Education* 12 (3) 4–28.

Shield, L. 2000. Overcoming Isolation: the loneliness of the long distance learner, EADTU Paris Millenium Conference: Wiring the Ivory Tower. Keynote Address.

Shield L., C. Rodine, M. Hauck and B. Haezewindt. 1999. The FLUENT Project: Creating richer online communities to support the distance language learner. Proceedings of ComNEd 99.

Shield L., M. Hauck and M. Kötter. 2000. Taking the distance out of distance learning. In P. Howarth and R. Herrington (eds) *EAP Learning Technologies*. Leeds University Press: Leeds.

References

Shuell, T. J. 1988. The role of the student in learning from instruction. *Contemporary Educational Psychology* 13 276–295.

Simpson, O. 2000. *Supporting Students in Open and Distance Learning.* London, Kogan Page.

Skehan, Peter. 1998. *A Cognitive Approach to Language Learning.* Oxford: Oxford University Press.

Smith, M. and Salam, U. 2000. Web-based ESL courses: A search for industry standards. *CALL-EJ Online* 2 (1).

Stevens, A. and S. Hewer. 1998. From policy to practice and back. Paper presented at the 1st Leverage Conference, Cambridge. http://greco.dit.upm. es/~leverage/conf1/hewer.htm

Stevenson, K., U. Muda, C. Karlsson, A. Szeky, P. Sander and T. Read. 2000. Developing an ODL quality assurance model using students' expectations of tutor support needs: an outcome of the Socrates funded CEESOC Project. *European Electronic Journal of Open and Distance Learning* 2000; 3: 23–29.

Sutton, L. A. 2001. The principle of vicarious interaction in computer-mediated communications. *International Journal of Education Telecommunications* 7 (3).

Tait, A. 2000. Planning student support for open and distance learning. *Open Learning* 15 (3) 287–299.

Tammelin, M. 1997. Turning a classroom into a virtual learning space: Lessons learned along the way. In Cornell, R. and K. Ingram (eds) *An international survey of distance education and learning: From smoke signals to satellite III.* Berlin: International Council for Educational Media and Orlando, FL: University of Central Florida, 12–17.

Tammelin, M. 1998. From Telepresence to Social Presence: The role of presence in a network-based learning environment. In Tella, S. (ed.) *Aspects of Media Education: Strategic imperatives in the information age.* Media Education Centre, Department of Teacher Education, University of Helsinki. Media Education Publications 8.

Tammelin, M. 1999. Teaching and studying environmental communication via a telematics-mediated course. In Nikko, T. and Nuolijärvi, P. (eds) Talous ja kieli III. Seminaari 9.10.5.1996. Helsingin kauppakorkeakoulu. Helsingin kauppakorkeakoulun julkaisuja B-17, 57–70.

Thompson, M. 1998. Distance learners in higher education. In Gibson, C. (ed.) Distance Learners in Higher Education: Institutional responses for quality outcomes. Madison, Wisconsin: Atwood Publishing.

Thorpe, M. 1995. The challenge facing course design. In Lockwood, F. (ed.) *Open and Distance Learning Today.* London: Routledge.

Thorpe, M. 2001. Evaluating the use of learning technologies. In E. Burge and M. Haughey (eds) *Using Learning Technologies: International perspectives on practice.* London: Routledge

Tight, M. 1996. *Key Concepts in Adult Education and Training.* London: Routledge.

Tu, C.-H. 2000. On-line learning migration: From social learning theory to social presence theory in CMC environments. *Journal of Network and Computer Applications* 23 (1) 27–37.

246

Tudor, I. 2001. *The Dynamics of the Language Classroom*. Cambridge: Cambridge University Press.

Tuijnman, A. 1999. Lifelong learning policies in a new technological era. In Mitter, S. and M.-I. Bastos (eds) *Europe and Developing Countries in the Globalised Information Economy*. London: Routledge.

Tuovinen, J. E. 2000. Multimedia distance education interaction. *Educational Media International* 37 (1) 16–24.

Tyler, S., M. Green and C. Simpson. 2001. Experimenting in Lotus Learning Space. In F. Lockwood and A. Gooley (eds) *Innovation in Open and Distance Learning: Successful development of online and web-based learning*. London: Kogan Page.

University of Wisconsin-Extension. 2000. Quality Distance Education (QDE): Lessons learned. http://www.uwex.edu/disted/qde/factors.html

Vanijdee, A. 2001. *Language Learning Strategy Use, Interaction with Self-Instructional Materials, and Learner Autonomy of Thai Distance Language Learners*. Unpublished PhD thesis, Reading University.

Vanijdee, A. 2003. Thai distance English learners and learner autonomy. *Open Learning* 18 (1) 75–84.

Van Lier, L. 1996. *Interaction in the Language Curriculum: Awareness, autonomy and authenticity*. London: Longman.

Van Lier, L. 2002. Ecology, contingency and talk in the postmethod classroom. *New Zealand Studies in Applied Linguistics* 8 1–21.

Victori, M. and W. Lockhart. 1995. Enhancing metacognition in self-directed learning. *System* 23 (2) 223–34.

Vrasidas, C. and M. McIsaac. 2000. Factors influencing interaction in an online course. In M. G. Moore and G. T. Cozine (eds) *Web-based Communications, the Internet and Distance Education*. Pennsylvania, The American Center for the Study of Distance Education. pp. 62–72.

Warschauer, M. 2000. The changing global economy and the future of English teaching: *TESOL Quarterly* 34 (3) 511–535.

Warschauer, M., H. Shetzer and C. Meloni. 2000. *Internet for English Teaching*. Alexandria, VA: Teachers of English to Speakers of Other Languages, Inc.

Weller M. J. and R. D. Mason. 2000. Evaluating an Open University web course: Issues and innovations. In Asensio, M., Foster, J., Hodgson, V. and McConnell, D. (eds) *Networked Learning 2000*. Lancaster: Lancaster University.

Weller, M. 2002. *Delivering Learning on the Net: The why, what & how of online education*. London: Kogan Page.

Wenden, A. 1987. Conceptual background and utility. In A. Wenden and J. Rubin (eds) *Learner Strategies in Language Learning*. Englewood Cliffs, NJ, Prentice-Hall. pp. 3–13.

Wenden, A. 1999a. An introduction to metacognitive knowledge and beliefs in language learning: Beyond the basics. *System* 27 (4) 435–441.

Wenden, A. 1999b. Metacognitive knowledge and language learning. *Applied Linguistics* 19 (4) 515–537.

White, C. J. 1993. *Metacognitive, Cognitive, Social and Affective Strategy Use in Foreign Language Learning: A comparative study*. Unpublished PhD thesis, Massey University, New Zealand.

White, C. J. 1995a. Autonomy and strategy use in distance foreign language learning: research findings. In Wenden, A. and L. Dickinson (eds) *System Special Issue on Autonomy* 23 (2) 207–221.

White, C. J. 1995b. Note taking strategies and traces of cognition. *RELC Journal* 27 (1) 89–102.

White, C. J. 1995c. Strategy choice and the target language: a comparative study of learners of French and Japanese. In *Australian Review of Applied Linguistics. Special Issue. The Hard Work–Entertainment Continuum: Teaching Asian languages in Australia.* 12 169–182.

White, C. J. 1997. Effects of mode of study on foreign language learning. *Distance Education* 18 (1), 178–196.

White, C. J. 1998. Conceptions of distance learning. DEANZ Conference, *Best Practice, Research and Diversity in Distance Education*. Rotorua, New Zealand.

White, C. J. 1999a. Expectations and emergent beliefs of self-instructed language learners. In *Metacognitive Knowledge and Beliefs in Language Learning. System Special Issue* (27) 443–457.

White, C. J. 1999b. The metacognitive knowledge of distance learners. *Open Learning* 14 (3) 37–47.

White. C. J. 1999c. Towards a learner-derived theory of language learning through self-instruction. Applied Linguistics Association of New Zealand Symposium, University of Auckland, 25 September 1999.

White, C. J. 2000. The use of multiple textual forms in distance learning. *Journal of Distance Learning*: 18–26.

White, C. J., P. Easton and C. Anderson. 2000. Students' perceived value of video in a multimedia language course. *Educational Media International: Journal of the International Council for Educational Media*, 37 (3) 167–175.

Williams, M. L., K. Paprock, and B. Covington. 1999. *Distance Learning. The essential guide*. London: Sage.

Wilson, B. and M. Lowry. 2000. Constructivist learning on the web. In E. Burge (ed.) *The Strategic Use of Learning Technologies*. San Francisco: Jossey-Bass.

Young, J. R. 2000, May 12. The lowly telephone is central to some distance education courses [online]. *Chronicle of Higher Education*, 46. www.chronicle.com/chronicle/archive.htm

Author Index

Author index

Subject Index